Thomas Paine

AND THE CLARION CALL
FOR AMERICAN INDEPENDENCE

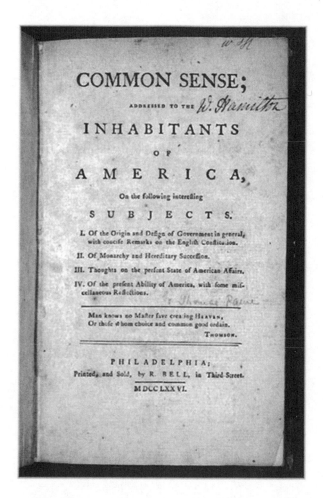

Original cover of Thomas Paine's *Common Sense*, the pamphlet that convinced Americans of the absurdity of hereditary rule. "Why," Paine had asked, "should someone rule over us simply because he is someone else's child?" It defied common sense.

Thomas Paine

AND THE
CLARION CALL
FOR
AMERICAN
INDEPENDENCE

HARLOW GILES UNGER

DA CAPO PRESS

Da Capo Press
Hachette Book Group
1290 Avenue of the Americas, New York, NY 10104
HachetteBooks.com
Twitter.com/HachetteBooks
Instagram.com/HachetteBooks

Printed in the United States of America

First Edition: September 2019

Published by Da Capo Press, an imprint of Perseus Books, LLC, a subsidiary of Hachette Book Group, Inc. The Da Capo Press name and logo is a trademark of the Hachette Book Group.

The Hachette Speakers Bureau provides a wide range of authors for speaking events. To find out more, go to www.hachettespeakersbureau.com or call (866) 376-6591.

The publisher is not responsible for websites (or their content) that are not owned by the publisher.

Print book interior design by Trish Wilkinson.

Library of Congress Cataloging-in-Publication Data has been applied for.

ISBNs: 978-0-306-92193-3 (hardcover); 978-0-306-92194-0 (ebook)

LSC-C

10 9 8 7 6 5 4 3 2 1

To my wonderful son Richard

Contents

List of Illustrations

Cover: Thomas Paine. William Sharp engraving, after 1793 portrait by George Romney. National Portrait Gallery, Washington, D.C.

Frontispiece: *Common Sense*

Acknowledgments

MY DEEPEST THANKS AND APPRECIATION TO GARY BERTON, A consummate Thomas Paine scholar who is Coordinator of the Institute for Thomas Paine Studies and Secretary of the Thomas Paine National Historical Association. Mr. Berton was most generous in reviewing the manuscript of this book and sharing his extraordinary knowledge of Thomas Paine's life and his enormous number of written works. In addition, Mr. Berton's automated authorship analyses ensured a level of accuracy in this work unavailable to previous researchers.

My sincere thanks as well to my editor Robert Pigeon for the care, skills, and time he invested in this and all my books. More than an outstanding editor, Robert is a gifted teacher who for more than a decade has never ceased to help me improve my work. Thanks, too, to others who have helped me with my work for many years, including Lissa Warren, John Radziewicz, and Kevin Hanover. I am also grateful to Hachette Book Group publicity director Joanna Pinsker; marketing associate Odette Fleming; Cisca Schreefel, manager of editorial production; Trish Wilkinson, designer; Martha Whitt, copy editor; and the Hachette Book Group sales team. In addition, I send my deepest thanks to website developer Tom Bowler for his steadfast friendship and for his magnificent work—both technically and artistically—on my various websites, including harlowgiles unger.com. Lastly, many aides and scholars at archival organizations in the United States, Britain, and France gave freely and willingly of their time and knowledge to help me with research for this book, and I thank them all.

Chronology

1737   Born February 9, Thetford, England.

1744   Attends Thetford Grammar School until 1749.

1750   Apprentice to his father as stay maker.

1753   Enlists on *King of Prussia* privateer.

1758   Works as stay maker; marries in 1759.

1760   Wife dies; he quits stay making.

1761   Visits London; studies at Royal Society; becomes exciseman; fired five years later.

1766   Teaches at a London academy; resumes studies at Royal Society.

1768   Resumes work as exciseman in Lewes, Sussex; begins writing news articles.

1771   Remarries.

1772   Writes twenty-one-page petition to Parliament for higher wages for excisemen.

1773   Lobbies Parliament; meets Benjamin Franklin.

1774   Fired as exciseman; separates from wife; bankruptcy; sails to America.

1775   Edits, writes for *Pennsylvania Magazine*; fighting breaks out at Lexington, Massachusetts.

1776   Writes *Common Sense*; inspires American fight for independence; Congress declares independence; he enlists in American Army; appointed General Greene's aide-de-camp; retreat to the Delaware; writes *American Crisis I*; inspires victory at Trenton.

1777   Appointed Secretary to the Committee on Foreign Affairs in Congress.

1778   Flees with Congress to Lancaster, Pennsylvania, then York; writes more *Crisis* essays to boost American morale; the Deane Affair.

1779   Resigns from Congress.

1780   Clerk of Pennsylvania Assembly; leads Pennsylvania abolition movement; starts subscription for army; *Crisis Extraordinary* details fiscal plan for America; dispute over western territories.

1781   To France with John Laurens; returns with $500,000 in silver and shipload of military stores; helps organize Bank of North America; victory at Yorktown.

1783   Treaty of Paris; British evacuate New York; "The times that tried men's souls are over."

1784   New York awards Paine a farm; Pennsylvania and Congress give him cash.

1785   Invents, builds model of revolutionary single-arched iron bridge.

1787   Sails to Europe to promote his bridge; visits Paris, London; returns to Thetford; United States approves Constitution.

1788   Builds iron bridge in England.

1789   Storming of the Bastille; Paine returns to Paris; joins revolutionaries.

1790   Conflict with Burke; erects iron bridge in Paddington; forwards key to Bastille to President Washington; begins writing *Rights of Man*.

1791   Completes *Rights of Man*; revisits Paris, returns to London to provoke social, political changes.

1792   British charge Paine with seditious libel; he flees to France; declared honorary French citizen; elected to French National Assembly; leads fight to save king from execution; British court tries and finds him guilty of sedition *in absentia*.

1793   Execution of French king; Paine writes Part I of *Age of Reason*; arrested for trying to prevent king's execution; imprisonment in the Luxemburg Palace in Paris.

1794 Finishes writing *Age of Reason* in prison; chance avoidance of execution; Robespierre executed; Paine released from prison; restored to Convention.

1796 *Age of Reason* published; English prosecution of *Age of Reason*; writes accusatory letter to Washington.

1797 Goes to live with printer Nicolas de Bonneville and family; works with Fulton; advises Irish-independence leaders; meets with Bonaparte; influence on French government policies.

1802 Sails to Baltimore; President Jefferson's welcome; shunned by Federalists; attacks by Federalist newspapers.

1803 Moves to New York; *Age of Reason* reduces his influence; counterattacks with *Letters to the Citizens of the United States*; Mme. Bonneville arrives.

1804 Settles on New Rochelle farm; 1805 assassination attempt on Paine; writes *Prospect Papers*.

1806 In failing health; denied right to vote.

1809 Writes last will; dies in New York City, June 8; buried on New Rochelle farm, June 10.

1819 Paine's remains stolen, removed to England, and lost.

Note: The author has occasionally modernized spellings, punctuation, grammar, and syntax in eighteenth- and nineteenth-century letters, manuscripts, and publications for clarification purposes and without knowingly altering the intent of the original author. Readers may find the original language, spellings, and punctuation in the works cited in the notes. Italicized words within quotations are those of the speaker or author of those words. Unless otherwise noted, illustrations were obtained from the Library of Congress or sources in the public domain.

My country is the world and my religion is to do good.

—Thomas Paine, *Rights of Man*

INTRODUCTION

Thomas Paine's words leaped off the page, embracing readers—indeed, whole peoples—inspiring them to change their lives, their governments, their kings, even their gods. In an age when spoken and written words were the only forms of communication, Paine's words roused men to action like few others. They exposed as myth that birth predetermines one's rights and privileges. And they implanted a revolutionary new concept in the minds of men: that all men are created equal.

Paine's words resounded in palaces, homes, and hovels, along city streets and country roads; they toppled tyrants, empowered peasants, provoked revolutions; they changed the social fabric of the Western world, the course of history, the course of man. They resonated around the world then and now.

Other *philosophes* in the Age of Enlightenment—Locke, Rousseau, Voltaire, and the like—had aroused intellectuals and literate political leaders, but Thomas Paine addressed Everyman: literate or not, poor, rich, noble, ignoble. . . .

"Why," Paine demanded to know, "why should someone rule over us simply because he is someone else's child?" He answered his own question, calling the notion absurd, saying it defied common sense.

In 1776, Paine's words were heresy. After all, hadn't God himself granted kings the absolute right to rule? Rulers believed it; churches and clergymen believed it; most of the governed believed it. Thomas Paine did not, and untold thousands of ordinary people around the globe who read or heard his simple truths soon agreed. In America, commoners picked up their muskets and did the unthinkable by rebelling against royal rule, and in the decade that followed, the French followed suit. A century later, royal rule by divine right was on its way to extinction across the face of the earth.

"I know not whether any man in the world has had more influence on its inhabitants or its affairs for the last thirty years than Tom Paine," America's John Adams asserted. "Call it then the Age of Paine."[1]

George Washington agreed. As his army of simple farmers lay shivering on the banks of the Delaware River after fleeing across New Jersey from British troops, he ordered Thomas Paine's words read aloud to the troops.

"These are the times that try men's souls," Paine had written. "The summer soldier and the sunshine patriot will, in this crisis, shrink from the service of his country; but . . . tyranny, like hell, is not easily conquered . . . the harder the conflict the more glorious the triumph."

Like a master preacher, Paine sent his explosive words boring into every mind and soul, until Washington's troops rose as one. All but frothing at their mouths with fury, they boarded rafts to cross the ice-choked Delaware River in the dead of night, and at dawn, with Paine firing his musket in concert with theirs, they stormed into Trenton, New Jersey, and overwhelmed a larger, better-armed force of German mercenaries. After months of humiliating defeats, the victory at Trenton lifted the morale of an entire people and convinced the American army it could win the war of independence.

"Without the pen of Paine," John Adams exclaimed, "the sword of Washington would have been wielded in vain." Washington agreed, pointing out that Paine's words had left few Americans "at a loss to decide upon the propriety of a separation [from Britain]."

A decade later, Paine's words had the same effect in France, and, still later, in Britain. As he told Jefferson, he held certain truths to be self-evident, among them that "the laws of Nature and Nature's God" had created all men equal and entitled them to certain unalienable rights. Envisioning a worldwide confederation of free men, he defined those rights in a major work he called *Rights of Man*, which he dedicated in part to Washington, the hero of the American Revolution, in part to Lafayette, the hero of the French Revolution.

The most widely read political writer of his generation, Paine proved himself more than a century ahead of his time, conceiving and demanding unheard-of social reforms that became integral elements of modern republican societies: among them, government subsidies and public housing for the poor, free universal public education, pre- and postnatal care for women, and universal social security, with government payments to everyone fifty years or older. He outraged the rich with a call for an inheritance tax, property taxes on the lands of aristocrats, and a progressive income tax to reduce inequality between rich and poor. And he called for an end to slavery and to monarchy itself.

"It requires some talents to be a common mechanic," Paine scoffed, "but to be a king requires only the animal figure of a man."

A warm, jovial man and sometime poet, Thomas Paine won likeminded friends in the highest ranks of British, American, and French society. In America, his close friendships with Benjamin Franklin and Thomas Jefferson produced elements of the *Declaration of Independence*; his friendship with James Madison colored the *Bill of Rights*. In America, Congress gave him a cabinet post; Pennsylvania made him a citizen; and New York State gave him a 277-acre farm north of New York City, where his talents as an inventor produced advanced forms of iron bridges and helped Robert Fulton develop one of the first steam engines to power boats.

With America free and independent, Paine went to France to join Lafayette and other political liberals in stripping the monarch of absolute powers and establishing a French republic, with a constitution that used as its basis Paine's *Rights of Man*.

Hailed as much in France for *Common Sense* as he had been in America, he won election to the French National Assembly, where he opposed capital punishment and argued against execution of the French king. Thirsting for royal blood, outraged radicals tossed Paine in prison to await the guillotine. Facing death, he worked on his magnum opus: *The Age of Reason*. In it he extended the principles of liberty he had espoused in *Common Sense* and *Rights of Man* to religion, calling it a human invention designed, like monarchy, to terrify and enslave man.

His attack on religion, however, turned much of the Western world against him. Former friends and admirers shunned him; devout Christians despised and rejected him and his writings; an assassin's bullet only barely missed its mark. And when the man Americans had once hailed as Father of all Founding Fathers fell sick and died in 1809 at seventy-two, few noticed, and even fewer cared. As a further insult to his legacy, an irrational Englishman ripped his bones out of the earth and shipped them to England, where they were lost. A series of fires subsequently consumed most of his papers.

But neither fire nor censors succeeded in silencing his words. Revealed once more in the pages that follow, Thomas Paine's words continue to try men's souls.

Chapter 1

CRIES OF PAINE

E VEN WHEN HE WAS SIX, THOMAS PAINE SCOFFED AT THE RITUAL of silence in his father's Quaker meetinghouse as defying common sense. While sitting in pews all day awaiting the word of God, all he and his father and the other Quakers heard were shrieks of pain from the nearby whipping post, blending in ghastly harmony with pleas for water from captives of the stocks and the pillory in the alley hard by the Quaker place of worship.

The voice of God?

Hardly!

"I believe in one God and no more," Paine professed later in life. "I do not believe in . . . any church that I know of. My own mind is my own church. All national institutions of churches . . . appear to me no other than human inventions set up to terrify and enslave mankind, and monopolize power and profit."[1]

Born in Thetford, England, in January 1737, Thomas Paine was the only surviving child of Joseph Paine (or Pain or Payne, as it was often spelled when people wrote phonetically). Although unsure of the spelling of his name, he was sure about his scorn for Quaker beliefs that included the concept of predestination, which, for him, would mean a life scratching out a bare living making corset stays—the thin, semi-rigid strips of wood, horn, ivory, metal, or whalebone to insert in women's corsets. For those women who could afford corsets, stays stiffened them into body casts that they believed compressed their waists into wasp-like sensuality.

The Paines—it was Thomas who settled on the spelling—lived in a cottage that included the father's stay-making shop as well as living quarters. They depended on a nearby plot of land they leased from the Duke of Grafton to provide the family with enough to eat. Paine's mother Frances was a devout Anglican who taught her son the goodness of God for having placed George II, Prince Elector of the Holy Roman Empire, on the British throne and placing the Paines in the thrall of the Duke, who owned all the land within eyesight and beyond. She held no dissenting beliefs of her own and insisted that her son be baptized and confirmed in the Anglican Church, but she yielded to her husband by allowing Thomas to attend Quaker meetings with his father. She agreed with but one of her husband's many Quaker beliefs: their son would have to learn the Bible—all of it.

And learn it he did.

Indeed, his amazing mind and prodigious memory absorbed almost every word of the Old and New Testaments, an astonishing amount of which he could recite the rest of his life—along with anything and everything else he read and chose to remember.

"It was my good fortune to have an exceeding good moral education," he recalled, "and a tolerable stock of useful learning. Though I went to the grammar school, I did not learn Latin because I had no bent to learn

1. A street in eighteenth-century Thetford, a town seventy miles north of London known best for its public hangings during Lent each year.

languages, but this did not prevent me from being acquainted with the subjects of all the Latin books used in the school. The natural bent of my mind was to science," he recalled—with which he might well have included mathematics, physics, mechanical design, astronomy, and "some talent for poetry."

At eight, Paine penned his first rhymes after burying a dead bird in his father's garden:

> *Here lies the body of John Crow,*
> *Who once was high and now is low;*
> *Ye brothers Crow take warning all,*
> *For as you rise, so must you fall.*[2]

Although he spent seven years in the classroom, he absorbed what proved to be his most important childhood lessons walking to and from school in springtime, when he witnessed productions of the Thetford Lent Assizes. The Assizes were a ghastly annual ritual of public trials and executions that lured throngs of gleeful spectators from the entire countryside—even from London, ninety miles to the south.

"Why is it that scarcely any are executed but the poor?" Tom Paine asked his parents, without eliciting a response that satisfied his curiosity.[3]

Each year, the Assizes sent scores of petty criminals to their deaths, sometimes tied to a stake and burned alive, sometimes hanging by the neck from a scaffold on the hill that Paine climbed to school each day. Those sentenced to hang did not die easily. Indeed, they entertained cheering throngs by squirming, kicking, and convulsing in a macabre dance of death after executioners had hauled them into the air with ropes looped about their necks. Left to hang for an hour, some managed a few final spasms as encores that drew more hurrahs from the crowd before the final, eternal curtain closed on their lives.

Ironically, the Thetford Lent Assizes sent no murderers to die, only thieves—some of them children—guilty of larceny.

When Paine was thirteen, Thetford court sentenced seventeen-year-old Amy Hutchinson to death for allegedly poisoning her husband. "Her face and hands were smeared with tar, and having a garment daubed with

2. The Thetford Lent Assizes drew crowds from as far off as London to witness the annual public hangings at Lent. Thomas Paine's primary school stood only yards away, forcing the children to witness executions as they walked to school.

pitch, after a short prayer the executioner strangled her and twenty minutes after, the fire was kindled, and [she] burnt half an hour."[4]

The court sent other children to the gallows for a variety of crimes, but usually punished petty larceny on the ducking stool, in the pillory or stocks, or with a public whipping. There was, however, no clear line between petty crimes that warranted public humiliation or torture and those that earned a public hanging. Penalties were at the discretion of the Lord Chief Justice, who sat beneath a painting of "Lady Justice." At her feet an inscription urged the court to "Judge righteously, and plead the cause of the Poor and Needy. *Proverbs* 31 and 9."

After Voltaire visited Thetford, he called the British a people who murdered by law, and Paine often cried in his bed at night after witnessing someone he knew fall victim to the intractable decision of the Lord Chief Justice.

The law did far more than murder individuals, however. The English government used it to try to crush the spirits of the British people. As Paine would write later, "The Constitution of England is so exceedingly complex that the nation may suffer for years together without being able to discover in which part the fault lies."[5] In tiny Thetford, for example, the law gave the Duke of Grafton absolute rule over the 2,000-odd commoners who lived on and worked his lands under leases that extracted such high annual rents as to leave them barely enough income to feed

3. The pillory and stocks stood outside young Thomas Paine's Quaker meetinghouse, adding a chorus of moans and groans to Sunday services.

their families from the sale of what they produced. But it was God's will, all good Englishmen agreed.

The Duke not only owned all the land, he appointed all local officials and Thetford's two members of Parliament. The Duke dictated what children could learn in school and at church, what books and newspapers adults could read, and what preachers of various denominations could preach. Because most residents lived on the Duke's leaseholds, they were not property owners and could not vote. Indeed, they lived in constant fear of losing their only shelter for uttering a thought—political, religious, or other—that strayed from the Duke's opinions.

Why, Thomas Paine asked his parents, should anyone have powers to control others—even hang them—simply because he was firstborn in a particular household to a particular set of parents? To a child's mind too young to process abstractions, it defied common sense, and neither Paine's father nor his mother could explain Thetford's (or England's) political and social incongruities to their son. It was God's way, they uttered to his annoyance.

But why, he asked, did England even need a king? The Bible, he said, proclaimed, "The Lord shall rule over you."[6]

Thus, Thomas Paine grew up tormented by injustices he saw perpetrated in the name of the Duke, the monarch, the church, and God. By the time he was thirteen, he loathed them all and sought freedom and a better life at sea by running off to the coast.

"I happened to pick up a pleasing natural history of Virginia," he recalled later, "and my inclination from that day of seeing the western side of the Atlantic never left me."[7]

His father, however, knew the usual fate of youngsters who ran away from home to go to sea. He followed his son to the piers, arriving just in time to prevent his sailing on the privateer *Terrible*, under the command of the notorious Captain William Death [*sic*!].

"From this adventure," Paine admitted years later to the London printer and bookseller Thomas Clio Rickman, "I was happily prevented by the affectionate and moral remonstrances of a good father."[8] As it turned out, the *Terrible* lost 175 of its 200-man crew in an encounter returning from sea, including 19 of her 20 officers—among them, Captain Death.

Three years followed with Tom working as an apprentice stay maker in his father's workshop. At seventeen, however, he determined to quit the strictures of Thetford and its horrifying Lent Assizes for good. Although he still harbored fantasies of sailing to Virginia, he had only four options for doing so, the two easiest being to buy passage on a merchant vessel or slip a saber in his belt and sign on as an apprentice pirate. He lacked the pocket for the former, however, and the stomach for the latter. He also lacked the advanced schooling and special training needed to join the royal navy—a third way of sailing to America. That left him but one option: to sign on to a privateer as a "powder monkey" carrying gunpowder from the hold to the gun deck.

The outbreak of what would become the Seven Years' War between England and France gave him that chance. With war, every participating nation needed as many privateers as possible to impede and harass enemy shipping. The more privateers, the more men needed to man them, and Paine signed on the twenty-four-gun privateer *King of Prussia* with a crew of about 250. Though a novice, "a few able and social sailors," he said, quickly instructed "land men in the common work of a ship," and life at sea soon became routine—even boring at times.[9]

Eventually, *King of Prussia* found more than enough action, capturing at least six merchant ships and rescuing two others from French privateers. "Most of the men killed or wounded," Paine recalled, were not injured by cannonballs, but "by splinters from inside of the ship that fly in all directions."[10]

After two years, Paine had seen enough of sea life—and death. With enough saved from his seaman's earnings to live comfortably for a few months, he disembarked in favor of more stability and less bloodshed ashore. Although he settled in London rather than return to Thetford, his limited skills forced him to resume work in stay making. He used his idle time, though, expanding his knowledge at lectures on astronomy, Newtonian philosophy, and physics at London's Royal Society. Founded a century earlier as the "invisible college of natural philosophers," it became the Royal Society in 1661 after receiving a charter from Charles II. In the centuries that followed, it sponsored free lectures by the world's most renowned scientists. In 1687 it published Sir Isaac Newton's *Principia Mathematica* and a century later, in 1752, it hosted Benjamin Franklin as he conducted what was then the world's most famous experiment demonstrating the electrical nature of lightning.

During those years, it accumulated one of the world's largest libraries. Open free of charge to the public, it proved a wellspring of knowledge for Thomas Paine, who spent almost every waking moment devouring library offerings in astronomy, physics, philosophy, Greek and Roman history and mythology. To complement his studies, he bought two globes and an orrery, or mechanical model of the solar system. In staring into space at night, Paine concluded that the earth was "only one of a system of worlds . . . as large or larger than ours and each of them millions of miles apart from each other."[11]

Paine also attended public lectures outside the Society on complex subjects such as electricity, hydrostatics, mechanics, and, of course, astronomy. Transfixed by the "millions of worlds" in the sky, he developed an insatiable appetite for astronomy. In effect, Paine absorbed more than a university education—until he ran out of funds to continue living in London.

In 1758, he took a job as a master stay maker in Dover. A year later, he found a higher-paying job in the same trade in Sandwich, Kent, where he displayed a new talent as a part-time, open-air preacher, a common occupation of Methodists at the time. In September 1759, he married and opened his own stay-making shop, but within a year the shop failed, and a year after that his wife died.

"In July 1761," Rickman recalled, Paine grew "disgusted with the toil and little gain of his occupation and renounced it forever."[12]

Life was not going well for Thomas Paine.

In 1761, his late wife's father—an excise man, or sales-tax collector—found Paine a similar job in the brewing industry, and Paine, twenty-four by then, seized it rather than go into the military to earn his keep. By then, Britain and France and six other European nations were at war. Although Britain would eventually emerge as a victor of sorts and France a loser, the war left both nations bankrupt and overwhelmed by enormous debts.

England's Parliament reacted by imposing taxes that crushed the nation's domestic economy, sending 40,000 Englishmen to debtors' prisons for not paying their taxes and provoking widespread anti-tax riots. Paine's job as an excise-tax collector promised steady, easy work for equally steady wages that were nonetheless low, given the dangers of trying to collect taxes at that time. Paine's job required only that he visit each brewery once monthly to estimate the depletion of ale in each cask from the same time of the previous visit. He would then calculate the tax the brewer owed the government on that amount. Apart from the rioting that all taxes had provoked, excise taxes generated massive amounts of smuggling, with vicious assaults on excise men who stumbled on smugglers and tried arresting them. Although the excisemen caught several thousand smugglers every year, many suffered crippling injuries—even death.

To avoid injury, many excise men accepted bribes or, more frequently, resorted to "stamping"—an easy and less dangerous procedure by which they stayed home and estimated (usually underestimated) the depletion of brewer stocks rather than risk physical harm by showing up at the breweries. Caught stamping in the summer of 1765, Paine was fired.

Angry at what he considered unfair treatment, he again envisioned leaving for America, where colonist tax protests had also grown violent. After farmer protests in England had forced Parliament to rescind some tax increases, it had compensated for lost revenues by raising import and export duties in America. In March 1765, it tried adding a stamp tax in America—with what it thought was good reason. Soaring costs of military garrisons to protect American colonists against Indian attacks had inflated England's huge war debts, and Parliament—indeed, most Englishmen—believed Americans should pay for some of their own military protection. The stamp tax seemed the most innocuous way to make them do so.

In effect for decades in England, the stamp tax required the purchase and affixment of one or more revenue stamps—often less than a penny each—on all legal documents, periodicals, liquor containers, and a variety of industrial and consumer goods. All but negligible when added to the cost of any individual item, it nevertheless amounted to a considerable—and reliable—revenue source for the government when stamp collections on tens of thousands of documents and products poured into the treasury. British Chancellor of the Exchequer Lord Grenville estimated the stamp tax would pay for about 20 percent of troop costs in America, with duties on imports and exports covering the rest. Americans, however, called the stamp tax confiscation and staged enough riots in the months following enactment of the tax to force Parliament to rescind it before they had even collected a penny.

Embittered by his dismissal as an excise man, Paine thought of joining anti-tax protests either in Britain or America, but he had no money to travel or sustain himself—at home or abroad. Out of work and growing hungry, he again turned to open-air preaching, earning only pennies a day, but honing his skills as a public speaker. Indeed, he impressed one listener enough to be hired as an assistant teacher and tutor in a London academy.

"I remember him once speaking of the improvement he gained in the above capacities and some other lowly situations he had been in," his biographer Rickman quoted him as saying. "I have seldom passed five minutes of my life, however circumstanced," Paine had said, "in which I did not acquire some knowledge."[13]

Although he earned little, tutoring freed him to resume attending lectures at the Royal Society and elsewhere in London, expanding his already impressive knowledge of astronomy, philosophy, and physics before again running out of funds. In the first formal writing effort of his life, he wrote a contrite letter to the Board of Excise Men to try to get his job back: "I humbly presume to entreat your honors to restore me. . . . I will endeavor that my future conduct shall as much engage your honors' approbation as my former has merited your displeasure."[14] Paine was fortunate that the dangers of tax collection had created enough vacancies to force the Board to rehire him. But it sent him to Lewes, a busy market town of just over 4,000 on the coast south of London—all but overrun by smugglers. Paine's predecessors had made stamping the rule to avoid injury and, when caught, were fired. Paine's new jurisdiction also included Brighton, a larger, even more dangerous waterside community for excise men, about ten miles west of Lewes.

"Mr. Paine might perhaps have been in the habit of smuggling, in common with his neighbors," Rickman recalled in later years. "It was the universal custom along the coast and more or less the practice of all ranks of people, from lords and ladies, ministers and magistrates, down to the cottager and laborer."[15]

Paine found instant happiness in Lewes. The bustling county seat of Sussex, Lewes was a charming old town that sat high atop the gleaming white chalk cliffs overlooking the English Channel. Its crown jewel was sturdy Bray Castle, a fortification built by one of William the Conqueror's knights in 1069, three years after the Norman landing in nearby Hastings. Lewes proved the perfect town for the gregarious Tom Paine to stroll its narrow streets, stopping to chat with friendly shopkeepers who often stood outside their doors greeting passersby and inviting them to inspect their wares. Paine found a particularly warm welcome—and lodging— with a gentle Quaker tobacconist, who could not lure Paine to the Quaker meeting, but nonetheless formed a close friendship—and helped Paine find another wife.

In March 1771, Paine married Elizabeth Olive, a Quaker ten years younger than he, but so imbued by Quaker doctrines that she insisted on practicing sexual abstinence and refused to bed by Tom's side during their first year of marriage. He finally went to live elsewhere, but never commented on their separation, and he and his wife parted amicably when Paine later left Lewes. He allowed his wife to keep all their common property, and he remained silent about their relationship the rest of his life. He never divorced his wife nor she him, but once they separated, they never saw each other again.

"It is nobody's business but my own," he snapped at anyone who pried into his marital life. "I had cause for it, but I will name it to no one."[16]

He apparently confided in Thomas Clio Rickman, like Paine a dissenting Quaker and habitual poet. "This I can assert," Rickman attested later, "that Mr. Paine always spoke tenderly and respectfully of his wife; and sent her several times pecuniary aid, without her knowing ever whence it came."[17]

Son of a Quaker brewer and innkeeper in Lewes, Rickman published political and religious pamphlets. He and Paine would remain close lifelong friends, with Rickman later moving to London to become a bookseller and author. He would be the only one of Paine's many biographers who knew Paine intimately and maintained a relationship to Paine that approximated that of Boswell with Johnson. Even during his frequent travels, Paine maintained a steady correspondence with Rickman and, indeed, left Rickman his memoirs.

Of Paine's life in Lewes, Rickman noted that, as Paine's marriage deteriorated, he grew closer to "a very respectable, sensible, and convivial set of acquaintances who were entertained with his witty sallies and informed by his more serious conversations.

> In politics he was at this time a Whig and notorious for that quality which has been defined as perseverance in a good cause and obstinacy in a bad one. He was tenacious of his opinions, which were bold, acute, and independent and which he maintained with ardor, elegance, and argument.[18]

Not anticipating Paine's future celebrity, a mutual friend of Paine and Rickman and a participant in their many discussions and poetry competitions penned these lines about Paine:

> *Immortal Paine, while mighty reasoners jar,*
> *We crown thee General of the Headstrong War;*

Thy logic vanquished error, and thy mind
No bounds but those of right and truth confined.
Thy soul of fire must sure ascend the sky,
Immortal Paine thy fame can never die;
For men like thee their names must ever save
From the black edicts of the tyrant grave.

"During his residence at Lewes," Rickman related, "Paine wrote several excellent little pieces in prose and verse, and among them a song—later celebrated—on the death of General Wolfe," beginning

In a mouldering cave where the wretched retreat,
Britannia sat wasted with care;
She mourned for her Wolfe, and exclaim'd against fate
And gave herself to despair.[19]

"It was about this time," Rickman continued, "that he wrote 'Farmer Short's Dog Porter,' in the manner of a drama—a work of exquisite wit and humor."[20] Although Paine called it a "ridiculous" tale, it was one of the first of what would be Paine's many biting attacks on government and Britain's system of justice.

Farmer Short, Paine related in rhyme, had cast a vote in parliamentary elections that had angered three local judges. To exact revenge, they ordered the farmer's dog "Porter" arrested and condemned it to hang for frightening a hare so badly that "the hare, by running hard"

Thro' hedge and ditch, without regard,
Plunged in a pond and there was drown'd.

In condemning the dog to death, the judges cited as precedent the case of a man "who fires a gun for fun" and unknowingly kills a man. "D'ye think the other mayn't be tried?" Paine asks poetically.

Most sure he must, and hang'd, because
He fired his gun against the laws;
For 't is a case most clear and plain,

Had A not shot, B hadn't been slain;
So had the dog not chased the hare,
She never had drown'd—that's clear.

This logic, rhetoric, and wit,
So nicely did the matter hit,
That Porter, though unheard was cast,
And in a halter [noose] breathed his last.
The justices adjourned to dine,
And whet their logic up with wine.[21]

Apart from bitterly sarcastic poetry, in Lewes Paine wrote short articles for the local newspaper, honing his writing skills and acquiring some notoriety as a newspaper reporter. Besides local affairs, he also involved himself in the plight of fellow excise men, winning election as their spokesman to appeal to Parliament for higher pay. Paine produced the first in what would be a lifelong production of pamphlets—none, fortunately for readers, bearing as long a title as *The Case of the Officers of Excise; with Remarks on the Qualification of Officers and of the Numerous Evils Arising to the Revenue from the Insufficiency of the Present Salary. Humbly Addressed to the Hon. and Right Hon. Members of Both Houses of Parliament.*

Paine spent the winter of 1773 in London, approaching MPs to support his petition, but he picked a bad time to do so. Parliament had once again entangled itself in problems with unhappy American colonists. Although Parliament had calmed earlier American protests in 1766 by repealing the stamp tax, enactment of the Townshend Revenue Act the following year provoked far more violent protests. The new act imposed added duties on tea, glass, lead, paper, and paint, which, except for tea, were basic products for building homes, stores, and churches and for publishing books and newspapers. British troops occupied Boston to quell the protests, only to provoke still more violence. One protest grew so violent in 1770 that troops fired on a mob, killing five civilians and wounding eight others—an encounter American newspaper headlines inflated into "The Boston Massacre."

Chastened by the Boston killings, Parliament repealed all Townshend duties except one, on tea, and again searched for ways to pay government debts and the costs of its military establishment in North America. It was in no mood, therefore, to consider Paine's petition to raise the pay of the nation's excisemen. To make matters worse, the Board of Excise Men fired him for leaving his post to go to London without its permission. Still worse: the costs of his venture left him bankrupt and facing debtors' prison.

At the time, America's Benjamin Franklin was faring no better in England. Agent in London for Pennsylvania, Massachusetts, New Jersey, and Georgia, and postmaster general for colonial America, Franklin was, in effect, acting ambassador in Britain for the American colonies. Though he lacked diplomatic credentials, he had direct contact with the most important figures in government and commerce in both lands. Siding openly with American colonists after the Boston Massacre, he infuriated Parliament by publishing a satirical polemic in the *Public Advertiser* assailing British rule in America. Calling his article "Rules by Which a Great Empire May Be Reduced to a Small One," he listed twenty rules, one of which provided that provinces "not enjoy the same common rights" as the mother country.

"However peaceably your Colonies have submitted to your Government, shown their affection . . . and patiently borne their grievances, you are to *suppose* them always inclined to revolt, and treat them accordingly," Franklin's rules stated. "Quarter Troops among them, who by their Insolence may *provoke* the rising of Mobs, and by their Bullets and Bayonets *suppress* them."[22]

Parliament responded to Franklin's biting humor by firing him as postmaster general in America.

Neither Franklin nor Paine ever explained how they met—third parties refer to "a friend" as intermediary. But meet they did, with Franklin taking an immediate liking to Paine, especially after Paine showed deep understanding of Franklin's scientific work, which he had acquired listening to Franklin's Royal Society lectures. In addition, Paine's poetry and other writing had combined with his preaching, teaching, and listening to Royal Society lectures to enrich his own conversational skills—and impress Franklin still more. Franklin had founded a "Club for Honest Whigs" and enjoyed mentoring promising young men—almost as much as he enjoyed mentoring promising young women, if for different reasons.

4. Benjamin Franklin became Thomas Paine's patron in London and helped him migrate to America.

As he had six years earlier with the brilliant young American Benjamin Rush, who was studying at Edinburgh University Medical School, Franklin introduced Paine to literary friends and other "distinguished public characters" in London.

In December 1773 Parliament abruptly dismissed Franklin after he tried defending the protests of a Boston street mob that had dressed as American Indians, boarded three ships carrying tea from England, and dumped all 342 tea chests—about forty-six tons worth $1 million—into Boston Bay.

Just as Parliament dismissed Franklin, the Board of Excise Men acted to quiet Paine by sending a sheriff to auction his possessions—his household furniture, books, even his horse. Although the proceeds kept him out of debtors' prison, he remained penniless without prospects of work. Brimming with resentment at the injustices of the Board of Excise Men, of Parliament, and, of course, the king, Paine turned to Franklin for help.

As Franklin packed to leave for America, he consoled Paine—convinced him that America would provide a more comfortable intellectual, political, and ideological home. Offering to serve as Paine's patron, he helped Paine arrange passage to America and gave Paine letters of introduction to influential Americans who might help Paine establish himself in the New World. A founder of the prestigious American Philosophical Society, Franklin wrote to a range of members on Paine's behalf—scientists, thinkers, and other prominent Philadelphians—as well as members of his own family.

"The bearer Mr. Thomas Paine," Franklin wrote to Richard Bache, his English-born son-in-law in the marine insurance business, "is very well recommended to me as an ingenious young man. . . . If you can put him in a way of obtaining employment as a clerk, or assistant tutor in a school, or assistant surveyor . . . so that he may procure subsistence at least, till he can make acquaintance and obtain knowledge of the country, you will do well and much oblige your affectionate father."[23]

Six months later, on March 4, 1775, Paine sent Franklin this letter from Philadelphia: "Your countenancing me has obtained for me many friends and much reputation, for which please accept my sincere thanks."

He went on to describe his nine-week voyage across the Atlantic as "dismal and dangerous," with an outbreak of "the putrid fever"—probably typhus—which claimed five lives. Paine himself "suffered dreadfully with the fever" and had "very little hopes that the captain or myself would live to see America."

On arrival, a prominent Philadelphia physician, learning "that I was on your recommendation, provided lodging for me and sent two of his men with a chaise to bring me ashore, for I could not at the time turn in my bed without help. I was six weeks on shore before I was well."[24]

Once afoot again, Paine sought to present himself to New Jersey's colonial governor William Franklin, Benjamin Franklin's illegitimate son, but in the governor's absence, Franklin's other friends and relatives proved more than generous:

5. Thirty-nine-year-old Thomas Paine sailed to America under the patronage of Benjamin Franklin, who gave Paine letters of introduction to influential Americans.

I have been applied to by several gentlemen to instruct their sons on very advantageous terms to myself, and a printer and bookseller here, a man of reputation and property, Robt. Aitkin, has lately attempted a magazine, but having little or no turn that way himself, he has applied to me for assistance.[25]

Philadelphia's largest printer/bookseller at the time, Aitkin had recently visited his native Scotland and returned determined to expand into publishing—a common supplementary business of successful booksellers then. Already the printer for the Continental Congress, Aitken launched a new periodical, the *Pennsylvania Magazine*, but soon found himself so burdened by work he looked to hire an editor. Paine had more credentials than most, having been an avid reader of newspapers and magazines in Britain and contributor of short articles to a newspaper in East Sussex. Aitkin hoped that Paine, as a disciple of Benjamin Franklin, might help his magazine succeed.

Dr. Benjamin Rush, Philadelphia's most prominent physician at the time, met Paine "accidentally in Mr. Aitkin's book store," Rush recalled years later. "Soon after, I read a short essay with which I was much pleased . . . against the slavery of the Africans in our country and which I was informed was written by Mr. Paine."[26]

It was not, in fact, Paine's work, having appeared in the rival *Pennsylvania Journal*—after Paine had assumed editorship of *Pennsylvania Magazine*—but it reflected Paine's views in so many ways that Rush, recalling it so many years later, mistakenly believed Paine had been the author.*

"That some desperate wretches should be willing to steal and enslave men by violence and murder for gain is rather lamentable than strange," the explosive article began. "That many civilized, nay, Christianized people should approve . . . the savage practice, is contrary . . . to every principle of Justice and Humanity." The article asked Americans to consider "with what consistency they complain so loudly of [British] attempts to enslave them while they hold so many hundred thousands in slavery and annually enslave many thousands more." The article was signed "Justice and Humanity."[27]

At the time, most, if not all, authors signed their articles with pseudonyms, which not only made libel suits difficult to initiate, they protected authors against costly legal challenges and possible injury or death in duels with irate readers. "Vox Populi," "Aesop," and others were among the signatures of articles that appeared in Pennsylvania periodicals. Readers of the most controversial often assigned them to Paine—at times

---

*A computerized author-attribution analysis by the Institute for Thomas Paine Studies at Iona College, New Rochelle, New York, has "deattributed" the article from its list of writings by Paine. Not only is the style too clumsy to have been Paine's, he would never have referred to Christianity as "our religion" or as a "divine religion." See Author's Note, Appendix A, page 273.

6. Philadelphia's popular London Coffee House, where public officials and merchants met to buy and sell slaves.

incorrectly.* Paine often stopped at the popular London Coffee House and seethed with anger—openly at times—as he watched the bidding for slaves in the street outside. Even during Thetford's unholy Assizes, he had never seen humans sold like animals, and he expressed his horror to Rush, joining the doctor as an avowed Philadelphia abolitionist.

"I did homage to his principles upon the subject of the enslaved Africans," Rush recalled. "After this Mr. Aitkin employed him as the editor of his magazine."[28]

Paine found the opportunity to edit and write full-time irresistible. As he wrote to his friend Rickman, "An army of principles will penetrate

*Paine's biographer Thomas Clio Rickman railed at "a ridiculous notion . . . that Mr. Paine wrote not the works attributed to him; or if he did not, that he was greatly assisted. This silly stuff has been generally urged by his opponents. The contrary is the fact. Mr. Paine was so tenacious on this subject that he would not alter a line or word. . . . I remember when . . . I objected to the pun 'Madjesty' as beneath him. 'Never mind,' he said, 'they say Mad Tom of me, so I shall let it stand Madjesty.'" Thomas Clio Rickman, *Life of TP*, 65n.

where an army [of soldiers] cannot. It will succeed where diplomatic management would fail. It is neither the Rhine, the Channel, nor the ocean that can arrest its progress. It will march on the horizon of the world, and it will conquer."[29]

Paine prepared to send Benjamin Franklin a copy of *Pennsylvania Magazine*, which later became *American Monthly Museum* magazine. Writing from a perch "opposite the London Coffee House Front Street," he asked Franklin to contribute "anything you may judge serviceable."

"He had not above six hundred subscribers when I first assisted him," Paine added. "We have now upwards of fifteen hundred and daily increasing. This is only the second number [issue]."[30]

Paine predicated his projections for future growth on fostering controversy, selecting articles that reflected his revolutionary thinking on a range of social and political issues. One article he published accused men of tyrannizing women. "If we take a survey of ages and of countries," its intrepid author wrote, "we shall find the women, almost—without exception—at all times and in all places, adored and oppressed."

> Man, who has never neglected an opportunity of exerting his power in paying homage to their beauty, has always availed himself of their weaknesses. He has been at once their tyrant and their slave. . . . Even among people where beauty received the highest homage, we find men who would deprive the sex of every kind of reputation: "The most virtuous woman," says a celebrated Greek, "is she who is least talked of."[31]

Ecstatic in the impenetrable cloak of anonymity that pseudonyms provided authors, Paine spurred his pen across the manuscripts he received, an eighteenth-century Quixote attacking the world's ills, editing as he saw fit, often adding a word or more of his own—usually more. Another article he edited assailed dueling as barbaric and urged "that a law be passed declaring the act of sending a challenge, or reducing a person to defend his life with sword or pistol, to be a felony; and the killing of a person in a duel, to be punished as murder."[32]

As editor, Paine was careful to balance provocation with soothing poetry and intellectually stimulating pieces on science and mechanical

7. A Philadelphia bookseller offered Paine his
first job, editing the *Pennsylvania Magazine*.

innovations that allowed readers to skip political and social issues if they
chose. Some of Paine's own articles could be dull, bordering on the absurd
at times: "Tho Nature is gay, polite, and generous," one of his bland, but
calming, pieces began, "she is sullen, rude, and niggardly at home. . . . He
that would view Nature in her undress. . . ."[33]

He could not, however, ignore the growing conflict with Britain, and,
with that in mind, he published "Thoughts on a Defensive War," in which
the anonymous author wrote, "Whoever considers the unprincipled enemy we have to cope with will not hesitate to declare that nothing but
arms or miracles can reduce them to reason and moderation." After reading the article, Paine may have added a few thoughts of his own, revealing

himself to be a Quaker who would "gladly . . . lay aside the use of arms and settle matters by negotiation; but unless the whole will . . . I take up my musket and thank heaven he has put it in my power."[34]

The article charged the British government with having "lost sight of humanity," saying that the mother country had been guilty of "spilling the blood of her children." The House of Commons, it went on, had exhorted Britain's troops "to fight, not for the defense of their natural rights, not to repel the invasion or the insults of enemies, but on the vilest of all pretenses . . . property."[35]

8. Benjamin Rush, M.D., America's most renowned physician, struck up a friendship with Thomas Paine while browsing in a Philadelphia bookstore. Rush later helped Paine write his famous pamphlet *Common Sense.*

"Thoughts on a Defensive War" caught the attention of prominent Philadelphians—secessionists, reconciliationists, and Tories alike. "African Slavery in America" drew widespread criticism and denunciation—even death threats—while most Philadelphians ignored the article calling for women's equality, finding it too absurd to warrant comment.

Paine's magazine also caught the attention of scholars at Benjamin Franklin's American Philosophical Society. They not only bought subscriptions to his magazine, they invited him to join their society, but the cost was more than he could afford. Regardless of whether they embraced Paine's magazine or dismissed it as trash, Philadelphians bought it and read articles that variously enlightened, entertained, or enraged.

In addition to essays, Paine attracted readers with inspiring patriotic poetry:

> From the east to the west blow the trumpet to arms,
>   Thro' the land let the sound of it flee;
> Let the far and the near unite with a cheer,
>   In defense of our Liberty Tree.[36]

Thomas Paine's poetry, Benjamin Rush commented, gave *Pennsylvania Magazine* "a currency few works of that kind have since had in our country."[37]

By then, as Paine had boasted to Franklin, he had built the circulation of *Pennsylvania Magazine* to 1,500. Within a year, 150,000 readers across America would await his every word.

Chapter 2

COMMON SENSE

MASSACHUSETTS WAS ALREADY AT WAR WITH BRITAIN AND THE other American colonies were debating whether to follow suit when thirty-seven-year-old Thomas Paine arrived in America in late autumn 1774. The British army had just seized the weapons of Boston's provincial government, and the Massachusetts Assembly had fled to Suffolk County, where it issued resolutions urging citizens to arm themselves and form militias. In its final, most explosive resolution in Suffolk County, it declared Massachusetts independent of Britain.

In Philadelphia, delegates from twelve colonies gathered at what was the first-ever Continental Congress and endorsed the Suffolk County resolves. To further support Massachusetts, Congress formed a colony-wide Continental Association to end trade with Britain, including slave importation, a major source of British revenues.

By then, Paine and Dr. Benjamin Rush had met several times. Bonding by their common ties to Benjamin Franklin, they found much else in common as well: both came from working-class families in small communities and had climbed intellectual peaks by intense study—much of it on their own and much of it encouraged by Benjamin Franklin. Both Rush and Paine favored a degree of separation from Great Britain as an autonomous entity within the British Empire. Paine expressed his views more harshly than Rush, calling British enslavement of white America akin to white America's enslavement of black America.

Rush delighted in introducing Paine to political figures and social reformers and to his fellow members of the American Philosophical Society.

Paine was not only brilliant, he was a great conversationalist—a delight to be with.

Although Philadelphia was America's largest city with 30,000 people* and its most important port, it was relatively small physically, stretching barely two miles in any direction and an easy walk, with doorstep visits more common than not. It was not long, therefore, before Paine knew many politicians, including members of Congress. Paine drank little, dressed well except for a sprinkle or two of snuff on his front, and expressed deep interest in what everyone he met had to say. His gentle English accent—a melodious country lilt rather than Philadelphia's (or London's) harsh city twang—infused his words with poetic rhythms that mesmerized listeners, while his outsized nose and broad, ever-present smile gave him the appearance of a lovable clown. He had, though, one irritating habit—to some—of seldom pausing to let others respond, but most of his audience embraced what he had to say on a wide range of subjects.

In April 1775, George III ordered British troops into Boston "to arrest the principal actors and abettors in the Provincial Congress." His order dashed hopes of Paine, Rush, and other reconciliationists who had hoped the crown would grant American colonies autonomy within the British Empire. Empowered by the king's order, British troops set out from Boston to nearby Lexington where two "principal actors" in the Boston uprising—merchant-king John Hancock and activist Samuel Adams—had fled. From there the troops were to march on Concord where Patriot rebels had amassed an arsenal of weapons and ammunition.

Seven hundred British troops stomped into Lexington, where 200 locals—almost half the town's population—awaited on the village green shouldering muskets. Calling themselves "Minutemen," they ranged in age from sixteen to sixty-five and included eight pairs of fathers and sons, all farmers who stood side by side facing the dreaded redcoats. When a few Minutemen broke ranks and ran for cover behind nearby stone walls, the British moved in. Amidst the confusion and shouting that followed,

---

*In contrast, New York had 25,000 people, Boston 16,000, and Charleston 12,000. In Europe, London's population was 650,000 and that of Paris 560,000.

what a poet would later call "the shot heard 'round the world" rang out,* provoking a hail of gunfire from all directions. When the firing ended, eighteen Minutemen lay on the soft cold grass; eight dead, ten wounded. Although Minutemen injured only one British soldier, their shots triggered a revolution that would eventually send the world's greatest empire into irreversible decline.

The slaughter at Lexington outraged most Americans—none more than the continent's newest Patriot, Thomas Paine. "Britain is the parent country, say some," Paine raged. "Then the more shame on her conduct. Even brutes do not devour their young nor savages war on their families."

> No man was a warmer wisher for reconciliation than myself before the fatal nineteenth of April 1775, but the moment the event of that day was made known, I rejected . . . England forever and disdained the wretch that with the pretended title of FATHER OF HIS PEOPLE can unfeelingly hear of their slaughter and composedly sleep with their blood upon his soul.[1]

Rush agreed, admitting he had been a mere "spectator" to events before the shots at Lexington. "The battle of Lexington gave a new tone to my feelings," he asserted. "I considered the separation of the colonies from Great Britain inevitable."[2]

Nor did the exchange on Lexington Green end the fighting that day. British troops went on to Concord to find and destroy a Patriot arsenal. After an extensive search, the British commander concluded that Patriots had removed most of the weapons, and he ordered his men to return to Boston. On the way, they met a growing rain of sniper fire. Minuteman ranks had swelled into the thousands. Musket barrels materialized behind every tree, boulder, and stone wall, threatening the British with annihilation. The humiliated British troops wreaked revenge as they retreated to Boston, looting and burning houses, bayoneting anyone who stood in their way, civilian or military.

---

*The words are from "Concord Hymn," a poem by Ralph Waldo Emerson for the 1837 dedication of a monument commemorating the April 19, 1775, Battle of Concord, which followed the Lexington encounter.

"The same tyranny which drove the first emigrants from home pursues their descendants still," Paine railed.

> To say that reconciliation is our duty is truly farcical. The last cord now is broken. . . . There are injuries which nature cannot forgive; she would cease to be nature if she did. As well can the lover forgive the ravisher of his mistress, as the continent forgive the murderers of Britain.[3]

In the end, the British had no choice but to continue retreating back to Boston, which at the time was a near-island in Boston Bay, connected to the mainland by only a narrow strip of land called Boston Neck. Four days after Concord, the provincial assembly voted to raise an army of 13,600 men to lay siege to Boston. Within a month, Rhode Island, Connecticut, and New Hampshire had sent 8,500 men to join Massachusetts Minutemen on the hills surrounding Boston, leaving the British no clear escape from the town except by sea.

Three weeks later, a Second Continental Congress met in Philadelphia, with Massachusetts delegate John Adams proposing that Congress broaden the geographic participation of the forces laying siege to Boston. He convinced Congress to incorporate the troops into a "Continental Army" and appoint Virginia's George Washington as commander in chief. After Congress agreed, Washington set out for Boston.

Two days later—long before Washington could reach Boston—British troops there attacked a weak point in the American line, landing 2,400 troops on Charlestown peninsula across the bay and staging a bayonet charge up Breed's Hill and onto adjacent Bunker Hill. Although the British seized both hilltops and annihilated their American defenders, the victory proved all but meaningless, costing more than 1,000 British soldiers their lives—a disproportionately high number of them officers.

Two weeks later, when Washington arrived to take command of American troops, their number had grown to 14,500, positioned in an almost impenetrable ring on the hills surrounding Boston. Early in 1776, it became absolutely impenetrable after Colonel (later Major General) Henry Knox and his men moved forty-three cannon and sixteen mortars onto the heights surrounding Boston—enough to annihilate British forces in the city below.

9. After Massachusetts declared war with the British, the Second Continental Congress appointed Virginia's George Washington to assume command of a combined Continental Army in America's War of Independence.

With Washington's military advantage evident to all, one of Pennsylvania's political and social leaders, John Dickinson, convinced Congress to send King George an "Olive Branch Petition." A Quaker by birth, Dickinson expressed his hopes for restoring harmony with the king's government, reaffirmed American loyalty to the king, and pleaded with the king to prevent any more hostile acts by Parliament.

Paine scoffed at Dickinson's flirtation with the king, calling on "the warmest advocate for reconciliation to show a single advantage that this continent can reap, by being connected with Great Britain." He said American corn and other produce would "fetch its price" in any European market without British help. Mouthing a policy that would guide America for more than a century to follow, Paine argued that "the injuries we sustain by that connection are without number."

> Any submission to, or dependence on Great Britain tends directly to involve this continent in European wars and quarrels and sets us at variance with nations who would otherwise seek our friendship. . . . As Europe is our market for trade, we ought to form no partial connection with any part of it. It is the true interest of America to steer clear of European contentions, which she never can do . . . by her dependence on Britain.[4]

By the end of 1775, however, Paine and other advocates of independence had failed to change the minds of hard-core reconciliationists. The two sides had reached a stalemate—as had American and British military forces.

"I had put some thoughts on paper upon this subject and was preparing an address to the inhabitants of the colonies," Dr. Benjamin Rush recalled in his memoirs written long after Paine's death. Rush claimed that he had feared repercussions of such an article on his medical practice and turned to Paine, who had "nothing to fear from the popular odium to which such a publication might expose him. Paine could live anywhere, but my profession and connections tied me to Philadelphia where a great majority of the citizens and some of my friends were hostile to a separation from Great Britain and forbad me to come forward as a pioneer in that controversy."

Paine "readily assented to the proposal," Rush recalled, "and from time to time called at my house and read to me every proposed chapter of the proposed pamphlet as he composed it."[5]

"They cannot govern us," Paine insisted as he read the words he had written to Rush:

> To be always running three or four thousand miles with a tale or a petition, waiting four or five months for an answer, which when obtained requires five or six more to explain it . . . [is] folly and childishness. . . . Small islands not capable of protecting themselves are the proper objects for kingdoms to take under their care, but there is something absurd in supposing

a continent to be perpetually governed by an island. In no instance hath nature made the satellite larger than its primary planet. . . . England and America . . . belong to different systems: England to Europe, America to itself.[6]

Rush said he was so enthralled by Paine's writing that he urged Paine to send copies to Benjamin Franklin, to Samuel Adams, one of the instigators of the Boston uprisings, and to astronomer/mathematician David Rittenhouse, who had enormous influence over Philadelphia's intellectual community. Less outspoken than Samuel Adams, Rittenhouse was nonetheless "a friend to American independence." Adams, an excitable rabble-rouser out of Harvard, was enthusiastic, calling reconciliationists "puling, pusillanimous cowards"[7] and praising Paine for simplifying his language to permit ordinary Americans to understand complex political concepts.

Rush claimed that after reading Paine's finished work, he—Rush— had suggested changing its name from *Plain Truth* to *Common Sense.* He then sent Paine to see "a certain Thomas Bell, a Scottish printer and bookseller of a singular character . . . a thoughtless and fearless Whig and an open friend to independence. In a few weeks his [Paine's] pamphlet made its appearance."[8]

Common Sense exploded off the press, its words and phrases spreading gale-like across the American landscape, sweeping away centuries-old beliefs, collapsing pillars of western European social and political structure. Demand for the pamphlet outpaced the first printer's ability to produce it. A second printer went into action, then a third. Together, they sold 150,000 copies within a year. Everyone seemed to want a copy: political leaders, clergymen, merchants, bankers, farmers, tavern keepers and their drunken clients—even some who couldn't read. Those who could often stood in taverns reading it to their less literate companions. A black market developed, with two-penny copies selling for more than ten times that amount. After two years, at least 500,000 copies were circulating in America, Britain, France, and other parts of western Europe. More eyes pored over *Common Sense* when it appeared than any printed work besides the Bible. It was the greatest publishing success of the eighteenth century and, in many ways, the most important publishing event since Martin Luther's *95 Theses* provoked the Reformation.

Common Sense proposed a second Reformation—political rather than religious. Even Henry VIII, who diluted Roman Catholic Church power by substituting his own archbishop for the Pope, had not dared undermine the belief that God had placed him and other monarchs on their thrones. Paine argued that God had had nothing to do with it. In effect, he pronounced a heresy of the highest order. The majority of common and uncommon folk of every rank and order, in every palace, church, and home, feared God might strike them dead if they dared think thoughts other than those prescribed by church and crown. All had routinely accepted ignominies and injuries inflicted by church and state as God's will. Paine now addressed them as no one else in history, beginning with a warm, comforting, and reassuring introduction directed at "the good people of this country."

Recognizing that they were "grievously oppressed" by the King of England and Parliament, he assured them that they were "not alone in their suffering . . . the principles of all Lovers of Mankind are affected." In blasphemous language that left readers gasping, Paine called King George III a "royal brute" for "desolating the country with fire and sword [and] declaring war against the natural rights of all mankind."[9]

Challenging the king's right to rule America, Paine exposed as myth the concept of divine right of kings, the foundation of British and western European society for the previous millennium and a principle he called "the most barefaced falsity ever imposed upon mankind." The history of England contradicted it, he argued, in the continual "contest for monarchy and succession. . . ."

"Monarchy and succession have laid . . . the world in blood and ashes," he declared. "'Tis a form of government which the Word of God bears testimony against." If divine right of kings existed, he suggested, God would have chosen the best monarch rather than permit a bloodbath between rival candidates for the same throne—many of them brothers.[10]

Paine attacked monarchy as no man before him, calling it "ridiculous" and saying the king is "shut from the world" in his palace, "yet the business of the king requires him to know it thoroughly. . . . In the early ages of the world . . . there were no kings; the consequence of which was there were no wars."[11] He called the first kings "the principal ruffians of some restless gang, whose savage manners . . . obtained titles of chief among plunderers." Citing William the Conqueror, the first English king of sorts, Paine called him "a French bastard" who had landed at Hastings "with an armed banditti" and seized control of England "against the consent of the natives." The Norman Conquest, he said, "hath no divinity in it."[12]

Paine went on to assail hereditary succession as evil and absurd:

> Did it ensure a race of good and able wise men, it would have the seal of divine authority, but as it opens the door to the foolish, the wicked, and the improper, it hath in it the nature of oppression. Men who look upon themselves as born to reign and others to obey soon grow insolent.[13]

No one had ever written what Paine wrote in quite the way he wrote it. England's John Locke had hinted at the same a century earlier, but in language incomprehensible to any but learned scholars. Geneva's Jean-Jacques Rousseau had also assailed divine right of kings only a little more than a decade before *Common Sense*, and, although Paine said he had never read Locke, he had studied Rousseau's *The Social Contract* and borrowed much from it.

"L'homme est né libre, et partout il est dans les fers," Rousseau had charged in the opening words of *Le contrat social [The Social Contract]*. "Man is born free, but everywhere he is in chains." But Rousseau failed to show how to break such chains, proposing only that man should subject himself to "the general will" rather than royal rule—in effect, a dictatorship of the majority. As Paine put it, Rousseau had left "the mind in love with an object [liberty] without describing the means of possessing it."[14]

Although Rousseau conceded the inevitability of revolution, neither he nor Locke openly advocated it. Indeed, Locke was a staunch defender of the monarchy, advocating reforms only to check the monarch's power, not to overthrow him. Paine called for outright overthrow of the monarch and an end to monarchy, citing as his reasons "simple facts, plain arguments, and common sense.[15]

"The blood of the slain, the weeping voice of nature cries, 'TIS TIME TO PART,"[16] he thundered. Echoing Patrick Henry's stirring call to battle of a year earlier, Paine told Americans, "Resolution is our inherent character, and courage hath never yet forsaken us." Then, as Patrick Henry had done, Paine asked, "Wherefore, what is it that we want? Why is it that we hesitate?"

> From Britain we can expect nothing but ruin. . . . O ye that love mankind! Ye that dare oppose not only the tyranny but the tyrant, stand forth! Nothing can settle our affairs so expeditiously as an open and determined declaration for independence. . . . A government of our own is our natural right! [17]

Unlike Rousseau, Voltaire, Locke, and even Patrick Henry, Paine purposely left his name off the document, because, as he put it, "the object of attention is the doctrine not the man," and as he stated when he opened his discourse, the cause of Americans was "the cause of all mankind." He signed his pamphlet "Common Sense."

Although many Europeans embraced much of what Paine had to say—as they had embraced Rousseau—printers in France and other absolute monarchies "did not dare to publish . . . that monarchy is unlawful by the Old Testament," as Paine charged, reminding the world, as he had reminded his parents years earlier, "The Lord shall rule over you"—not the king.

French printers categorized it under "Affaires de l'Angleterre et de l'Amérique" ["British and American Affairs"] and called elements of it products of excessive "republican zeal."[18]

To demonstrate his devotion to "republican zeal," however, Paine instructed Thomas Bell and his other printers to funnel profits from American sales of *Common Sense* to Congress to help pay for the war.

Paine's simple words were those of a commoner—silent until then in the British and, indeed, the American worlds, where noblemen and landed gentry ruled. But America, if not Britain, he said, had progressed:

> America has now outgrown the state of infancy. Her strength and commerce make large advances to manhood, and science, in all its branches, has not only blossomed, but even ripened upon the soil. The cottages, as it were, of yesterday have grown to villages, and villages to cities. And while proud antiquity . . . parades the streets of other nations, their genius . . . comes hither.[19]

Common Sense shook the American, British, and European political worlds as words had seldom done, stirring functionaries, workers, farmers and other common folk, as well as political and religious leaders who had favored reconciliation. Men read it in their clubs, teachers read it to students, churchmen read it from their pulpits instead of sermons. And Benjamin Franklin, Thomas Jefferson, John Adams, Roger Sherman, and Robert Livingston all read it in preparing the final draft of the America's Declaration of Independence in June 1776. Few if any had ever thought of, let alone discussed, the questions Paine raised.

"I have heard it asserted by some," Paine argued, "that, as America hath flourished under her former connection with Great Britain, that the same connection is necessary towards her future happiness. We may as well assert that because a child has thrived upon milk, that it is never to have meat. . . . The commerce by which she hath enriched herself includes the necessaries of life and will always have a market while eating is the custom of Europe."[20]

Paine went on to scoff at arguments based on America's filial ties to Britain, saying simply: "It happens not to be true." He said, "the phrase *parent* or *mother country* hath been . . . adopted by the king and his parasites" to lure the gullible masses into unnatural fealty. "Europe, and not England, is the parent country of America," he declared.

The new world hath been the asylum for the persecuted lovers of civil and religious liberty from *every part* of Europe. Hither have they fled, not from the tender embraces of the mother, but from the cruelty of the monster. . . . We claim brotherhood with every European Christian.[21]

"Not even one-third of the inhabitants even of this province are of English descent," he reminded readers. Indeed, Benjamin Franklin had complained twenty-five years earlier, "Pennsylvania will in a few years become a German colony." As Paine wrote, there were upwards of 100,000 Germans in Pennsylvania, and half the population south of New England was of non-English stock.[22]

"I reprobate the phrase of parent or mother country applied to England only as being false, selfish, narrow, and ungenerous," Paine went on. "The first king of England (William the Conqueror) was a French-man. . . . By the same method of reasoning, England ought to be governed by France."[23]

Paine dared reconciliationists to present "a single advantage" to remaining tied to Britain. "But the injuries and disadvantages we sustain by that connection are without number." Any tie to Britain, he maintained, would involve America in European wars and quarrels and create unnecessary enemies who might otherwise be valuable trading partners. "Monarchical governments are never long at rest," Paine pointed out. "Europe is too thickly planted with kingdoms to be long at peace, and whenever war breaks out between England and any foreign power, the trade of America goes to ruin. . . . Neutrality would be safer."[24]

Calling Europe "our market for trade," Paine argued that any connection with Britain or any other nation would necessarily damage relations with other nations. George Washington would adopt Paine's words in formulating foreign policy as President of the United States in the 1790s.

But *Common Sense* was not about trade; it was a call to action, and America responded appropriately. Thousands who had favored reconciliation either changed their minds or held their tongues. As George Washington put it, "The sound doctrine and unanswerable reasoning . . . in *Common Sense* will not leave numbers at a loss to decide upon the propriety of a separation. . . . *Common Sense* is working a powerful change in the minds of men."[25]

As if to second Washington, Thomas Paine had written, "The sun never shined on a cause of greater worth. Everything that is right or reasonable pleads for separation."[26]

In London, members of Parliament read it and prepared for war. Even the king read it—only six months after refusing to read Dickinson's Olive Branch Petition. The monarch grew so enraged he ordered Parliament to strip Paine of his British citizenship.

Paine laughed, warning the king that America had at its command "the largest body of armed and disciplined men of any power under heaven."[27]

No single colony is able to support itself, but the whole, when united, can accomplish the matter. . . . Debts we have none. . . . Can we but leave posterity with a settled form of government, an independent constitution of its own, the purchase at any price will be cheap.[28]

Paine called on Congress to build a navy: "We ought to view the building of a fleet as an article of commerce . . . and protection. . . . No country on the globe is so happily situated or so internally capable of raising a fleet as America. Tar, timber, iron, and cordage are her natural produce. We need go abroad for nothing. . . . Hemp flourishes. . . . Our iron is superior to that of other countries. Our small arms equal any in the world. Cannon we can cast at pleasure. Saltpeter and gunpowder we are every day producing."[29]

Some called Paine reckless for building American expectations of easy victory. In fact, British commanders in America had enormous advantages with a well-equipped, well-trained, disciplined professional army and the support of the world's largest navy. The British could also count on fierce support from American Loyalists—about 20 percent of the white population at the time. The only disadvantages the British faced in trying to put down the American rebellion were their distance from Britain, the inexperience of their troops in the vastness and variety of the American wilderness, and the tendency of British officers to look with disdain on and underestimate the skills of Patriot citizen-soldiers.

Paine persisted in warning against any form of reconciliation, and Americans rallied about him—more so after a group of local farmers thwarted British attempts to land troops in North Carolina. At the end of February, a well-organized, well-armed Loyalist force in North Carolina had marched eastward to rendezvous with British troops landing at the port of Wilmington. A band of Patriot farmers armed only with outdated muskets waited in the thick forest surrounding the narrow Moore's Creek Bridge. As the Loyalists began to cross, the Patriots sprang from behind the trees and all but annihilated the Tories.

The victory at Moore's Creek Bridge drew tens of thousands of undecided colonists and reconciliationists into the fight for independence. News that more British ships had sailed from Britain toward Charleston to subjugate the South with German mercenaries further alienated Americans—especially in southern colonies, which had sought to stay aloof from the conflict that had enveloped distant New England.

Before ending his appeal in *Common Sense*, Paine proposed a new form of decentralized republican government for Americans, suggesting that an elected "continental conference" draw up a "continental charter," comparable to Britain's Magna Carta. The charter would leave most governance to the states and establish a new, elected Continental Congress responsible for national defense and elements of foreign affairs common to all states. The continental charter would also "secure freedom and property to all men, and . . . the free exercise of religion."

> But where, say some, is the King of America? I'll tell you, friend, he reigns above and doth not make havoc of mankind like the Royal Brute of Britain. . . . In America, THE LAW IS KING. For as in absolute governments the king is law, so in free countries, the law ought to be king and there ought to be no other.[30]

Instead of a signature, Paine ended *Common Sense* with a call for every American "to hold out to his neighbor the hearty hand of friendship and . . . bury in forgetfulness every former dissention."

> Let the names of Whig and Tory be extinct and let none other be heard among us than those of *a good citizen and resolute friend, and a virtuous supporter of the* RIGHTS *of* MANKIND *and of the* FREE AND INDEPENDENT STATES OF AMERICA.[31]

Many readers assumed Benjamin Franklin had written the unsigned pamphlet and its stirring final words. Others were certain the author could only be the Harvard-educated John Adams, of Massachusetts.

Paine sent the first copy of *Common Sense* to Franklin, who had now returned to Philadelphia. John Adams bought two copies, one for himself, the other to send to his wife, Abigail, at their farm outside Boston. By then, Franklin was calling Paine "my adopted political son," with Paine responding warmly, respectfully, and with reverence.

To Paine's—and Franklin's—annoyance, Philadelphia's Quaker leaders openly rejected *Common Sense*. They saw taking up arms—even against oppressive British rule—to be a violation of their pacifist beliefs. Quakers represented nearly half the state's population of about 500,000.

Astonished by their stand, Paine wrote a five-page addendum to *Common Sense*, scolding his Quaker critics for presuming to speak for "the whole body of Quakers . . . without proper authority for so doing" and for "dabbling in [political] matters which the professed Quietude of your Principles instruct you not to meddle with."

In explaining his call to arms, Paine said, "We feel for the ruined and insulted sufferers . . . with a degree of tenderness that hath not yet made its way into some of your bosoms."

> If the bearing of arms be sinful, the first going to war must be more so. . . . If ye really preach from conscience . . . convince the world thereof by proclaiming your doctrine to our enemies, *for they likewise bear ARMS*. Had ye the honest soul . . . you would preach repentance to *your* king; ye would tell the Royal Wretch his sins and warn him of eternal ruin. Ye would not spend your partial invectives against the injured.[32]

What Paine did not—indeed, could not—know at the time was that many of the Quaker leaders who called on their co-religionists to remain loyal to the British crown were in fact Loyalist spies, informers, and propagandists.

"The Quakers especially, are accused of rendering all sorts of services to the British army," Gérard de Rayneval would report to the French foreign minister two years later, when he became the French government's first minister to America.[33]

The Quakers, of course, were not alone in rejecting *Common Sense*. As Rayneval reported, "Scarcely one-quarter of the ordinary inhabitants of Philadelphia . . . favor the cause of independence. Commercial and family ties . . . seem to account for this."[34]

One Tory leader—the influential University of Pennsylvania president Rev. William Smith—guessed from the style of writing that Paine was author of *Common Sense*, and he attacked it as the "foul pages of interested writers and strangers intermeddling in our affairs." In a letter he addressed to "the People of Pennsylvania" in the *Pennsylvania Gazette*, Smith called for an end to American resistance. Signing his letter "Cato," he declared it evident "that the true interest of America lies in *reconciliation* with Great Britain on *constitutional principles*."

Upon such a footing, we may again be happy. Our trade will be revived. Our husbandmen, our mechanics, our artificers will flourish. Our language, our laws, and manners being the same with those of the nation with which we are again to be connected, that connection will be natural. . . . We have long flourished under our charter government. What may be the consequences of another form we cannot pronounce with certainty; but this we know: that it is a road we have not traveled and may be worse than it is described.[35]

Paine responded to Cato with four angry letters signed by the pseudonymous "Forester."

"To be nobly wrong is more manly than to be meanly right," Paine replied in his first "Forester" letter. "Remember, thou hast thrown me the glove, Cato, and either thee or I must retire. I fear not the field of fair debate. But thou hast . . . made it personal." Paine characterized Cato's letters as "gorged with absurdity, confusion, contradiction, and the most notorious and willful falsehood."

The present war differs from every other . . . that it is not carried under the prerogative of the crown . . . but under the authority of Parliament. It follows that even the King of England . . . could not ratify . . . a reconciliation, because . . . the King could not . . . repeal *acts* of Parliament. . . . There is no body of men more jealous of their privileges than the Commons: Because they sell them! Mark that, Cato.[36]

Cato, however, was not Paine's only critic.

John Adams, the fervent Massachusetts advocate of independence, warned that "'Common Sense,' by his crude, ignorant notion of a government by one assembly, will do more mischief in dividing the Friends of Liberty than all the Tory writings together.

"He is a keen writer but very ignorant of the science of government,"[37] Adams wrote in a pamphlet he called *Thoughts on Government*, originally written for the North Carolina Assembly after it had voted to declare independence from Britain and then sought Adams's guidance in establishing a government.[38]

10. An early admirer of Paine, John Adams, exclaimed, "I know not whether any man in the world has had more influence on its inhabitants or its affairs . . . than Tom Paine."

In reply to Paine, Adams agreed that a popularly elected government was essential to liberty, but warned that the sovereign unicameral legislature Paine had suggested in *Common Sense* was as susceptible to corruption and imperious action as any sovereign monarch. In a nation as "extensive" as America, Adams insisted, only a government with powers distributed among multiple branches limited by automatic checks and balances could ensure success for republican government. He suggested a bicameral legislature, an independent judiciary, and an executive armed with veto powers over legislation.

Adams's criticisms did little to discourage sales of *Common Sense*, however, or, for that matter, the warmth that had developed between the two men by then. Indeed, Adams joined Benjamin Franklin and Benjamin

Rush in writing glowing letters of introduction for Paine to influential figures in New York, where Paine went in mid-February 1776 to convince the provincial legislature to support the independence movement. By then, Massachusetts, North Carolina, South Carolina, and Georgia had authorized their delegates to the Continental Congress to vote for independence, with Virginia on the verge of following suit.

On March 17, British troops in Boston began boarding ships in the harbor and, ten days later, with about 1,000 Loyalists aboard, they abandoned the city, burned harbor fortifications, and sailed off to Halifax, Canada. Their departure left Massachusetts the first American colony free of British rule and gave General Washington and his Continental Army their first signature victory in America's War of Independence. Washington quickly pressed his advantage and marched about 10,000 troops 200 miles to the southwest to seize the important port city of New York.

Convinced for the first time that America's Continental Army could defeat the British and win the War of Independence, the Second Continental Congress convened in Philadelphia and on April 6 opened American ports to ships of all nations save Britain. On May 15, Congress urged all the American colonies to end royal rule and voted to seek military and financial aid from France, whose loss of Canada to the British in the Seven Years' War had left the French government lusting for revenge. Citing Paine's *Common Sense*, Virginia's Richard Henry Lee argued that neither France nor any other foreign country would provide aid unless America declared independence and transformed itself into a sovereign nation, able to deal reciprocally with other nations.

On June 7, therefore, he stood in Congress and resolved that the United Colonies "are and of right ought to be free and independent states, that they are absolved from all allegiance to the British Crown, and that all political connection between them and the state of Great Britain is, and ought to be, dissolved."[39]

A month later, on July 2, Congress agreed.

At that very moment, however, British transports were sailing into New York Bay with 10,000 troops. A month later their number had expanded to more than 30,000, and a month after that 20,000 of them poured onto Long Island, killing or wounding nearly one-third of Washington's army, taking two American field generals prisoner, and capturing most of the Continental Army's food supply. As thousands of American troops fled, Washington and his aides galloped off to the blare of British buglers sounding the call of hunters on a fox chase. "I never felt such a sensation before," said a Washington aide. "It seemed to crown our disgrace."[40]

Convinced they had crushed the impudent Americans, the British commanders, Major General Sir William Howe and his brother Admiral Lord Richard Howe, sent one of their captive American generals to Philadelphia with orders to Congress to revoke the Declaration of Independence and collectively swear allegiance to Britain. In the minds of the British high command, America's War of Independence was over.

Thomas Paine disagreed. Violating every principle of his Quaker heritage but determined to free America from the tyranny of monarchy, he picked up a musket for the first time in his life and galloped out of Philadelphia to confront the British army on the battlefield.

Chapter 3

THE TIMES THAT
TRIED MEN'S SOULS

T HOMAS PAINE BELIEVED HIS PEN WAS MIGHTIER THAN ANY SWORD, but the Declaration of Independence by Congress on July 4, 1776, inspired him to put aside his pen and defy his Quaker teachings by trying to wield a sword—or in his case, a musket. On July 9, before Washington's disastrous defeat in Brooklyn, Paine had volunteered for action with a Pennsylvania "flying camp" to fight and, if he had to, die for liberty.

Designed to "fly" as needed from one battle to another to support fellow troops, Paine's unit marched to reinforce defenses at Amboy (now Perth Amboy) New Jersey, opposite the southern tip of Staten Island, where British transports without number were sailing by and landing thousands upon thousands of troops on the northern shore of the island by New York Bay.

His commander had assigned Paine to estimate the size of British forces, and the author of *Common Sense* spent a month counting masts. He estimated the number of ships at more than 350, with the probable number of troops they discharged upwards of 30,000—more than enough, he feared, to annihilate Washington's little army of less than 10,000.

On August 27, Paine's fears became reality when 20,000 British and Hessian troops crossed the bay and stormed ashore in Brooklyn on southwestern Long Island, where the British all but annihilated the Patriot army. Only a thick nocturnal fog allowed a few thousand survivors to escape across the East River to New York Island (Manhattan) on August 29. Washington had posted the Connecticut militia to guard against a

British landing there and moved the main body of his troops to Harlem Heights, about six miles to the north. On the morning of September 15, five British ships sailed up the East River and pounded American emplacements. Within hours, 6,000 of the 8,000-man Connecticut militia standing guard against a British landing sprinted to the rear without firing a shot.

"Good God," Washington cried out. "Are these the men with which I am to defend America?"[1]

Meanwhile, Congress had responded to what they misinterpreted as an offer of a cease-fire by the British high command. It appointed the venerable Benjamin Franklin to go to Staten Island with John Adams and Edmund Rutledge of South Carolina to talk peace, only to have the Howe brothers demand revocation of the Declaration of Independence as a precondition to any talks. The three emissaries stomped out and returned to Philadelphia.

With the British too occupied in New York to bother attacking Amboy, Paine's flying camp of Pennsylvanians—those who didn't desert—moved northward to join Major General Nathanael Greene, who was organizing defenses at Fort Lee, New Jersey—a seemingly impregnable perch atop a sheer rock wall on the west bank of the Hudson River opposite New York Island (Manhattan).

Greene and Paine bonded immediately, with Greene naming Paine his aide-de-camp. They had much in common. Greene, like Paine, was a disaffected Quaker, a believer in a single, universal God and deeply suspicious of organized religion. And, like Paine, Greene had had but a smattering of schooling in his early years, but so regretted his lack of formal education that he became a voracious reader, accumulating a library of more than 250 books. Like Paine, Greene devoured the sciences, Roman and Greek history, political philosophy, and the law.

Unlike Paine, though, Greene came from a family of wealth and influence. One of six sons of Nathanael Greene, Sr., the amiable owner-founder of Nathanael Greene & Co., the younger Greene had grown up on a 200-acre farm in Greenwich, Rhode Island, across the bay from Newport. The Greenes were descendants of Rhode Island's original Quaker settlers who, led by Roger Williams, fled persecution by the Massachusetts theocracy.

11. Rhode Island merchant Major General Nathanael Greene was Thomas Paine's first military
commander and became one of Paine's close friends.

A devout Quaker, Nathanael Greene's father built a business empire that
included a forge and anchor works, a sawmill, warehouse and store, transport ships, and a commercial wharf—in addition to his farm.

In the winter of 1772, a British revenue schooner, the *Gaspée*, intercepted and seized one of Greene's transport vessels that was attempting to
smuggle twelve hogsheads* of West Indies rum into Rhode Island without
paying the required duty.

On June 10, a mob of five dozen Rhode Islanders (said to have been
paid by Greene) retaliated by burning the *Gaspée* after it ran aground near
Warwick. Greene compounded the British loss by suing the commander
of the *Gaspée* for illegal seizure of his (Greene's) transport vessel and its
cargo. He won a judgment of £600 in a Pawtucket court.

---

*A hogshead was a barrel with a capacity of about sixty-five gallons.

The loss of his ship and its cargo turned Nathanael Greene and his sons into active secessionists, with the soon-to-be-general, Nathanael Greene, Jr., helping to organize and lead a 1,000-man Rhode Island militia. Renamed the Army of Rhode Island, it marched to Boston to join George Washington's troops besieging the British occupation force. Promoted to general in the Continental Army, Greene merged his troops with Washington's army on the march to New York.

With his troop strength diminishing after the Brooklyn defeat, Washington sent Greene to Fort Lee, New Jersey, to recruit reinforcements while the main army withdrew from Manhattan northward to the Westchester County mainland. It was on his recruiting venture that Greene met Paine and named him his aide-de-camp—and, *ex officio*, his constant companion and friend. For Greene, like many others, to meet Paine was to form a warm and lasting friendship.

Meanwhile, British troops had anticipated Washington's retreat from Manhattan and attacked at White Plains. The Americans fled in disorder in three directions, with Washington leading a contingent of about 5,000 westward across the Hudson River to Fort Lee, where, by then, Greene and Paine had assembled a 2,500-man force.

"The enemy knowing the divided state of our army, conceived the design of penetrating into the Jersies," Paine wrote in the first of many dispatches he would send from the field to Philadelphia's *Pennsylvania Journal.* "Accordingly a large body of British and Hessian troops crossed the North [Hudson] River and landed about six miles above the fort [Fort Lee]. As our force was inferior to that of the enemy . . . the garrison was ordered to march."[2]

Like all of Paine's dispatches, he signed it "Common Sense."

As 6,000 enemy troops disembarked a few miles north, Greene's and Washington's combined force fled southward toward Newark.

"Finding their numbers greatly superior," Washington lamented to John Hancock, then-president of Congress, "it was thought prudent to withdraw our men. . . . We lost the whole of the cannon that was at the Fort, except two twelve pounders, and a great deal of baggage—between two and three hundred tents—about a thousand barrels of flour and other stores in the Quarter Master's department."[3]

In fact, the fall of Fort Lee combined with previous losses across the Hudson to cost Washington 3,000 troops (by desertion), forty-six cannons, 2,800 muskets, and tens of thousands of rounds of ammunition along with countless other supplies. Still worse, the Americans lost almost all their tools. Even if Washington's remaining troops chose to make a stand, they would have had nothing but their bare hands to build earthworks or other defensive positions.

A British officer at Fort Lee confirmed Washington's losses, adding gleefully that he had also found "some poor pork, a few greasy proclamations, and some of that scoundrel Common Sense man's letters, which we can read at our leisure, now that we have got one of the 'impregnable redoubts' of Mr. Washington's to quarter in."[4]

With winter approaching and the British in close pursuit, Washington's men staggered southward through sheets of icy autumn rains into Newark, where they encamped for the night. With British troops only two hours to the rear and fast approaching, the men of two brigades stunned Washington, Greene, and Paine by declaring their enlistment periods at an end. With that they promptly fled the camp and returned to their homes. The Continental Army that remained counted barely 3,000 men to carry on the War of Independence.

"The fortune of our arms was now at its lowest ebb," Paine wrote to the *Pennsylvania Journal*. "The number of the enemy was at least 8,000, exclusive of their artillery and light horse. . . . Our army, never more than 4,000, at one time [numbered] less than a thousand effective men.

"The retreat," he continued, "was censured by some as pusillanimous and disgraceful, but did they know . . . that this handful of Americans retreated slowly above 80 miles without losing a dozen men—and that suffering themselves to be forced into action would have been their entire destruction—did they know this they would never have censured it at all. They would have called it prudent. Posterity will call it glorious."[5]

That night in Newark, Paine sat by a fire, a drum wedged between his knees on which to write. All but trembling with rage, he began to pen a message he hoped would lift public morale and encourage the remaining troops to continue fighting. It would not be easy to write so complex a message in simple terms that all could understand, but *Common Sense* had not been easy and had nonetheless inspired tens of thousands of Americans to take up arms. Now he needed a message to keep them from throwing down their arms.

By then, wear and weather had left most of the remaining troops in rags, their shoes or boots worn thin or through. Those who could find blankets or even scraps of thick cloth wrapped themselves as best they could or huddled against a comrade or two to try to keep warm in the insistent autumn rain. Besides the dead or captured, sickness left 500 unfit for duty. Of seventeen officers in one regiment, only five stood fit enough to fight.

"I believe most men have more courage than they know of," Paine explained to *Pennsylvania Journal* readers. "I knew the time when I thought that the whistling of a cannon ball would have frightened me to death, but I have since tried it and find that I can stand it with little discomposure."[6]

From Newark, Washington's army retreated south to Brunswick, where he expected the New Jersey militia to reinforce his army, but when it failed to appear, Washington's hopes for victory all but collapsed. He had no choice but to retreat westward toward Trenton and cede the territory behind him in eastern New Jersey to the British. Along the exhausting route west, Paine ended each day scribbling notes by a campfire, hoping his words in Philadelphia's newspaper would succeed where musket balls in battle had failed.

"None can say that our retreat was precipitous," he wrote:

> We were near three weeks in performing it. Twice we marched back to meet the enemy . . . and had not some of the cowardly and disaffected inhabitants spread false alarms in the country, the Jerseys would have never been ravaged. Once more we are again collected and collecting. Our new army is recruiting fast.[7]

With British troops advancing to within sight of Philadelphia, Congress fled to Baltimore and on December 12 all but conceded defeat. Even Washington was discouraged, writing to his brother, "It is impossible to give you any idea . . . of my difficulties—and the constant perplexities and mortification I constantly meet with."[8]

Paine's dispatch to the *Journal* reported, "Our army reached Trenton on the 4th of December, continued there until the 7th and then, on the approach of the enemy, it was thought proper to pass the Delaware River."[9]

To try to halt the British pursuit, Washington ordered his men to seize all river craft within fifteen miles of his position. Left without means to cross the river, the British commander ordered 3,000 Hessian mercenaries to remain in Trenton to maintain a watch on the Americans on the opposite bank. He then led his British troops to more comfortable quarters at nearby Princeton to wait for the river to freeze and allow his troops to cross on foot to wipe out Washington's crippled army and end the Revolution.

"Our numbers [are] quite inadequate," Washington complained to his cousin who, in the general's absence, had agreed to supervise Washington's plantation at Mount Vernon, Virginia, south of Alexandria. "Your imagination can scarce extend to a situation more distressing than mine," Washington wrote. "Our only dependence now is upon the speedy enlistment of a new army. If this fails us, I think the game is pretty well up, from disaffection and want of spirit and fortitude. The inhabitants instead of resistance are offering submission."[10]

The game seemed pretty well up elsewhere as well. An expedition into Canada that Washington had authorized had met with disaster earlier in 1776 with the death of the American commanding general, 100 American troops dead or wounded, and more than 300 taken prisoner.

"I thank God that I fear not," Paine wrote as he crouched for warmth by a campfire in the Pennsylvania woods near the Delaware River. "I see no real cause for fear. . . . By perseverance and fortitude we have the prospect of a glorious issue."

> By cowardice and submission, the sad choice of a variety of evils . . . a ravaged country . . . a depopulated city . . . habitations without safety, and slavery without hope . . . our homes turned into barracks and bawdyhouses for Hessians, and a future race to provide for, whose fathers we shall doubt of. Look on this picture and weep over it! And if there yet remains one thoughtless wretch who believes it not, let him suffer it unlamented.[11]

With the defeat of American forces on two fronts, Congress appointed a Committee of Secret Correspondence to seek foreign aid. Committee chair Richard Henry Lee of Virginia wrote to his younger brother Arthur Lee, an attorney in London, asking him to gauge European attitudes towards American independence efforts. Not long after Lee had written his letter, a curious Frenchman, Achard de Bonvouloir, reached Philadelphia and contrived to meet with members of Congress. Claiming to be a merchant from Antwerp, Belgium, Bonvouloir told congressional leaders that he personally could not discuss French military aid, but that he believed the French court was "well-disposed" toward the Americans. Indeed, he said he saw "no obstacles" to private transactions in which American merchants bought arms and other supplies from French merchants in exchange for produce—tobacco, rice, and the like.

In fact, Bonvouloir was the French army's most accomplished intelligence officer, sent by Foreign Minister Charles Gravier, Comte de Vergennes, in response to Arthur Lee's inquiries. Intent on avenging his nation's defeat by the British in the Seven Years' War, Vergennes charged Bonvouloir with assessing the depth of secessionist intent and strength of secessionist forces and the type of military aid that might help ensure American victory. Left near bankruptcy by the Seven Years' War, France could ill afford to engage Britain in all-out war herself, but by providing surreptitious aid to prolong the American Revolution, the French could tie down and wear out the British military in the American provinces and eventually open the way for a French force to invade and reclaim Canada.

Bonvouloir returned to France and assured Vergennes that American secessionists were prepared to fight to the death of the last man to gain independence. If he or the foreign minister had any doubts of American Patriot commitment, Thomas Paine laid those doubts to rest in *Common Sense*, which had now reached France and other parts of Europe, albeit untranslated but easily understood by the well educated who spoke English.

"I offer nothing more than simple facts, and common sense," Paine had told Americans earlier and now told the world. "Volumes have been written . . . on the struggle between England and America . . . and the period of debate is closed. Arms, as the last resource, decide this contest."[12]

Knowing that the costs to France of sending outdated but functional war materiel to the Americans would be all but negligible, Vergennes planned to convert Paine's words in *Common Sense* into action. At the time, French military depots were bulging with obsolete arms and ammunition from the Seven Years' War. Although technological advances had rendered much of the artillery all but useless in modern warfare on the vast open plains of Europe, much of it was more than adequate for close-quarter combat in the hills and forests of the American wilderness.

Encouraged by Bonvouloir's visit, the Committee of Secret Correspondence in Congress voted to send one of its own to France—the shrewd Connecticut merchant-banker* Silas Deane—to buy 100 field pieces and arms, ammunition, and clothing for 25,000 men. Congress, in turn, pledged to pay all the costs of his purchases, of course, plus Deane's expenses and a commission of 5 percent—a standard arrangement then. Deane was also to try to recruit engineers and artillery experts from the French officer corps to serve in the Continental Army.

Like most merchant-bankers in Congress, Deane's motive for supporting independence had more to do with ending British taxation than promoting independence. The war that ensued, however, presented him with an irresistible moneymaking opportunity that he could cloak in patriotism. Indeed, America's leading banker Robert Morris, a partner with Deane in many business ventures, encouraged him: "It seems to me that the present oppert'y [opportunity] of improving our fortunes ought not to be lost, especially as the very means of doing it will contribute to the service of our country at the same time." And as Deane prepared to leave for France, Morris added, "If we have but luck in getting the goods safely to America, the profits will be sufficient to control us all."[13]

---

* Merchant-bankers were tradesmen peculiar to America's barter system. Without hard money to buy tools, for example, a farmer would pledge a certain portion of his future crop to the merchant, who, in turn, paid for and "loaned" tools to the farmer, much as a banker lends money today. Repaid with a portion of the farmer's crops, the farmer kept his tools while the merchant-banker resold the crops he received for other goods or, if possible, for cash. Either way, he functioned as both merchant and banker, hence the term that was common in eighteenth-century America.

By then, Paine had finished writing what he hoped would reprise the thunder he had unleashed with *Common Sense*. The central theme of *Common Sense* had been equality of man and freedom to live one's life as one chose—a theme powerful enough to have helped provoke the outbreak of revolution. Now he sought to dispel the fear that temporary setbacks in battle had instilled in the hearts and minds of many Americans—on the front lines as well as in homes, schools, churches, and Congress. After crossing the Delaware with Greene and Washington, he asked for and received permission to make the thirty-mile trek southward to Philadelphia and the *Pennsylvania Journal* press to supervise publication of his new essay.

Meanwhile, Deane had arrived in Paris and learned that Vergennes had already developed a complex plan for secretly arming American revolutionaries. Even before Bonvouloir returned from America, Arthur Lee had met the notorious French playwright Pierre-Augustin Caron de Beaumarchais, creator of such brilliant works as *The Barber of Seville* and *The Marriage of Figaro*,* among others. As a master weaver of intricate plots, Beaumarchais had insinuated himself into real-life palace intrigues, using his status as a playwright to cross international borders and fix royal problems for his patron, the French king.

Once he grew aware of the Frenchman's ties to the French court, Lee expounded the American cause, pointing out that Americans shared the deep French hatred for the British. Lee said an investment of £100,000 or £200,000 to support the Americans would ensure not only an American victory over the British but the return of Canada to France. Inadvertently or by design, Arthur Lee had uttered the magic words etched on Vergennes's heart: "Le retour de la Nouvelle France"—"the return of New France (Canada)."

Lee also promised Beaumarchais that France would reap all the rewards of trade that had enriched England for a century. "Go to France,

---

*Later, in 1786, Wolfgang Amadeus Mozart converted the wildly popular *Marriage of Figaro* into an opera, using an Italian libretto by Lorenzo Da Ponte, based on the Beaumarchais play. In 1816, Gioachino Rossini converted *The Barber of Seville* into an opera of the same name, using an Italian libretto by Cesare Sterbin.

12. French playwright Pierre-Augustin Caron de Beaumarchais arranged secret shipments of French arms to American rebels and ensured America's first victory in the War of Independence at Saratoga, New York.

Monsieur," Lee urged Beaumarchais. "Tell your ministers that I am prepared to follow you to confirm . . . the statement of the case."[14]

Immediately after meeting with Arthur Lee, Beaumarchais assured Vergennes, "The Americans will triumph, but they must be assisted in their struggle."[15] With that, Beaumarchais sent a passionate essay to the king entitled "La paix ou la guerre"—"Peace or War." A little-known landmark in American history, the document steered France toward a Franco-American alliance that would ensure the birth of a new nation.

"The quarrel between America and England will soon divide the world and change the system of Europe," Beaumarchais predicted in his document for the king. "I am obliged to warn Your Majesty . . . if the English triumph over the Americans, their victory will embolden them to expand their empire by seizing the French West Indies.

"*We must help the Americans*," he concluded.

With France unable to afford war—with Britain or anyone else—Beaumarchais proposed sending the Americans enough military and financial aid to put them "on an equal—but not superior—level of strength with England." In doing so, France could help prolong the conflict in America indefinitely, exhausting both the Americans and British and putting both at the mercy of France—"without compromising ourselves."[16]

While Beaumarchais was promoting Arthur Lee's request for French aid, Thomas Paine had reached the *Pennsylvania Journal* in Philadelphia, and, on December 19, the printer launched a run of 18,000 copies of Paine's essay each in the form of an eight-page pamphlet entitled "*The American Crisis, Number 1*, by the Author of *COMMON SENSE*."

In it, Paine lashed out at Britain's King George III, calling him "a common murderer" and "highwayman."

"If a thief breaks into my house," Paine posited, "if he burns and destroys my property, and kills or threatens to kill me, or those that are in it . . . am I to suffer it?"

> What signifies it to me, whether he who does it is a king or a common man; my countryman or not my countryman; whether it be done by an individual villain, or an army of them? . . . Let them call me rebel and welcome, I feel no concern from it; but I should suffer the misery of devils, were I to make a whore of my soul by swearing allegiance to one whose character is that of a sottish, stupid, stubborn, worthless, brutish man.[17]

Paine sought to assure Americans that "God Almighty" would not surrender America to military destruction or allow Americans to perish. He called up the image of Joan of Arc, the courageous French girl who had inspired "a few broken forces" in fifteenth-century France to repel "the whole English army."[18] Paine hailed both the officers and men of Washington's army for staging their retreat across the Delaware "with a manly and martial spirit. It is a great credit to us that, with a handful of men, we sustained an orderly retreat for near an hundred of miles, brought off our ammunition, all our field pieces, the greatest part of our stores, and had four rivers to pass. . . . The sign of fear was not seen in our camp."[19]

Paine wrote in the simplest terms to allow even unschooled Americans to understand. Those who could not read—and there were many—listened, as others read the words aloud.

> I bring reason to your ears in language as plain as A, B, C. I hold the truth to your eyes. . . . Not a place upon earth might be so happy as America. Her situation is remote from all the wrangling world, and she has nothing to do but to trade with them. . . . I am as confident, as I am that God governs the world, that America will never be happy till she gets clear of foreign dominion.[20]

Remembering the troops crouched by fires in the vast darkness about him by the Delaware, Paine explained why the enemy had left New England and carried the fight into the middle provinces.

"The answer is easy," he wrote. "New England is not as infested with Tories. . . . Every Tory is a coward; for servile, slavish, self-interested fear is the foundation of Toryism; and a man under such influence, though he may be cruel, never can be brave."[21]

As Paine supervised the printing of *The American Crisis* in Philadelphia, the Continental Congress was considering capitulation only six months after declaring American independence. Washington knew he needed a quick, dramatic strike against the British to revive American morale and save the Revolution.

"We are all of the opinion . . . that something must be attempted to revive our expiring credit," his aide Colonel Joseph Reed advised the general. "Our affairs are hastening fast to ruin if we do not retrieve them by some happy event."[22]

Reed had not told Washington anything he hadn't known or planned. "Christmas day at night, one hour before day is the time fixed for our attempt on Trenton," he whispered to Reed. "For heaven's sake keep this to yourself, as the discovery of it may prove fatal to us."

As Christmas approached in 1776, Paine returned to camp, having borrowed a horse and filled his saddlebags with copies of his new pamphlet. Greene and Washington read passages of his essay, and, aware of how *Common Sense* had roused American spirits in favor of independence, Washington believed the new essay would lift army spirits and help stem the defeatism that had infected Congress and Americans generally.

"I turn with the warm ardor of a friend to those who have nobly stood, and are yet determined to stand the matter out," Paine's words seemed to fulfill Washington's hopes. "I call not upon a few, but upon all, not in this state or that state, but in every state: rise up and help us. . . . better to have too much force than too little, when so great an object is at stake."

> Let it be told to the future world that in the depth of winter, when nothing but hope and virtue could survive, that the city and the country, alarmed at one common danger, came forth to meet and to repulse it. . . . It matters not where you live, or what rank of life you hold, the evil or the blessing will reach you all. . . . The rich and the poor, will suffer or rejoice alike. The heart that feels not now is dead . . . his children will curse his cowardice. . . . 'Tis the business of little minds to shrink; but he whose heart is firm, and whose conscience approves his conduct, will pursue his principles unto death.[23]

When Washington had finished reading Paine's essay, he issued a copy to each of his officers on Christmas afternoon, with orders to read it to their men. As day turned into night, their voices filled the air across the camp as they read Paine's words aloud, chanting solemnly all but in unison:

> THESE are the times that try men's souls. The summer soldier and the sunshine patriot will, in this crisis, shrink from the service of their country; but he that stands by it now, deserves the love and thanks of man and woman. Tyranny, like hell, is not easily conquered; yet we have this consolation with us, that the harder the conflict, the more glorious the triumph. What we obtain too cheap, we esteem too lightly: it is dearness only that gives every thing its value. Heaven knows how to put a proper price upon its goods; and it would be strange indeed if so celestial an article as FREEDOM should not be highly rated. Britain, with an army to enforce her tyranny, has declared that she has a right (not only to TAX) but "to BIND us in ALL

CASES WHATSOEVER" and if being bound in that manner, is not slavery, then there is not such a thing as slavery upon earth. Even the expression is impious; for so unlimited a power can belong only to God.[24]

Paine signed his essay "Common Sense," a pseudonym that political figures in Britain and America now recognized as Paine's, but a name that America's common man, in battle or not, embraced as kin. Even the most pious troops had never heard a sermon so stirring: "God may bless you . . . it matters not what rank of life you hold . . . the blood of . . . children will curse cowardice . . . God Almighty will not give up . . . O! ye that love mankind, stand forth . . . Ye that dare oppose not only the tyranny but the tyrant, stand forth! . . . Show your faith . . . that God may bless you."[25]

The passage—"These are the times that try men's souls"—resounded in homes, churches, schools, taverns, and public gatherings across America. They became watchwords that remain part of America's heritage today, reaching a thunderous climax with seven words sounded on the banks of the Delaware River for the first time in the history of man: THE FREE AND INDEPENDENT STATES OF AMERICA.[26]

As Christmas night stretched into the early hours of December 26, 1776, Washington's troops—many damaged by the long retreat and biting cold—rose as one. Inspired, reinvigorated by Paine's promise of victory, they moved to the river's edge where, one by one—2,400 in all, including Paine—they boarded a flotilla of small boats carrying only arms, ammunition, and three days' rations. With Washington himself in the lead boat, they pushed off into the ice-choked waters through a storm of rain and sleet and crossed to a landing area north of Trenton.

Nine hours after Paine's call to glory, they formed two columns and surged into Trenton, Paine among them, his words still ringing in their ears, his musket firing beside them. Outraged by the British king's having hired Hessian mercenaries to slaughter Americans, they stormed up King Street, firing at anything that moved.

The Hessians were still abed in quarters near the top of King Street, sleeping off Christmas night festivities, certain that a lookout was unneeded against the ragtag Americans in so fierce a storm. Stepping outside for a brief moment, a Hessian officer saw the Americans approaching.

13. Inspired by Thomas Paine's call to action, George Washington led his troops across the Delaware River on a daring dawn attack on Hessian troops in Trenton, New Jersey.

"Der Feind! Der Feind!" he cried out. "The enemy! The enemy!"

"Heraus! Heraus!"—"Turn out! Turn out!"

The terrified Hessians raced out into the snowstorm in nightclothes toward artillery emplacements at the top of King Street. Washington, however, had anticipated the threat and sent a fifty-man squad to circle to the rear of town and capture the two cannons that stared down the street at the advancing Americans. The two officers who led the daring raid fell wounded defending the cannons—one of them a distant Washington cousin, Captain William Washington; the other, Lieutenant James Monroe, who had temporarily abandoned university studies in Virginia to enlist in the Virginia militia. General Washington decorated and promoted both young men for their heroism in ensuring one of the signal military victories in American history: the surrender of the entire 1,000-man Hessian force and cession of Trenton to the Americans.

Elated, Washington pressed on to Princeton, where he hoped to catch the British encampment off guard. By then, however, the fall of Trenton had alarmed the British high command in New York, which ordered

General Earl Lord Cornwallis to march into New Jersey to reinforce British troops in Princeton. But in one of the most clever maneuvers of his military career, Washington ordered his troops to set up a mock encampment, complete with tents and burning campfires well outside Princeton, then steal away quietly into the night toward the town. As Cornwallis ordered his troops to surround what he believed to be Washington's encampment, Washington's men trapped the British force in Princeton and forced it to cede the town, surrender its arms, and retreat eastward to Brunswick, leaving much of western New Jersey in Patriot hands.

With Washington's improbable victories at Trenton and Princeton, American spirits soared—civilians and soldiers alike. News of the victories spread across the American landscape, across the Atlantic to Britain, across the English Channel to Europe, along with Thomas Paine's stirring exhortation, "These are the times that try men's souls."

"Ce sont les temps qui tentent les âmes des hommes," read the widely published translation in France, where royalty and commoner united in celebrating the humiliation of their centuries-old enemy.

In America, Congress returned to Philadelphia; confidence replaced fear in American minds and hearts. And, after receiving praise from various members of Congress, Paine, too, returned to Philadelphia and began writing more essays to advance America's fight for freedom.

"Perhaps you thought America was taking a nap," Paine mocked Admiral Richard Viscount Howe in a second essay, *The Crisis II*, which he addressed "To Lord Howe".

"We have learned to reverence ourselves and scorn the insulting ruffian that employs you," Paine barked at Britain's military leaders.

> Your avowed purpose here is to kill, conquer, plunder, pardon, and enslave, and the ravages of your army . . . have been marked with as much barbarism as if you had openly professed yourself the prince of ruffians; not even the appearance of humanity has been preserved.[27]

Paine called Britain the "greatest offender against God on the face of the whole earth. Blessed with all the commerce she could wish for, and furnished . . . with the means of civilizing both the eastern and western world, she has made no use of both." He accused Britain of ripping out "the bowels" of every country it had conquered—India, Africa, the West Indies—and intending to do the same in America.

"By what means do you expect to conquer America?" Paine asked. "If you could not effect it in the summer when our army was less than yours nor in the winter when we had none, how are you to do it? In point of generalship, you have been outwitted and in point of fortitude outdone."

> Like a game of draughts [checkers], we can move out of one square to let you come in, in order that we may afterwards take two or three [pieces] for one; and as we can always keep a double corner for ourselves, we can always prevent a total defeat.[28]

Paine mocked Lord Howe, pointing out that Washington's triumphs at Trenton and Princeton had reduced British authority in New Jersey to a "small circle of territory. . . . I laugh at your notion of conquering America," Paine wrote. "The dead only are conquerors because none will dispute the ground with them."[29]

Paine's constant reference to America, however, was quixotic. America was a geographic entity of sorts, but there was no America in the political sense. It had no geographical boundaries, no government, no foreign minister or ambassadors abroad, and no status in the capitals of any nations on earth. And without status as a sovereign nation, Paine's "America" could not deal with foreign powers. Congress, therefore, voted to transform its Committee of Secret Correspondence into a Committee on Foreign Affairs, and, with none of its members known to European leaders, it voted to appoint a salaried secretary whose name was known abroad to correspond with foreign leaders. John Adams moved to appoint Thomas Paine, internationally renowned for his "ready pen." Although Adams had disagreed strongly with Paine's proposal for a unicameral legislature in the new American republic, he had cited Paine's *Common Sense* as "a very meritorious production written with elegant simplicity."[30]

Benjamin Franklin agreed, and Congress elected Thomas Paine, the stay maker from Thetford, England, Secretary to the Committee on Foreign Affairs by a vote only one short of unanimity, with a salary of seventy dollars a month—in effect, the first American Secretary of State.

"I felt myself obliged to Pain [*sic*] for the pains [*sic*!] he had taken and for his good intentions to serve us," John Adams explained condescendingly twenty-five years later, after a bitter falling-out with Paine over religious beliefs. "I saw he had a capacity and a ready pen, and, understanding he was poor and destitute, I thought we might put him into some employment where he might be useful and earn a living."[31] Despite being the most widely circulated writer in the nation, Paine had dug his own pit of poverty by assigning all proceeds from his writing to Congress for the war effort—including *Common Sense*. He would never receive a penny for any of his work in the fight for American independence.

"When I bring out my political and anecdotal works," he explained to his friend Clio Rickman, "I shall sell them; but I must have no gain in view. . . . They are with me a matter of principle and not a matter of money. . . . In a great affair, where the good of man is at stake . . . I should lose the spirit . . . of it were I conscious that I looked for reward."[32]

Officially responsible for keeping committee records and drafting member correspondence, Paine took advantage of chronic member absences by usurping powers not delegated to him and, in the absence of any committee members, drafting original letters and even restating his title as "Secretary for Foreign Affairs."

"The appointment," Clio Rickman concluded, "gave Mr. Paine the opportunity of seeing into foreign courts and their manner of doing business and conducting themselves."[33]

Having sparked a revolution in America, Thomas Paine now envisioned setting the rest of the world ablaze.

Chapter 4

AMERICAN CRISIS

WITH BRITISH AND AMERICAN FORCES LICKING THEIR WOUNDS IN the bitter cold of winter quarters, George Washington issued a proclamation on January 25, 1777, requiring those who had been "so lost to the interest and welfare of their country as to . . . take oaths of allegiance . . . [to] the King of Great-Britain . . . [to] take the oath of allegiance to the United States of America." He said those refusing would be treated "as common enemies of the American States."[1]

Paine by then had returned to Philadelphia to assume his duties as Secretary to the Committee on Foreign Affairs and to write more *American Crisis* essays. Like the Army, Congress had shut down for the winter, and Paine, inspired by Washington's proclamation, dated *Crisis III* "April 19, 1777," to mark the second anniversary of the Battle of Lexington and the outbreak of the War of Independence.

"Every attempt, now, to support the authority of the king and Parliament of Great Britain over America is treason against every state," Paine echoed Washington's proclamation. "Men must now take one side or the other and abide by the consequences. . . . He that is not a supporter of the Independent States of America . . . is, in the American sense of the word, A TORY . . . and becomes A TRAITOR."[2] Paine habitually capitalized words for emphasis.

Paine urged that, in addition to requiring a loyalty oath, America should collect "a tax of ten, fifteen, or twenty per cent per annum . . . on all property."

Although Congress had no authority to promulgate either Washington's proclamation or Paine's proposals, Pennsylvania's assembly did. On June 18, it passed a law requiring residents to take the following oath or forfeit their property and state citizenship:

> I (name) do solemnly and sincerely Declare and Swear . . . that the State of Pennsylvania is and of right ought to be a free and Sovereign State and independent State—and I do forever renounce all Allegiance, Subjection, and Obedience to the King or Crown, of Great Britain, and I do further swear . . . that I never have since the Declaration of Independence . . . assisted, abetted, or in any wise countenanced the King of Great Britain, his generals, fleets, or armies . . . and that I have . . . demeaned myself as a faithful citizen and subject of the United States, and that I will at all times maintain and support the freedom, sovereignty, and Independence thereof.[3]

North Carolina followed suit.

Paine repeated certain pronouncements from *Common Sense*, reminding readers that Britain "for centuries past has been nearly fifty years out of every hundred at war" and that "by having Britain for our master, we become enemies to the greatest part of Europe. . . . By being our own masters . . . we have Europe for our friend and the prospect of an endless peace."[4]

Paine was closer to the truth than he may have realized. As *Crisis III* circulated across America, Pierre-Augustin Caron de Beaumarchais's *La paix ou la guerre* had won the eye and heart of the French king and, just as important, the eye and heart of the king's hawkish foreign minister the Comte de Vergennes. While insisting that France had to avoid another costly war with Britain, Vergennes asked Beaumarchais to develop a plan to help the Americans without leaving a trace of French government involvement. Beaumarchais obliged with a plot worthy of any of his greatest plays.

He proposed that the French royal treasury give him 1 million livres (about $4 million today) to establish a private company with a Spanish name—Hortalez et Cie.—that would conceal French involvement from the British. Hortalez & Cie. would then use half the money to buy obsolete surplus arms from the French military. In effect, the transaction would immediately channel half the king's money back into the royal treasury via the war ministry while ridding the army of surplus materiel that was useless for European warfare. Hortalez & Cie. would then lend the other half of the king's money to the American government to buy more war supplies from the king's army and repay the loan by filling the empty French arms ships with the equivalent value of tobacco, rice, indigo, lumber, and other commodities. Once they arrived in France, Beaumarchais would sell the American commodities in French markets, recouping the money the king had loaned him plus interest and substantial profits for himself.

Even as Secretary to the Committee on Foreign Affairs, Paine knew nothing of the Beaumarchais scheme. He suspected something amiss in Paris, however, when dozens of retired French army officers began appearing at the door of Congress demanding commissions in the Continental Army. Many skirted Philadelphia and reported directly to George Washington's tent expecting a commission from the great man himself.

In an angry letter to Congress, Washington protested "the distress I am . . . laid under by the application of French officers for commissions in our service. This evil . . . is a growing one . . . they are coming in swarms from old France and the Islands. . . . They seldom bring more than a commission and a passport, which, we know, may belong to a bad as well as a good officer. Their ignorance of our language and their inability to recruit men are insurmountable obstacles to their being ingrafted into our Continental battalions; our officers, who have raised their men, and have served through the war upon pay that has hitherto not borne their expenses, would be disgusted if foreigners were put over their heads."[5]

When Congress failed to act, Washington sent another angry note to congressional leader Richard Henry Lee asking "what Congress expects I am to do with the many foreigners they have at different times promoted to the rank of field officers. . . . These men have no attachment nor ties to the country . . . and are ignorant of the language they are to receive and give orders in . . . and our officers think it exceedingly hard . . . to have strangers put over them, whose merit perhaps is not equal to their own, but whose effrontery will take no denial."[6]

14. Thomas Paine exposed Connecticut's Silas Deane as a profiteer in the purchases of arms and ammunition from France and the recruitment of officers.

Washington's second letter had its desired effect. Congress stopped granting military commissions to foreigners unless Washington himself requested it—as he had for the Marquis de Lafayette and several others.

To bring Deane's spending sprees and recruitment activities under control, Congress appointed Benjamin Franklin and Arthur Lee to go to Paris to form a three-man commission to negotiate treaties of commerce and amity with France and other foreign countries—a task that would keep Deane occupied in sectors other than recruiting and require support from either Franklin or Lee for Deane to commission any officers or make any purchases for Congress.

Coming from London, Arthur Lee arrived in Paris before Franklin and discovered that Deane had hired as his assistant a British spy and that the two had enlisted foreign officers by promising commissions well

15. Working as a secret agent for America's Continental Congress, Arthur Lee notified his brother Richard Henry Lee and Thomas Paine of Silas Deane's profiteering on American arms purchases in France.

above their former ranks at much higher salaries—in return for "appropriate gifts." Still worse, Deane had insinuated himself into the French government scheme with Beaumarchais to send surplus French arms to American Patriot forces. As several Beaumarchais ships loaded with arms and ammunition were about to sail for America, Deane demanded "commissions" from Beaumarchais to "facilitate" secret reception of arms in American ports. Deane's aide, meanwhile, sent word to London of the Beaumarchais shipments, allowing the British navy to track two of the ships and sink them.

Arthur Lee wrote of his suspicions about Deane to his brother Richard Henry Lee, who shared them with Paine. Then, in late 1777, Paine received a letter from the Franklin-Deane-Lee commission to the Committee on Foreign Affairs announcing a grant of 2 million livres from the French crown. "Such was the king's generosity he exacted no conditions or promise of repayment. He only required that we should not speak to anyone of our having received their aid." In December, the commissioners reassured Paine and the committee "that no repayment will ever be required from us for what [France] has already given us either in money or military stores."[7]

At the same time, however, an agent from Beaumarchais appeared at the doors of Congress with a bill for 4.5 million livres for arms shipments—along with a letter from Deane attesting to the legitimacy of the debt. Outraged by Deane's conflicting messages, Paine urged Lee to demand that Congress recall Deane.

From the time of Deane's appointment, Paine had suspected his motives, and not long after the presentation of the Hortalez bills, a series of angry letters arrived from Arthur Lee, warning, "Things are going on worse and worse every day." He charged Deane with "neglect, dissipation and private schemes" and accused Deane of working with Thomas Morris, Robert Morris's troubled half-brother, to "plunder . . . the public money."[8]

In early December 1777, Congress resolved that "Silas Deane be recalled from . . . France and that the Committee on Foreign Affairs . . . take proper measures for speedily communicating the pleasure of Congress herein to Mr. Deane." Paine did as instructed and wrote to Deane—not mentioning that Congress had made a second resolution "for choosing a commissioner" to replace Deane.[9]

Even as Congress tried resolving the Deane Affair, disaster struck American military forces on two fronts. Earlier in 1777, British General John Burgoyne had led a force of 7,700 British and Hessian troops across the Canadian border southward along Lake Champlain. In but four weeks, the British had chased poorly equipped American defenders southward to Saratoga, New York, only forty miles from Albany, near the vital intersection of the Mohawk and Hudson Rivers.

On a second front, General Richard Howe's force of 15,000 troops had sailed to the northernmost rim of Chesapeake Bay, streamed ashore unopposed at Head of Elk (now Elkton, Maryland), and marched to Brandywine Creek, the only natural barrier of sorts on the way to Philadelphia.

The tide of battle on the northern front, however, changed dramatically when fishermen in Portsmouth, New Hampshire, spotted the tip of a mast on the horizon offshore—then another mast and a French flag. As cheering townsmen rushed to the docks, the 300-ton *Mercure*, one of the three Beaumarchais ships, landed. Together, townsmen—men, women, and children—joined French sailors in offloading 12,000 muskets, fifty brass cannon, powder and ammunition, 1,000 tents, and clothes for 10,000 men onto a wagon train that began rolling westward toward Bennington, Vermont. As the first wagons arrived there, militiamen refilled their powder horns and, with new weapons in their hands, repelled the advance of a 1,000-man British force, killing 200 and capturing 700. By mid-October, the rearmed and reinvigorated Americans had marched the forty miles to Saratoga, New York, where they out-gunned and out-maneuvered General John Burgoyne's army, forcing 5,700 British troops and their fabled General "Gentleman Johnny" to surrender.

Outside Philadelphia, meanwhile, Washington and his ill-equipped army of 10,000 waited by Brandywine Creek, hoping the two other Beaumarchais arms shipments would arrive and give the Americans the arms to halt the advance of Howe's army. The ships never arrived. They were the two that had been sunk by the British.

With his men already at a disadvantage, Washington inadvertently added to their woes by miscalculating British strength and intentions and concentrating his troops and firepower opposite the center of the British line at Chadd's Ford. As the battle raged, British General Lord Cornwallis slipped away all but unseen through a thick forest with 8,000 British and Hessian troops. Marching northwest, they crossed Brandywine Creek at its narrowest point, far from the battle at Chadd's Ford, and looped around and behind the American Army's right flank, almost encircling Washington's entire force.

As paralyzing British fire swept across American lines from three directions, Washington's men turned about and fled in panic, leaving half his army dead or dying. British troops closed in from three sides—south, west and north—then moved toward Philadelphia, reaching the outskirts in early September.

With cannon fire belching in the distance, Paine hurriedly—and somewhat hysterically—tried to bolster American morale, scribbling *Crisis IV*: "It is not a field of a few acres of ground but a cause that we are defending.

And whether we defeat the enemy in one battle or by degrees, the result will be the same."

> Look back at the events of last winter and the present year: there you will find that the enemy's successes always contributed to reduce them. What they have gained in ground they paid so dearly for in numbers that their victories have in the end amounted to defeats. We have always been masters at the last push and always shall while we do our duty.

Paine addressed part of *Crisis IV* to General Howe—as he had addressed his brother Admiral Howe in *Crisis II*. Instead of mockery, however, Paine spewed only bitter words: "You, sir, are only lingering out the period that shall bring with it your defeat. . . . We are not moved by the gloomy smile of a worthless king, but by the ardent glow of generous patriotism. We fight not to enslave but to set a country free and to make room upon the earth for honest men to live in; and we leave to you the despairing reflection of being the tool of a miserable tyrant."[10]

As the belching British cannon fire drew closer, Paine desperately tried to rally Philadelphians to fight, as he had the troops at Trenton: "Gentlemen of the city and country," Paine's words seemed to soar above the cannon roars: "It is in your power by a spirited improvement of the present circumstance to turn it to a real advantage. Howe is now weaker than before and every shot will contribute to reduce him . . . you may save yourselves by a manly resistance."

To help organize them, Paine raced across town to the home of Major General Thomas Mifflin, a Philadelphia merchant who, though a Quaker, had quit the Continental Congress in 1775 to serve as an aide-de-camp to George Washington in the Continental Army. Mifflin, however, rushed home following the Brandywine disaster to evacuate his family. When Paine asked him if he would take command "if two or three thousand men could be mustered" to defend the city, Mifflin "declined," a downhearted Paine wrote to Benjamin Franklin, "and nothing was done."[11]

On September 19, Congress fled Philadelphia, with most members scattering toward their respective homes. Virginia's Richard Henry Lee rallied nearly twenty members of Congress—enough to form a quorum—and

16. Congressional leader Richard Henry Lee established a close working relationship with Thomas Paine after Paine was appointed Secretary to the Committee on Foreign Affairs.

they fled together to Lancaster, Pennsylvania, about eighty miles to the west, where they hoped to reestablish an American government and some of its functions.

"At 3 this morning," a startled John Adams scribbled in his diary after finding himself alone, "[I] was waked . . . and told that the members of Congress were gone, some of them a little after midnight." He and another delegate sent for their horses "and rode off after the others," eventually finding delegates from New York and New Jersey gathered at a tavern in Trenton, New Jersey.

"So many disasters," he moaned as he penned his recollections of the day. "Oh, Heaven! Grant us one great soul!" Adams pleaded. "One leading mind would extricate the best cause from that ruin which seems to await it for the want of it. We have as good a cause as ever was fought for."[12]

Rather than try to search for other remnants of Congress, Adams decided to return home and surrender to the inevitable. "It was my intention to decline the next election and return to the bar," he explained.

> I had been four years in Congress . . . I was daily losing the fruits of seventeen years industry. . . . My children were growing up without my care in their education. All my emoluments as a member of Congress . . . had not been sufficient to pay a laboring man upon my farm. Young gentlemen who had been clerks in my office . . . were growing rich. I thought, therefore, that four years drudgery and sacrifice . . . were sufficient . . . that another might take my place.[13]

After the rout at Brandywine, Washington's Continental Army had little choice but to cede America's largest, most important city to the British, rendering the previous winter's triumphs at Trenton and Princeton almost meaningless. "On Friday the 26th [September 1777]," Paine wrote to Franklin, "a party of the enemy, about 1500, took possession of the city."[14]

More humiliations were to come.

Paine was able to remain in the city unnoticed for a few days, but on September 29 he fled and "set off for camp without well knowing where to find it. I was three days before I fell in with it."[15]

To try to prevent further advances by Howe's army, Washington staged what devolved into a suicidal counterattack near Germantown, just outside Philadelphia. "I set off for German Town [sic] at about five next morning," Paine reported to Franklin. "The skirmishing with the pickets began soon after." By the time he reached "within five or six miles" of Germantown, Paine passed wagons carrying wounded troops back to camp. A few miles further the number of wounded grew into what he called a "crowd," with a wounded colonel warning Paine "that if I went further on that road I would be taken. . . . I never could learn . . . the cause of the miscarriage."[16]

The cause became evident later: Washington had sent two separate columns for a two-pronged pincer attack on the British, with each column following what a schematic diagram showed as two parallel roads to Germantown. In reality, one road followed a longer serpentine course, allowing the column on the straighter, shorter road to reach Germantown before its twin column.

Faced with an impenetrable wall of British fire and no support from the second column, the first column retreated. As night fell, a dense fog enveloped the area, and the retreating column collided with the second American column, which was still advancing along the longer road. With each American column mistaking the other for enemy soldiers, the two columns fired at each other. Caught between American and British fire, the trapped column lost 700 men, with 400 more taken prisoner as they retreated into British lines. The British had crushed the American Army and put the American government to flight. To all intents and purposes, the American Revolution again seemed near an end.

The next morning, Paine shared breakfast with Washington and found the commander in chief shaking his head, "at the same loss with every other to account for the accidents of the day. . . . I stayed in camp two days after the German Town action," Paine continued his letter to Franklin, "then set out to rejoin Congress," which had abandoned Lancaster after only a day and fled twenty-five miles farther west across the Susquehanna River to York. At the time, York was but a tiny outpost of civilization where Paine and the remnants of Congress faced extreme physical discomforts of frontier life while trying to address deep concerns about the course of the war—and George Washington's leadership.

The loss of Philadelphia—the nation's political, cultural, and social center—left every member of Congress in despair, along with most Americans. Many in Congress, including Virginia's influential Richard Henry Lee, muttered about replacing Washington with the British-born Horatio Gates. While Washington and his men foundered at Brandywine and Germantown, Gates had galloped to a stunning victory against the British in Saratoga, New York.

Paine by then had rejoined the remnants of Congress and, incensed over the growing criticisms of Washington, he began preparing a fifth *Crisis* essay defending the commander in chief—then thought better of it. Realizing he could not develop a plausible defense for Washington's losses at either Brandywine or Germantown, he spent the next few days traveling the eighty miles to the Valley Forge encampment. He found the troops still building huts. He described them in a letter to Franklin as "a family of beavers, every one busy, some carrying logs, others mud, and the rest fastening them together. The whole is a curious collection of buildings in the true rustic order."[17]

Far from providing Paine with a defense of Washington's prowess as a military leader, the encampment did just the opposite. Poised on what appeared to be a strategically perfect, elevated plateau, the Valley Forge encampment provided lookout points to spot the approach of enemy troops from Philadelphia to the east and a gentle slope on the west along which Washington's men could retreat in good order from an overwhelmingly larger enemy force. In every respect it seemed to provide perfect winter quarters—save one essential: water.

The camp had no springs. The water that fed the actual forge at Valley Forge was in a valley stream below and would have to be carried up the hill in buckets by hand. The result was an encampment of misery, with troops plagued by hunger, thirst, frostbite, filth, and despair. Valley Forge seemed one more blunder by the commander in chief—certainly nothing for Paine to write about. Indeed, it was enough to make him join, albeit reluctantly, those who questioned Washington's military leadership skills.

Many members of the Second Continental Congress of 1775 had favored Gates as commander in chief over Washington because of his broader military experience, but enough members opposed putting a Britisher in command of American rebels to prevent his appointment. Now, however, those who had favored Washington over Gates reconsidered their earlier decision and voted to establish a Board of War, with Gates as president, to supersede Washington as director of military operations, and a Gates aide, Irish-born Colonel Thomas Conway, as inspector general.

Rumors arose that Conway was to lead a cabal to replace Washington with Gates as commander in chief of the Continental Army. Indeed, Conway had written to Gates appealing to the Englishman's ambitions and heaping scorn on Washington. "Heaven has been determined to save your country," Conway flattered Gates, "or a weak general and bad counselors would have ruined it."[18]

Washington grew infuriated when he learned of the rumored plot, saying it was not the only "secret, insidious attempt that has been made to
wound my reputation. There have been others equally base, cruel, and
ungenerous. . . . All I can say is that [America] has ever had, and I trust
she will ever have, my honest exertions to promote her interest. I cannot
hope that my services have been the best; but my heart tells me they have
been the best I can render."[19]

Overall responsibility for the cabal to displace Washington remains
unclear. Although Conway was arch-facilitator, the plot may well have
originated in the War Ministry in London, which generated most British
espionage plots. "General Gates was to be exalted on the ruin of my reputation and influence," Washington related, "and General Conway, I know,
was a very active and malignant partisan, but I have reason to believe that
their machinations have recoiled most sensibly upon themselves."[20]

The cabal came to a quiet end when Congress, suspecting British complicity, ordered Conway demoted and transferred to an insignificant post
along the Hudson River valley;* Gates and the Board of War resigned,
with Gates returning to his former post as commander of the Northern
Army. Congress restored Washington as supreme commander, giving him
near-dictatorial powers and abandoning the concept of directing the war
by committee.

Rather than write an essay that would provoke arguments over the
competence of the commander in chief, Paine tried to combat pervasive
American despair in the winter of 1778 by turning public attention back
to the enemy, painting a portrait of British commanding general Howe
as the personification of evil. He began *Crisis V* as he had *Crisis II*, in the
form of another letter "To Gen. Sir William Howe."

"To argue with a man who has renounced the use and authority of
reason," Paine wrote to Howe, "is like administering medicine to the
dead. . . . Enjoy, sir, your insensibility of feeling and reflecting. It is the

---

* Conway resigned from the Army soon after. Challenged to a duel by General John
Cadwalader, a fierce Washington loyalist, Conway suffered a serious wound and, believing he was going to die, he sent Washington a letter of apology. After recovering
from his wound, he left America in disgrace and rejoined the French army.

prerogative of animals." He accused Howe of having "made your exit from the moral world" in favor of "conduct so basely mean . . . every nation on earth, whether friends or enemies, united in despising you. . . . The laws of any civilized country would condemn you to the gibbet without regard to your rank or titles."

Turning his focus to British government policies, he said that the English language lacked the words "to express the baseness of your king, his ministry and his army. They have refined villainy till it wants a name."

> Never did a nation invite destruction upon itself with the eagerness with which Britain has done. Bent upon the ruin of a young and unoffending country, she has drawn the sword that has wounded herself to the heart. . . . England finds that she cannot conquer America, and America has no wish to conquer England. You are fighting for what you can never obtain, and we defending what we never mean to part with. . . . Let England mind her own business and we will mind ours. . . . Go home, Sir, and endeavor to save the remains of your ruined country.[21]

In assailing Howe, Paine realized he had failed to address the deep fears the loss of Philadelphia had implanted in many Americans. The success he had scored with *Common Sense* and *Crisis I* had left Americans ready to charge into the lists abrim with hope for victory. Ending his angry letter to Howe in mid-page, he wrote an addendum aimed at reviving American spirits. Entitled *Common Sense to the Inhabitants of America*, it praised Americans for introducing freedom and individual liberties to the world and told them that their struggle was "the most virtuous and illustrious revolution that ever graced the history of mankind." He tried softening the impact of the British occupation of Philadelphia, saying the city's importance to America had diminished.

"It had long ceased to be a port," he said of Philadelphia. "Not a cargo of goods had been brought into it for more than a twelve-month, nor any fixed manufactures, nor even ship-building carried on in it." He said it was "absurd" to believe "that the soul of all America was centered there and would be conquered there." He mentioned nothing of the Conway Cabal, nothing of the humiliating losses at Brandywine and Germantown, nothing of the horrors at Valley Forge; he made only one brief reference to Washington and his "unabated fortitude." Instead, he focused on lifting reader spirits, writing of their struggle as "the most virtuous and illustrious revolution that ever graced the history of mankind."

"We have equaled the bravest in times of danger. . . . We never had . . . so fair an opportunity of final success as now." [22]

Having omitted almost any mention of Washington, he sent the general "my sincerest wishes for your happiness in every line of life" and assured Washington, "I shall never suffer a hint of dishonor or even a deficiency of respect to you to pass unnoticed." By writing to Washington, Paine sought to reduce tensions that appointment of a Board of War had created between leaders of Congress and the commander in chief. He also sought to assure Washington that he, Paine, had had nothing to do with either the Board of War or the Conway Cabal. And, he added, "I never heard either Col. R[ichard Henry] Lee or [Lee's brother] Col. F[rancis Lightfoot] Lee [a member of Congress] express a sentiment in your disfavor," Paine assured Washington. "I likewise take the liberty of mentioning to you that at the time some discontents from the Army and the country last winter were doing you great injustice, I published the fifth [number] of the *Crisis*, in which I hoped . . . to shame them out." [23]

By then, France had recognized the United States as an independent country and Congress named Benjamin Franklin America's first minister plenipotentiary to any foreign land. On February 2, 1778, French and American representatives in Paris signed two treaties—one, commercial, the other military pledging mutual defense against attack by third-party nations. Shortly afterwards a French army and navy set off across the Atlantic to support the American war effort against Britain.

Fearing a return of French influence in North America, the British government in London responded by sending a peace commission to seek reconciliation with the Americans and issue formal pardons to those Americans—George Washington among them—whom Britain had hitherto condemned as traitors. When the commission arrived in America, it was too late.

By then, Washington had discovered the source of the distresses at Valley Forge. Quartermaster General Thomas Mifflin, a Philadelphia-area merchant before the Revolution, had sought to profit from his office by ordering supplies bound for Valley Forge redirected to his own warehouses, where the goods were sold to the highest bidders, more often than not, bids that far exceeded the prices Congress could pay.

When Washington confronted Mifflin, he resigned and Congress reassigned him to an obscure military post where he could do no harm. Washington then persuaded his trusted friend, Rhode Island Major General Nathanael Greene—also a merchant in private life—to accept the Quartermaster General's post. Within days, Valley Forge had a surplus of clothing, food, and other supplies, and when, on May 1, 1778, an aide rode into Washington's headquarters at Valley Forge with news of the two treaties with France, he proclaimed an official day of "public celebration," beginning with religious services and followed by "military parades, marchings, the firings of cannon and musketry." Washington ordered an enormous banquet served up to the entire camp and invited Thomas Paine to sit beside him at a table for the camp's officers.[24]

So when Britain's Carlisle Commission arrived in America, Washington had not only filled the bellies of his troops, his officers had brought the men back to fighting shape, and Congress had received copies of the treaties that Franklin and his commission had negotiated with France.

News that a French fleet was sailing to America with an invasion force alarmed the British high command, which decided to abandon Philadelphia and consolidate its northern armies at the main British base in New York City. As British troops and their long wagon train left Philadelphia and moved northward through the blistering New Jersey summer heat, Washington ordered his troops off the Valley Forge plateau to try to harass the British rear. Although the British had a day's head start, a week of heavy rains combined with searing heat and suffocating humidity to slow the huge British convoy and allow the Americans to catch up. Exhausted by the daily trek, both armies encamped for what they hoped would be a long, restful sleep at Monmouth Courthouse in central New Jersey.

At dawn the next morning, however, Washington ordered his troops to attack, triggering a day of wearying heroics by both sides, with indecisive results at day's end. As darkness set in, Washington's troops bedded down for the night, and, as they slept, the British quietly slipped away to Sandy

Hook, a spit of land on the northern New Jersey shore at the entrance to New York Bay. Transport ships waited to carry them away to New York, ceding New Jersey to the Americans. Washington claimed victory in a letter to his brother John, calling the battle at Monmouth Courthouse "a glorious and happy day." It had cost the British "at least 2000 of their best troops," he declared. "We had 60 men killed."[25]

Elated by Washington's success, Paine responded to Britain's peace offer with another of his *Crisis* essays—*No. VI*—in the form of a letter "To the Earl of Carlisle, General [William] Clinton, and William Eden, Esq., British Commissioners at New York." Calling their proposal "tedious and unmeaning," Paine told them, "Your cargo of pardons will have no market."

> Remember you do not command a foot of land on the continent of America. Staten Island, [New] York Island [Manhattan], a small part of Long Island, and Rhode Island circumscribe your power. . . . The treaty we have formed with France is open, noble, and generous. . . . In France we have found an affectionate friend and faithful ally. In Britain, we have found nothing but tyranny, cruelty, and infidelity.

Paine went on to threaten Britain with incendiary attacks—in effect, terrorist attacks—on the British homeland if it continued the war. In contrast to America's wealth spread across a continent, its minerals below ground, its lumber and furs hidden in impenetrable forests, Britain's wealth lay in cities, large towns, manufactures, and fleets of merchantmen. "The ships in the Thames may certainly be as easily set on fire," he warned. "The East India House and the Bank neither are nor can be secure from this sort of destruction . . . a fire at the latter would bankrupt the nation." In effect, Paine declared war on Britain, threatening it with terrorism at home. In demanding that Britain cease its provocations in America, he pointed out how easily a single American warrior with "the same language, the same dress . . . with the same manners as yourselves can pass from one part of England to another unsuspected. . . ."

"Say not when mischief is done," he thundered, "that you had not warning."[26]

Although the Carlisle Commission had cited France as the "natural enemy" of Britain and, therefore, of all British subjects, Paine mocked its contention. "The Creator of Man did not constitute them the natural enemies of each other," said Paine. "He has not made any one order of beings so. Even wolves may quarrel, still they herd together. . . . We hold out the right hand of friendship to all the universe."[27]

Paine followed publication of *Crisis VI* with a seventh in the series, this one addressed "To the People of England," mocking them on the one hand while asking "why . . . you have not conquered us? Who or what has prevented you? You have had every opportunity . . . your fleets and armies have arrived in America without an accident. No uncommon fortune has intervened." He answered his own question:

> It has been the crime and folly of England to suppose herself invincible. . . . Their recluse situation, surrounded by sea, preserves them from the calamities of war and keeps them in the dark. . . . They see not, therefore they feel not. They tell the tale that is told them and believe it. . . . They are made to believe that their generals and armies differ from those of other nations. . . . They suppose them what they wish them to be . . . They feel a disgrace in thinking otherwise.[28]

Writing in a personal style as if addressing an individual Englishman, he explained that he had left England for America with no thoughts of taking up arms for American independence. He conceived himself happy and wished everybody else to be so.

"But when the country . . . was set on fire about my ears, it was time to stir. It was time for every man to stir." Off the battlefield, he said he saw his essays as a service to both sides in the conflict, "setting forth to the one the impossibility of being conquered and to the other the impossibility of conquering."[29]

Paine said he was at a loss to understand Britain's motives for going to war with America. The lure of foreign conquests, he said, is usually the added resources and commerce of the conquered lands. But, he protested, "you enjoyed the whole commerce before. The country and commerce were both your own when you began to conquer . . . as they had been [for] a hundred years before. . . . What then, in the name of heaven could you

go to war for?" It was the type of indisputable Paine logic that characterized so many of his writings.

Paine warned the English people that "your present king and ministry
will be the ruin of you and you had better risk a revolution and call a
Congress than be thus led on from madness to despair and from despair
to ruin. America has set you the example, and you may follow and be
free."[30] As with all his articles, he signed it with the pseudonym known all
but universally across America, Britain, and Europe: "Common Sense."

By the time he had finished *Crisis VII*, Admiral Jean-Baptiste-Charles-
Henri-Hector, Comte d'Estaing, Marquis de Saillons, and a French fleet of
sixteen warships had entered Delaware Bay carrying, among others, Sieur
Conrad Alexandre Gérard, the first minister plenipotentiary from France
and, indeed, the first such representative of any foreign nation in America.
A thirty-year veteran of the French foreign service, his appointment was
meant as both an honor to the Americans and a snub to the English. Also
aboard was Silas Deane, returning to America as ordered by Congress.

Instead of resolving the conflict over French aid to America, however,
Deane expanded it, telling Congress he had "placed my papers and yours
in safety [in] Paris and left in full confidence that I should not be detained
in America." He followed his statement to Congress with a long essay
in the December 5, 1778, issue of the *Pennsylvania Packet* claiming he
alone had been responsible for arranging the three initial Beaumarchais
arms shipments. Paine countered with documentary evidence to show
that Deane had, in fact, had nothing to do with the supplies Beaumarchais had shipped to America on the first three ships. "The supplies he so
pompously plumes himself upon," Paine wrote of Deane, "were promised
and engaged . . . before he [Deane] ever arrived in France."[31]

Deane went on to assail the Lee brothers—Arthur and William in
Europe and Richard Henry Lee in America—for interfering with his,
Deane's, mission by collaborating with Britain and obstructing Deane's
efforts to obtain French military aid.

Outraged by Deane's baseless accusations against the Lees, Paine struck
back with a pair of letters to the *Pennsylvania Packet* defending the Lees
and exposing as much as he knew about Deane's malfeasance.

"Would anybody have supposed that a gentleman in the character of
a commercial agent and afterwards in that of a public minister would

return home after seeing himself recalled and superseded and not bring with him his papers and vouchers?" Paine asked in his first letter, which he addressed "To the Public on Mr. Deane's Affair."

"Neither has he yet accounted for his expenditure of public money, which . . . might have been done by a written statement of accounts. . . . Why did Mr. Deane leave his papers in France?" What did Deane mean by "a safe place," Paine asked acerbically. "Mr. Deane has not only left the public papers and accounts behind him, he has given no information to Congress where or in whose hands they are. . . . There is something in this concealment of papers that looks like embezzlement!"

A man may leave his own private affairs in the hands of a friend, but the papers of a nation are of another nature and ought never be trusted with any person whatever out of the direct line of business. Mr. Deane might have been taken at sea . . . have died or been cast away. . . . Many accidents might have happened by which those papers and accounts might have been totally lost, the secrets got in the hands of the enemy.[32]

What Paine saw as malfeasance, however, Robert Morris, John Jay, and the powerful merchant-bankers who dominated Congress saw as legitimate profit opportunities in any and all financial transactions they brokered between governments. Paine argued that such profiteering was criminal behavior. Why else, Paine asked, would Deane refuse to respond to congressional questioning, using as his excuse, *"a man could not legally be compelled to answer questions that might tend to incriminate himself."* [His italics.]

Those who expressed outrage at Deane's conduct, however, were a minority in Congress and in Philadelphia it seems—with good reason. Few members of Congress had not profited from munitions contracts. Although Paine joined David Rittenhouse, Charles Willson Peale, and a handful of others in forming a citizens committee to investigate and combat public corruption, its inquiries proved useless. Only a handful of Patriots like Patrick Henry and Paine himself had been serving the nation without direct or indirect compensation. The Deane Affair disgusted them, but almost every merchant, banker, and plantation owner—in and out of Congress—who could profit from the war did just that quite openly. After Paine uncovered the financial connections that Robert Morris, the US Superintendent of Finance, had established with Deane, he expressed his shock to Congress.

"To what degree of corruption must we sink," Paine demanded to know, "if our delegates and ambassadors are to be admitted on a private partnership in trade?"

> Such a connection unfits a delegate for his duty in Congress by making him a partner with the servant over whose conduct he sits as one of his judges. . . . Only let this doctrine of Mr. Morris's take place and the consequences will be fatal to both public interest and public honor. Why not as well go halves with every quartermaster and commissary in the Army? . . . No wonder that Mr. Deane should be so violently supported by the members [of Congress] and that myself, who has been laboring to fish out and prove the partnership offense so dangerous to the common good, should be made the object of daily abuse.[33]

Morris fired back, asserting his right to profit from his office and denying the government's right "to inquire into what mercantile connection I have had or now have with Mr. Deane, or with any other person."

> As I did not, by becoming a delegate for the State of Pennsylvania [in Congress] relinquish my right of forming mercantile connections, I was unquestionably at liberty to form such with Mr. Deane. Whether . . . I have been led to form any . . . new concerns with him since his arrival here is a matter which the public are in no ways interested to know.[34]

Paine's revelations about Deane and Morris enraged Washington, if few others. "Speculation, peculation, and an insatiable thirst for riches seem to have got the better of every other consideration and almost every order of men," the general railed. "Party disputes and personal quarrels are the great business of the day whilst the momentous concerns of an empire . . . are but secondary considerations and postponed. . . . I am alarmed and wish to see my countrymen roused."[35]

Washington, however, either ignored or had differentiated between types of speculation according to his own personal ethical values. As one of America's most prominent land speculators, he had claimed thousands of acres as his own in the wilderness west of the Appalachians and had seen nothing unethical about scooping up raw land in Pennsylvania and Ohio to satisfy his own thirst for wealth and that of his relatives and close friends. Indeed, far from being considered unethical, speculation, if not peculation, was a primary—and honored—occupation for almost all of America's Founding Fathers and all other leading merchants, bankers, and landowners. Lands in the wilderness were there for the taking—and those who could take did take. Even Benjamin Franklin returned from France with an unexplained shortage of £100,000 in congressional funds. When a member of Congress had the audacity to question the discrepancy, Franklin replied with scripture: "Muzzle not the ox that treadeth out his master's grain."[36] No one in Congress ever mentioned the shortage again.

Of all the Founding Fathers, only nineteen-year-old Lafayette left a fortune behind in his native France to volunteer in the fight for American independence—and suffered a serious wound at Brandywine for his sacrifice. As for Paine, far from thirsting for riches, he donated the wealth he could have amassed from the sale of *Common Sense* and the *Crisis* essays to the nation—and he received nothing but scorn for his generosity from merchant-bankers such as Morris, Deane, and John Jay. Instead of provoking outrage at Deane, Paine's accusations provoked outrage at himself for criticizing what for most congressmen was a cherished way of life. One member of Congress went so far as to assail Paine in the press, writing under the pseudonym of "Plain Truth," and stopping only after Paine threatened to sue him for "publishing a false, malicious libel tending to injure the Secretary for Foreign Affairs."[37]

Although "Plain Truth" abandoned his attack on Paine in the press, others picked up his cudgel and wielded it against Paine in the street. "The poor fellow got a beating from an officer . . . for having wrote the piece," Francis Lightfoot Lee lamented to his brother Richard Henry Lee a few days before Christmas 1778. On his way home, Paine had encountered a group of merchants and clothing makers returning from a festive evening of contract exchanges at the Army clothier-general's home. After one snarled, "There comes Common Sense," a second—the most inebriated

. of the lot—lunged at Paine, cursing and shouting, "I shall common sense him," as he shoved Paine into a gutter.[38]

Deane, meanwhile, sailed away to France safely, freed by Congress of all wrongdoing. In fact, he had left his papers with his aide, George Lupton, the British spy, who, with Deane's secretary Edward Bancroft, copied the papers and sent them to their British government contacts in London. When Deane arrived back in Paris, however, a number of his investments in illicit arms deals had collapsed. Forced to find a haven with a lower cost of living, he moved to Ghent, Belgium, then to London, where he joined a myriad of American hustlers selling shares in phantom American farmlands or manufacturing projects.*

In addition to brutalization on the streets, Paine suffered public humiliation for having exposed Deane's malfeasance. While Congress had all but embraced the departed Deane as a hero for his alleged success in obtaining French aid, Deane's allies in Congress—Jay, Morris, and others—hurled accusations at Paine for violating the rules of Congress by disclosing secret information in his written criticisms of Deane. Jay charged that by writing that the arms and ammunition on the three original Beaumarchais ships "were promised and engaged . . . before he [Deane] ever arrived in France," Paine had violated his oath "to disclose no matter . . . he shall be directed to keep secret."

Jay then addressed Paine: "You may withdraw!"[39]

Shocked by Jay's command, Paine complained to a friend, "I prevented Deane's fraudulent demand being paid, but I became the victim of my integrity."[40]

Jay thus condemned Paine to be the first public official dismissed by the new nation's federal government. After Paine had left the hall, John Penn of North Carolina, a Jay ally, moved that "Thomas Paine be discharged from the office of secretary of the Committee on Foreign

---

*In 1789, he is said to have boarded a ship for the United States, but grew ill as the ship waited in port for repairs and died. Other reports had him dying in a small English town. And still other reports dismissed the place he died, saying only that his aide Bancroft had poisoned him to prevent his revealing Bancroft's own nefarious activities.

Affairs."[41] Congress and America, it seemed, wanted nothing more to do with Thomas Paine or his notions of what was or was not common sense.

Rather than be dismissed, Thomas Paine quit, firing a memorial at Congress declaring, "I cannot in duty to my character as a freeman submit to be censured. I have evidence which I presume will justify me, and I entreat this house to consider how great their reproach will be should it be told they passed a sentence upon me without hearing me and that a copy of the charge against me was refused to me."[42]

Congress spent the following days debating whether to hear Paine, with Jay's ally Gouverneur Morris* arguing against hearing a man he called "a mere adventurer from England. . . . Are we reduced to such a situation," he asked Congress, "that our servants . . . shall beard us with insolent menaces and we shall fear to dismiss them without granting a trial forsooth?"[43]

Morris's open attack on Paine marked the beginning of an unnecessary and mutually injurious conflict that would hurt both men. Quite simply—if the workings of any mind are ever simple—Morris, from the very first, resented Paine's successful intrusion in the American Revolution and the deliberations of Congress. He considered Paine a vulgar lower-class English laborer—a corset maker and political radical consumed by an exaggerated sense of self-importance, meddling in matters that were none of his business and, in any case, beyond his competence.

"Paine . . . seems to become every hour more drunk with self-conceit," Morris grumbled. He accused Paine of proclaiming *Common Sense* as having started the American Revolution. "I frankly acknowledge," Morris added, "that I urged his dismission from the office he held of Secretary to the Committee on Foreign Affairs."[44] In effect, Morris sought to have Paine sent home to England.

Scion of wealthy landowners with roots reaching back to the seventeenth-century Dutch settlement in New Amsterdam (later, New York), Morris spent his childhood on his family's majestic 2,000-acre estate north of New York City. He earned a bachelor's degree and master's

---

*Gouverneur Morris was a close friend and a frequent business partner of Robert Morris, but they were unrelated.

degree from New York's King's College (later Columbia) before gaining admission to the New York bar in 1775, when he was twenty-three. Elected to the New York Provincial Assembly, he held beliefs and interests which, curiously enough, coincided with those of Paine in many areas. Like Paine he was a fierce opponent of slavery, and he favored religious freedom. A strong supporter of independence, he won appointment to the Continental Congress and, later, the Constitutional Convention.

Unlike Paine, however, Morris was "an aristocrat to the core," arguing at the Constitutional Convention that "there never was nor ever will be a civilized society without an aristocracy."[45] Thus, Morris's vision of the government and individual liberties in an independent America differed widely from Paine's. Both favored a strong central government, but Morris believed in restricting voting rights to male property owners, with unlimited terms for the President, lifetime appointments to the US Senate, and unfettered capitalism. Paine's vision ensured equality of all men—and women—in all respects, including universal suffrage, universal public education, universal health care, social security, and almost all the individual benefits promised by twentieth-century socialism.

Incensed at his cavalier treatment by Morris, Paine sent Congress a second letter of resignation declaring, "I have betrayed no trust. . . . I have revealed no secrets. . . . I have convicted Mr. Deane of error, and in so doing I hope I have done my duty."[46]

Four days of angry debate followed over whether to accept Paine's resignation, during which South Carolina's Henry Laurens, who had succeeded John Hancock as President of Congress, resigned in disgust after admitting he had kept Paine informed of all proceedings. A wealthy South Carolina rice grower and slave trader who had studied in England as a young man, Laurens, like Paine, became an avid amateur astronomer and one of many notable Paine friends from the American Philosophical Society.

After accepting Laurens's resignation, Congress accepted Paine's as well, severing Paine's last formal connection to the American government. Having contributed the last pennies of his earnings to Congress to buy arms and ammunition, he left himself without enough to buy himself a loaf of bread; he stepped out of Congress onto the streets of Philadelphia all but destitute.

Chapter 5

CAN NOTHING BE DONE
FOR POOR PAINE?

Bereft of worldly goods as he was, Paine had nonetheless amassed a wealth of friends who rallied about him. Always ready to offer him a room and a meal, they often found themselves lodging and feeding him for days—and giving or lending him as much money as he needed and they could afford.

"I feel myself so curiously circumstanced that I have both too many friends and too few," Paine wrote to former President of Congress Henry Laurens, the South Carolina rice king. "What they have had from me they have got for nothing, and they consequently suppose I must be able to afford it."

> I know but one kind of life I am fit for and that is a thinking one, and, of course, a writing one. . . . I think I have the right to ride a horse of my own, but I cannot now even afford to hire one, which is a situation I never was in before. . . . I take the liberty of communicating to you my design of doing some degree of justice to myself, but even this is accompanied with some present difficulties.[1]

Paine told Laurens he intended collecting all his writings, including *Common Sense*, and publishing them in two volumes octavo, the most common size of modern books—about eight to ten inches tall and about six inches wide.* He said he had "no doubt of a large subscription," but

---

* Octavo refers to folding of each large paper sheet three times, producing eight leaves and sixteen pages.

needed to borrow money to buy paper for the printer. "I would rather wish to borrow something from a friend or two. . . . I have hitherto kept all my private matters a secret, but as I know your friendship and you a great deal of my situation, I can with more ease communicate with you than to another."[2]

Former Pennsylvania governor Owen Biddle, an officer in the war and another of Paine's friends at the American Philosophical Society, rescued Paine with a clerk's job and a salary that gave him full freedom to write and join Philadelphia's political mix—although not enough money to buy membership in the Society. Invited to volunteer in a number of citizens committees, however, Paine eagerly accepted. Such committees not only put him in contact with Philadelphia's influential social and political elite, they gave him a voice in confronting the most intractable social, economic, and political problems facing the city, state, and nation—including inflation.

Early in 1779, the coldest winter in recorded American history at the time struck the American Northeast and inflicted hardships on Washington's army that surpassed those suffered at Valley Forge the previous year. A violent snowstorm intensified the suffering. According to Washington, it "so blocked up the roads that it will be some days before the scanty supplies in this quarter can be brought to camp." He said many troops had gone four or five days without meat or adequate supplies of bread.[3]

Pennsylvania President* Joseph Reed, whom Paine first met in Washington's tent the night before the Battle of Trenton, asked Paine to help promote a private subscription to subsidize the war effort. Paine corralled a few friendly merchants, warning them that "the rich will suffer most by the ravages of an enemy," and that it was "not only duty but true policy to do something spirited."[4] He convinced large numbers to hold fundraisers; even his avowed enemy Robert Morris participated, and, with Paine pledging $500 he could not afford, they pledged a total of £300,000 (just over $500,000 then). Morris and the others then founded America's first government-owned bank—the Bank of Pennsylvania—to handle the

---

*When each colony declared independence and became a sovereign entity, most chief executives assumed the title of "President" instead of "governor."

funds. Touched by Paine's efforts to secure American independence, the board of the newly established University of Pennsylvania awarded Paine an honorary master's degree.

Impressed by his work, Pennsylvania's assembly appointed him its clerk, providing him with enough income and comfort to resume writing. To Paine's delight, on the same day the assembly elected him clerk, it introduced America's first act abolishing slavery, introducing it with a preamble largely written by Paine himself. With a total population of just over 300,000, Pennsylvania had about 6,000 slaves.

"We esteem it a peculiar blessing granted to us," read Paine's preamble, "that we are enabled this day to add one more step to universal civilization by removing . . . the sorrows of those who have lived in undeserved bondage and from which, by the assumed authority of the Kings of Great Britain, no . . . relief could be obtained."[5]

The arrival of a British fleet off the Carolina coast near Charleston the following winter induced Paine to write *The American Crisis No. VIII.* Addressed to "The People of England," his essay reminded the British that "five years have nearly elapsed since the commencement of hostilities, and every campaign . . . has lessened your ability to conquer." He warned that England had yet to experience "the miseries of war," but recent forays along the British coast by Captain John Paul Jones and his small fleet of marauders had "signaled a shift in the course of the war . . . and invasion shall be transferred to the invaders. America is beyond the reach of conquest," he boasted.[6]

To his embarrassment, Paine learned a few days later that Charleston had fallen, in one of the worst American defeats of the war. The British captured the entire 5,400-man American garrison and its commanding general, along with four American warships.

"They have unwisely aggravated us into life," Paine returned fire in *Crisis IX* at the beginning of June. Because of long intervals between engagements, he said, Americans had had a tendency to grow "drowsy" and, disposed as they were to peace, they had slipped into "a dangerous calm.

"Afflicting as the loss of Charleston may be," he asserted, "if it universally rouses us from the slumber of twelve months past and renews the spirit of former days, it will produce an advantage more important than its loss. . . . It is not the conquest of towns . . . or garrisons . . . that can reduce a country so extensive as this. . . . This piece-meal work is not conquering the continent."

As he had in so many other editions of *Crisis*, Paine tried rallying American spirits at another low point of the Revolutionary War: "Charleston is gone," he admitted, blaming an insufficient supply of provisions. "The man that does not feel for the honor of the best and noblest cause that ever a country engaged in and exert himself accordingly is no longer worthy of a peaceable residence among a people determined to be free."[7]

Shortly after Paine had written *Crisis IX*, Washington complained to Congress about its continuing failure to fund the military, saying the Army faced a crisis that "in every point of view is extraordinary." Paine spent the next three months exploring methods of providing Washington with the funding he needed. Marching in and out of the Statehouse and meeting with members of the state assembly and members of Congress, he developed a plan he described in a pamphlet he released in early October 1780, *The Crisis Extraordinary, on the Subject of Taxation.*

Directed at leaders in Congress and state governments rather than the British or American public, he compared taxes and populations in England (seven million people, exclusive of Scotland and Ireland) and America (three million). Before the Revolutionary War, England had collected £11,642,653 in taxes, or £1.13s.3d "per head per annum, men women and children," which he called enough to have defrayed "all her annual expenses of war and government within each year."

In contrast, he continued, the cost of war to America's three million men, women, and children was costing £2 million a year, or an average of only thirteen shillings and four pence per person—a pittance that made paying taxes seem eminently palatable. When divided among the states, the cost to Pennsylvanians would be a mere three shillings, five pence per person—about the same tax England levied on two bottles of rum. The peace establishment at the end of the war, he predicted, would cost an additional £750,000 or a mere five shillings per person annually.

"Suppose Britain was to conquer America," he posited. "Our share would be six million pounds."[8] Paine admitted he had no firm plan for obtaining the funds, but suggested raising at least half from import duties and letting the individual states "devise means to raise the other half."[9]

Years would pass, however, before Congress and the states could reach agreement on converting his proposal into actual taxes. In the meantime, American forces needed cash urgently to pursue the war. Although 5,000 French troops had landed at Newport, Rhode Island, the Americans had lost Savannah as well as Charleston. Paine agreed to write to French Foreign Minister Comte de Vergennes for loans of £1 million a year for the duration of the Revolution.

Paine also had another plan, and wrote to his former military commander Nathanael Greene asking whether "a person possessed of a knowledge of America and capable of fixing it in the minds of the people of England [could] go suddenly from this country to that and, keeping himself concealed . . . were he to manage his knowledge rightly . . . produce a more general disposition for peace than by any [other] method."

> It was in a great measure owing to my bringing a knowledge of England with me to America that I was enabled to enter deeper into politics, and with more success than other people; and whoever takes the matter up in England must in like manner be possessed of knowledge of America.[10]

He was certain that all Britain—her people, even her government—had tired of war, but the difficulty was "how they are to come down from the high ground they have taken?" Paine apparently thought he could slip into England as unknown as he had been in America when he arrived, then hide behind a pseudonymous cloak, much as he had hidden behind the signature of "Common Sense" in advocating American independence in Philadelphia.

"I do not suppose that . . . [American] independence is . . . more unpopular in England than . . . it was in America before . . . *Common Sense*. . . . I had a considerable share in promoting the declaration of independence in this country. I likewise wish to be a means of promoting it in that country."[11]

Paine's plan to go to England appalled Greene, who warned Paine that unlike Philadelphia, London teemed with government informers—especially among printers and booksellers. Fearing he would hang if caught, Paine seemed to abandon his plan and turned his attention back to American domestic affairs. Among other major domestic disputes in

Congress was the disposition of the unsettled territories west of the Appalachian Mountains, beyond the recognized thirteen state borders. With little else of import to divert his attention, Paine studied the question—and embarked on a venture that would cost him more than a few influential American friends.

In 1690, a royal charter had granted the Virginia Company all the lands extending to the "Southern [i.e., Pacific] Ocean," stretching northwest to the Great Lakes. In pre-Revolutionary War years, a coterie of powerful Virginia families—the Washingtons, Lees, Randolphs, and others—had surveyed and staked out claims to hundreds of thousands of acres of Virginia Company lands, with the intention of dividing them into sections for resale to settlers.* In 1763, a royal proclamation had redefined Virginia's borders as extending to, but not beyond the heads of, all rivers emptying into the Atlantic, but as tax protests enveloped America, the British punished Virginia's protest leaders by abolishing the Virginia Company and claimed all its lands for Quebec.

With the Declaration of Independence, Virginia reclaimed those lands, allowing its citizens to reclaim their holdings. But other states objected, and with no other issues in which to involve himself, Paine wrote a pamphlet he called *Public Good*. In it he cited legal precedents to prove that all territories beyond the limits of the thirteen provinces that had belonged to the crown before the Revolution now belonged to the American government, i.e., Congress, and not to any of the states or individual land speculators. Although *Public Good* had no immediate practical effects, it revived a dispute that would continue to surface until 1787, when Virginia ceded the territory to the United States under the terms of the Northwest Ordinance.

Before Paine published *Public Good*, Virginia had been planning to present Paine with a handsome gift for his services during the Revolution. It not only rescinded the gift, one of its sponsors, Richard Henry Lee, who had been Paine's closest ally in Congress, all but dismissed Paine as a friend, as did the other members of the powerful Lee family. Paine's *Public*

---

*A "section" of land consisted of 640 acres, with thirty-six sections making up a township in early America.

Good angered many of Paine's other Virginia friends, including Thomas Jefferson, James Madison, and George Washington, all of whom had laid claims to lands in the wilderness that Paine now proposed they cede to Congress. Essay by essay, Paine was gradually wearing out his welcome in America—so much so that by the time he applied for membership in the American Philosophical Society, he had alienated so many former friends that they combined to reject his application.

When, therefore, Lieutenant Colonel John Laurens, a close aide to General Washington and son of Paine's friend Henry Laurens, asked Paine to come with him to Paris on a mission for Congress to obtain funding for the war, Paine gladly accepted. Congress had selected Laurens for the mission because he was not only familiar with the military details and complexities of the war as a Washington aide, he had studied law in Geneva and spoke French fluently. To further punish Paine for publishing *Public Good*, however, Congress refused to pay for Paine's passage, and Laurens (or perhaps his father) paid Paine's costs.

In early February, Thomas Paine and John Laurens sailed from Boston on the monthlong journey to Lorient on the southern coast of Brittany. In contrast to the frost that had recently gripped his social relationships in Philadelphia, Paine met a hero's welcome when he set foot on French shores. As he disembarked, a crowd of cheering Frenchmen stood at the pier with the commandant of Lorient and the mayor of nearby Nantes to greet and honor the man and his written works. Once in Paris, Paine basked in the warm friendship of his aging patron Benjamin Franklin, America's ambassador to France. Paine still hoped to make a quick visit to England incognito despite friendly advice to the contrary and the certainty that he faced certain death if authorities there identified him. Franklin stepped in to forbid his friend from going, and Paine yielded.

It was not a difficult decision given the accolades he received with every step he took in Paris. Remaining there for the next ten weeks, he tried to help John Laurens and Benjamin Franklin wrangle military and economic aid from the French government, but the lack of diplomatic credentials from Congress and his inability to speak French limited his participation. As it was, Laurens and Franklin obtained just under £2 million in hard money—gold and silver—along with "large amounts" of arms, clothing, and ammunition.

When Laurens and Paine returned to Boston, money in hand, they learned that Washington's army was moving south with the French army into Virginia. Their goal: to trap a British force under Cornwallis on a cape that dead-ended at Yorktown. Laurens abruptly left Paine and galloped off to join his commander, leaving Paine to lead sixteen teams of oxen and an armed guard to Philadelphia to deliver the gold and silver from France to Congress.

"I had to bear my own expenses and that of a servant he [Laurens] had left with me and two horses for three hundred miles," Paine complained, "and I was obliged to borrow a dollar at Bordentown to pass the ferry with."[12] Rather than trust the funds from France to the local Bank of Pennsylvania, Congress yielded to the proposal of US Superintendent of Finance Robert Morris to charter a national bank to hold the funds. Accordingly, Congress chartered the Bank of North America—America's first central bank—which pledged the full faith of the government to insure all deposits against loss.

By the time Paine reached Philadelphia with the gold and silver, the city had learned of Silas Deane's malfeasance and subsequent flight from Paris. "Silas Deane has run his last length," Paine smiled as he told Benjamin Franklin's nephew when he arrived. "In France he is reprobating America and in America he is reprobating France." Deane was indeed calling on American leaders to "abandon the alliance with France, relinquish independence, and once more become subject to Britain." Paine said that the publication of Deane's letters had so embarrassed his former friends in Congress that those who had set upon Paine for criticizing Deane in 1779 now embraced him.

"Mr. Robert Morris assured me that he had been totally deceived in Deane," Paine laughed as he wrote, "but that he now looked upon him to be a bad man, and his reputation totally ruined. Gouverneur Morris hopped round on one leg,* swore they had all been duped, himself among the rest, complimented me on my quick [in]sight and by God [Morris said] . . . nothing carries a man through the world like honesty."[13]

---

*Morris lost his right leg in 1780 when a carriage ran over him as he allegedly fled from an irate husband who discovered and objected to Morris's sexual rendezvous with the man's wife.

The restoration of Paine's reputation in Congress followed a week of universal joy in America following the surrender of Lord Cornwallis and the British army at Yorktown on October 19, 1781. Paine's own joy, however, was short-lived as he realized his service to America had again left him penniless. Adding to his distress was word that his printers had pocketed countless thousands of pounds of profits from the sale of writings he had ordered donated to Congress to help pay for the war. Still worse, Thomas Bell, the original printer of *Common Sense*, had published and kept all proceeds from an unauthorized second edition with what he claimed to be "large additions" by Paine himself.

"It is seven years this day since I arrived in America," Paine wrote to George Washington after Yorktown, "and tho' I consider them as the most honorary time of my life, they have nevertheless been the most inconvenient and even distressing. From an anxiety to support . . . the cause of America . . . I declined the customary profits which authors are entitled to."

He told Washington he had anticipated America would reciprocate his generosity but was stunned to encounter the contrary.

"Almost everybody knows, not only in this country but in Europe, that I have been of service to [America], yet so confined have been my private circumstances that for one summer I was obliged to hire myself as a common clerk for my support," Paine said. He thought that having dealt "generously and honorably" toward America, America would reciprocate. Instead, he found himself in "a very unpleasant situation" and was at a loss to understand why. "Everybody I meet treats me with friendship; all join in censuring the neglect and throwing the blame on each other, so that their civility disarms me as much as their conduct distresses me. But in this situation I cannot go on."

Paine said he now planned to go either to France or Holland, where he said "I have literary fame, and I am sure I cannot experience worse fortune than I have here."[14]

Washington was as stunned reading Paine's letter as Paine was in writing it. The commanding general appealed for help to Superintendent of Finance Robert Morris. Gouverneur Morris conferred with Paine, and, embarrassed for having publicly defended Silas Deane's malfeasance, the two Morrises met with Washington. On February 10, 1782, the three

17. What Paine saw as malfeasance, Robert Morris, seen here, and other powerful merchant-bankers in Congress considered legitimate opportunities to profit from arms transactions they brokered between governments.

signed what amounted to a proclamation ordering the Secretary of Foreign Affairs to hire Paine as a writer at $800 a year to fill the "necessity of informing the people and rousing them into action."[15]

On April 18, 1783, Washington announced the formal end of the war with Britain and, on the following day—the eighth anniversary of the massacre on Lexington Green—Paine published what would be his last *Crisis*—*Crisis XIII*, or one for each state.

"The times that tried men's souls are over," Paine declared, "and the greatest completest revolution the world ever knew, gloriously and happily accomplished." Paine looked to America's future as well as the past, pleading for national unity—"a Union of the States"—with each of the newly independent states subsuming its sovereignty to a supreme national government.

"On this our great character depends," he declared. "It is this which must give us importance abroad and security at home. It is through this only that we are, or can be, nationally known in the world; it is the flag of the United States which renders our ships and commerce safe on the seas, or in a foreign port. . . . All our treaties . . . are formed under the sovereignty of the United States, and Europe knows us by no other title. The division of the empire into states is for our own convenience, but abroad this distinction ceases. . . . In short, we have no other national sovereignty than as United States."

Besides national unity, he said, independence carried with it the responsibility "to enlighten the world and diffuse a spirit of freedom and liberality among mankind. . . . The remembrance of what is past . . . must inspire her."[16]

Paine said the American struggle and the Declaration of Independence had been most responsible for his becoming a full-time writer. "If in the course of more than seven years, I have rendered . . . service, I have likewise added something to the reputation of literature by freely and disinterestedly employing it in the great cause of mankind." With the war ended, he said, he would "always feel an honest pride in the part I have taken and acted and a gratitude to nature and providence for putting it in my power to be of some use to mankind."[17]

And, as in the past, he signed it with his widely revered American pseudonym, "Common Sense."

Well, almost revered. Paine had, unfortunately, alienated a raft of state leaders across the South who remained intent on eternalizing slavery and repelling central government encroachments on state sovereignty. Earlier, of course, he had alienated Virginians with his pamphlet *Public Good*, which called for transfer of Virginia's wilderness lands to the central government.

With the end of the war in 1783, therefore, came an end to Paine's evident usefulness to America. With no need for him to rouse the people, Congress ended his employ as a writer—and the $800-a-year salary Washington believed he had obtained for Paine. Paine appealed for a government pension for his wartime services, saying, "I neglected myself for years . . . to serve others," and that a pension would determine whether he could afford to "remain in the rank of a citizen of America or whether I must wish her well and say to her Adieu."[18]

But Congress had no funds. Indeed, before it could even consider Paine's appeal, several hundred Pennsylvania troops, their bayonets fixed, marched on the Statehouse demanding overdue back pay, and forcing members of Congress to flee Philadelphia to the safety of nearby Princeton, New Jersey. Their departure, with their families and those of congressional hangers-on, left Philadelphia all but deserted.

With all its horrors, the war had generated deep friendships and warm camaraderie, and although the gregarious Paine had accumulated a large coterie of friends of all ranks, peace now sent them all home, dispersing across the land or, in the case of Congress, fleeing to Princeton. Left friendless in Philadelphia, Paine grew lonely and suddenly longed for the long ago and the England he had known as a child in Thetford with his parents and school chums. Without money, however, he had no way of leaving Philadelphia, let alone crossing the sea to England. An officer he had befriended during the evacuation of Philadelphia had promised he would always be welcome, and with no means to survive in Philadelphia, he walked the thirty-odd miles to Bordentown, New Jersey, and the home of Colonel Joseph Kirkbride.

To Paine's surprise, George Washington tracked him down. "I have learned . . . that you are at Bordentown. Whether for the sake of retirement or economy, I know not. Be it for either, for both or whatever it may, if you will come to this place and partake with me, I shall be exceedingly happy to see you."

In fact, Washington was as stunned as Paine by the failure of Congress to pension the author of *Common Sense*. Still ebullient and uncharacteristically lighthearted over the outcome of the war, he invited Paine for an extended stay at his new headquarters at Rocky Hill, New Jersey, five miles from Princeton. "Your presence may remind Congress of your past services to this country," Washington enthused, "and if it is in my power to impress them, command my best services with freedom, as they will be rendered cheerfully by one who entertains a lively sense of the importance of your works and who, with much pleasure, subscribes himself Your sincere friend."[19]

Washington's patronage had immediate effects. In the spring of 1784, New York's Senate awarded Paine a 277-acre, confiscated Tory farm in New Rochelle, New York, just north of New York City. Worth more than £1,100, the fine farmhouse would provide him with a home in America, and a tenant farmer on the property would provide Paine with steady income. With the farm, also, came the state's formal recognition that Paine's literary works had "inspired the citizens of this state . . . in the rectitude of their cause and . . . contributed to the freedom, sovereignty, and independence of the United States."[20]

Elated, Paine sent Washington his thanks for "the friendship you have shown me and the pains you have taken to promote my interests."[21] Paine considered himself an accomplished poet and lyricist and composed a song to honor Washington. Written to the melody of *Rule Britannia*, Paine called his song *Hail Great Republic*. The first of its six stanzas read:

> *Hail great Republic of the world,*
> *Which rear'd her empire in the West,*
> *Where fam'd Columbus' flag unfurl'd,*
> *Gave tortured Europe scenes of rest;*
>
> *Be thou forever great and free,*
> *The land of Love and Liberty.*

Washington was indefatigable in promoting Paine's interest, writing to Richard Henry Lee in Congress, "Unsolicited by and unknown to Mr. Paine, I take the liberty of hinting the distressed situation of that gentleman.

That his Common Sense and many of his Crisis . . . had a happy effect upon the public mind, no one . . . will deny. That his services hitherto have passed unnoticed is obvious and that he is chagrined and necessitous I will undertake to aver. Does not common justice then point to some compensation?[22]

Washington then wrote to James Madison in the Virginia legislature: "Can nothing be done in our assembly for poor Paine? Must the merits and services of *Common Sense* continue to glide down the stream of time, unrewarded by this country?"

> His writings have had a powerful effect on the public mind. Ought they not then meet an adequate return? He is poor! He is chagrined! And almost if not altogether in despair of relief. . . . I am sure you will not only move the matter but give it your support.[23]

Rarely had Washington been so publicly emotional about anything but military affairs.

He wrote to Governor Patrick Henry on Paine's behalf and Edmund Randolph, one of Virginia's members in Congress and soon to become Virginia's governor. James Madison responded with a motion in the Virginia Assembly that the state give Paine a parcel of confiscated Tory land worth more than £4,000.

The era of *Common Sense*, however, lay seven years in the past; a new generation had replaced the heroes of '76 in state legislatures. To many Virginians in that younger generation, Paine threatened their way of life as a champion of emancipation and a strong central government, with powers to tax property and seize what had been state-owned lands in the western wilderness.

Indeed, even while visiting Washington at Rocky Hill, Paine had had the audacity to issue a "Letter to America" suggesting a standing army and navy—one of the British threats that had provoked the Revolutionary War. "It is only by acting in union," he now insisted, "that the usurpations of foreign nations on the freedom of trade can be counteracted and security [be] extended to the commerce of America."[24]

Virginia's assembly summarily rejected Madison's proposal to pension Paine, although Pennsylvania awarded him £500, and the American Philosophical Society reversed four earlier decisions and admitted Paine to its hallowed membership. The refusal of other states to honor Paine added to Washington's outrage at the cavalier attitude with which much of the nation now dismissed the heroes of the Revolution. Even with Washington standing in the wings, Congress halved the $6,000 that Paine's support-ers had proposed. The $3,000 grant, however, proved enough. Coupled with his state grants of property and money, Paine finally emerged from the shadows of poverty and could now claim the comforts of a relatively settled man.

Paine thanked Washington again and then seemed to withdraw from public life, first at his friend Colonel Kirkbride's home in Bordentown, New Jersey, where Paine acquired a small property of his own to escape the frenzied life of Philadelphia thirty miles away. After Congress resettled in New York, however, Paine moved to the farm he had been granted in New Rochelle, New York, about twenty miles from where Congress was sitting. Although he fully intended to retire from politics, his farm lay close enough to the political maelstrom to permit his issuing occasional essays to try to influence the course of events in his adopted land.

In the meantime, he would pursue dreams that his years of military and political warfare had forced him to postpone. A habitual sketcher of mechanical inventions born of his imagination, Paine now planned on becoming a full-time tinkerer and converting devices born of his imagi-nation into reality. He had described some of his imaginary inventions in

18. Thomas Paine's house in New Rochelle, New York, in a nineteenth-century photograph by Mercure Dan-iel Conway, author of the definitive two-volume Paine biography.

letters to his patron Benjamin Franklin, whose imagination and passion for tinkering were wilder and more fertile than Paine's and who had returned to Philadelphia in the fall of 1785.

"I send you the candles I have been making," Paine wrote to Franklin describing what he called smokeless candles. "In a little time after they are lighted the smoke and flame separate, the one issuing from one end of the candle and the other from the other end."[25] Franklin asked Paine to visit on January 1, 1786, but after testing the smokeless candles, Franklin convinced Paine they had no commercial value.

Not so with Paine's designs for iron bridges that he envisioned spanning rivers from shore to shore without piers to limit or interfere with riverboat traffic. Paine believed single-arched, shore-to-shore iron bridges would also eliminate the collapse of bridges in northern climes, where deep winter frosts formed ice so thick it often crushed bridge piers, collapsing the overhead span and leaving would-be travelers on either side unable to cross. Without bridges, Americans had no choice but to cross on costly ferries.

Paine had seen an arched single-span iron bridge on his visit to Paris in 1781, and, indeed, John Wilkinson, an English ironworker–turned-inventor, had built the world's first such bridge across the River Severn in Coalbrookdale, about 150 miles northeast of London. At about 100 feet across and designed to span narrow streams, it lacked the strength to stretch across America's great rivers, but Paine realized after careful calculations that a single-arched bridge could cross a river of any width if he shaped the arch as part of a perfect circle with a large enough diameter.

To make taller, wider bridges strong enough to carry traffic, he envisioned building them in sections, each a partial arch of two parallel, curved girders tied to each other by short, supportive steel ribs, creating a strong, web-like ensemble. To form the finished bridge, he planned connecting the arches end to end to form a colossal single arch in the form of a perfect semicircle. Paine copied actual spiders' webs in designing elements of his arch, citing such webs as one of nature's strongest structures, built with a minimum of materials. Paine won the enthusiastic support of Lewis Morris, a signer of the Declaration of Independence and owner, with his half-brother Gouverneur Morris, of the 2,000-acre Morrisania estate and

19. The River Wear bridge. Modern reconstruction of the world's first single-arched iron bridge at Coalbrookdale, England. Reflection illustrates Thomas Paine's theory that a single-arched iron bridge could span rivers of any width if the arch were shaped as part of a perfect circle.

farm in the Bronx. Morris envisioned a bridge across the tidal waters of the Harlem River as a swift, direct overland route for produce from Morrisania to markets on the southern tip of New York Island. Morris grew so enthusiastic about the bridge that, in addition to financial support, he turned one of Paine's cherished wishes into reality by presenting Paine with a gift horse that Paine would grow to adore and call "Button."

To gain national attention for his bridge, Paine rode to Philadelphia, rented a warehouse, hired a mechanic to assist him, and built a model made of cherrywood in thirteen sections—one for each state. As four big men stood atop the span "without the least injury to it, or signs of any," curiosity seekers lined up to see Paine's engineering wonder. Men of note followed—even national figures such as Dr. James Hutchinson, David Rittenhouse, Lewis and Gouverneur Morris, of course, and Paine's proud patron Benjamin Franklin.

Fearful the wooden model would not hold the combined weights of overland freight, Paine reached into his own pocket to finance construction of a model made of cast iron, which Benjamin Franklin agreed to exhibit at his home with the wooden model. Elected President of Pennsylvania's Executive Council by then, Franklin urged Paine to invite the entire Council to view the bridge and consider underwriting its construction across the Schuylkill River, the first of its kind in the Americas.

Deeply moved by Franklin's support, Paine responded, "I have the pleasure of submitting to you . . . two models for a bridge, one of wood, the other of cast iron . . . for the purpose of showing my respect to you as my patron in this country as for the sake of your opinion and judgment thereon."

> The European method of bridge architecture, by piers and arches, is not adapted to many of the rivers in America on account of the ice in the winter. The construction of those I have the honor of presenting to you is designed to obviate the difficulty of leaving the whole passage of the river clear of the encumbrance of piers.

Paine said he had designed the wooden model for "my good friend General [Lewis] Morris for a bridge over the Harlem River [in New York], but I can't help thinking that it might be carried across the Schuylkill [River, Philadelphia]." Paine recognized that the models were too large "to be admitted" in Franklin's house, "but will stand very well in the garden."[26]

After knowledgeable builders urged Paine to substitute wrought iron for the more brittle cast iron, he produced a second iron model and displayed it to the world in the Statehouse yard on January 1, 1787. The renowned scientist David Rittenhouse joined Benjamin Franklin as Paine's patron and sponsor. He had first met Paine in 1776 when he reviewed—and heartily endorsed—an advance copy of *Common Sense*. Rittenhouse had subsequently befriended Paine, helping him expand his knowledge of astronomy, the science that had and would continue to influence Paine's thinking about God and the Creation.

"Our world," Paine realized after long discussions with Rittenhouse, "if we compare it with the immensity of space in which it is suspended like a bubble or balloon in the air, is infinitely less in proportion than the smallest grain of sand is to the size of the world or the smallest particle of dew to the whole ocean and . . . is only one of a system of worlds of which the universal creation is composed."[27]

The long discussions among Paine, Rittenhouse, and Franklin invariably explored their ideas on creation. "From whence," Paine asked, "could arise the solitary conceit that the Almighty, who had millions of worlds equally dependent on His protection, should quit the care of all the rest and come to die in our world because . . . one woman had eaten an apple."

> Are we to suppose that every world in the boundless creation had an Eve, a serpent, and a redeemer? In this case, the person who is irreverently called the Son of God and sometimes God Himself would have nothing else to do than to travel from world to world in an endless succession of deaths with scarcely a momentary interval of life.[28]

As Franklin and Rittenhouse burst into laughter at Paine's absurd postulates, Franklin inevitably brought their talks back to the practical—at that time, the construction of Paine's chimerical bridge. To build that actual bridge across the Schuylkill River near Philadelphia, Paine estimated he would need 520 tons of wrought iron at a cost of $330,000—more than Pennsylvania's entire annual state budget.

Although members of the state assembly praised the structure, they refused the absurdly large financial resources Paine would need to build it. Nor could Franklin and Rittenhouse coax private investors to support the project. Franklin and Rittenhouse were as disappointed as Paine, and Franklin urged Paine to go to England and Europe to seek endorsements from learned societies—the Royal Academy of Sciences in London, for example, and the Académie des Sciences (Academy of Sciences) in Paris. Both were aggressive in obtaining financial support for the experimental advances they endorsed in science and architecture.

Franklin's suggestion came at a propitious time for Paine, who had just received a letter from his seventy-eight-year-old father in Thetford, with strong hints he was sending his son a final farewell. "I had, a few days ago, the great pleasure and happiness of a letter from you," Paine responded, "the first and only one I have received since the beginning of the war in 1775 to the present time. Never hearing from you or of you or any of my relations, I had determined coming to England the ensuing winter, and I yet hope to have the happiness of seeing you once more after so long a separation."[29]

As Paine contemplated returning to his native land and perhaps a last reunion with his father, the American economy began to collapse following a rupture of trade talks with Britain. The break followed the failure of America's loose-knit Confederation Congress to force all thirteen American states to abide by the Treaty of Paris that had ended the Revolutionary War. The treaty had required American states to compensate Tory property owners for uncompensated confiscation of their American properties and to force American subjects to pay their prewar debts to British merchants. With the British unwilling to negotiate with each state individually, Congress took charge of American negotiations, but it lacked powers to force states to abide by every tentative agreement it reached.

The British grew so exasperated, they abandoned negotiations, leaving American farmers without markets for their produce or income with which to pay their mortgages, let alone feed their children. Farmers, craftsmen, and other economically distraught Americans called for dissolution of the Bank of Pennsylvania and the Bank of North America and demanded that state governments print paper money with which farmers could pay their taxes and debts. With 95 percent of Americans working in agriculture, the American economy was based on barter, with personal IOUs—in effect, nonstandard paper money of sorts—ensuring the equitability of each transaction.

Merchants—almost all of them creditors—opposed paper money and, in Rhode Island, shopkeepers closed their doors rather than accept such payments. When the legislature responded by making it illegal *not* to accept paper money, some merchants fled the state. Debtors rioted and broke into shops to force shopkeepers to accept paper money—to no avail.

The discontent spread quickly to other states. Farmers—thousands of them veterans who had yet to be paid for wartime services—were first to rebel. Out of money, most had no protection against seizures of their properties for nonpayment of debts or taxes. Hundreds of farmers saw their lands and homes confiscated and their livestock and personal possessions—including tools of their trade—auctioned at prices too low to clear their debts. Hysterical wives and children watched helplessly as sheriffs' deputies dragged farmer-husbands and fathers off to debtors' prisons, where they languished indefinitely—unable to earn money to pay their debts.

Enraged farmers across the nation took up rifles and pitchforks to protect their properties, firing at sheriffs and others who ventured too near. Reassembling their wartime companies, they set fire to jails, courthouses, and offices of county clerks, threatening to ignite a second American revolution—this one against their own state governments. In western Massachusetts, former captain Daniel Shays, a destitute farmer struggling to hold on to his property, convinced his neighbors that local lawyers and judges had conspired with Boston merchants, bankers, and state legislators to raise taxes and seize farms for nonpayment of taxes. Calling on farmers to "close down the courts!" Shays led a force of 500 men to Springfield to shut the state supreme court and seize the federal arsenal. As his cry echoed across the state, mobs of farmers shut courthouses in six other towns.[30]

In New Hampshire, farmers marched to the state capitol at Exeter, surrounded the legislature, and demanded forgiveness of all debts, return of all seized properties to former owners, and equitable distribution of property. A mob of Maryland farmers with similar demands burned down the Charles County courthouse, while Virginia farmers burned down the King William and the New Kent County courthouses.

Paine now feared that Gouverneur Morris had been right, that Americans—and perhaps ordinary men everywhere—were incapable of governing themselves. The individual liberties Paine so cherished and worked to establish in America were devolving into anarchy. Even Washington began to believe in the truth of Gouverneur Morris's pronouncement: "There never was nor ever will be a civilized society without an aristocracy."[31]

When he had written *Common* Sense, Paine warned Americans that the euphoria of military victory and independence would eventually give way to uncertainty and the necessity of selecting a government to rule the new nation. There were but three choices: a popularly elected congress, military rule, or mob rule. The first was failing, and military rule became impossible after General George Washington, his officers, and all but eighty troops left the military. As the nation fell under the thrall of the mob, Morris and other powerful men in Congress saw Thomas Paine and his radical ideas as the source of the spreading anarchy and plotted to force his departure from America. Thomas Paine put down his sketch pads and wrenches and unsheathed his pen to confront both his political enemies and the unruly mob that awaited in the national arena in Philadelphia.

Chapter 6

MONEY IS MONEY;
PAPER IS PAPER

A FTER THE MOB HAD CHASED CONGRESS FROM PENNSYLVANIA, members of the Pennsylvania State Assembly who hadn't fled decided to yield to popular dissent and consider revoking the Bank of Pennsylvania's charter.

There was no hard money or specie—gold, silver, Bank of England notes, etc.—to underwrite commerce in farm country. It simply did not exist. There were too few people to warrant the Bank of England shipping any to the American wilderness. Issuance of paper money by the state, on the other hand, would simply systematize and standardize the value of paper IOUs that already circulated. In theory, at least, state-issued paper money would convert every handwritten IOU for, say, a pound of a particular commodity into a standard printed note with a monetary value.

Thomas Paine, however, believed that paper money was not only worthless, but legalized theft. "Money is money and paper is paper!" he warned the mobs of Americans burning down courthouses in cities along the Atlantic coast.

"All the inventions of man cannot make them otherwise," he snapped. "The alchemist may cease his labors, and the hunter after the philosopher's stone go to rest if paper can be metamorphosed into gold and silver or made to answer the same purpose in all cases." Calling paper "a means for debtors to cheat their creditors," Paine began writing a long essay defending the Bank of Pennsylvania, but when he realized he would not finish it in time to influence the assembly, he went to Philadelphia to confront assemblymen personally. He faced nothing but a chorus of angry shouts of "common nonsense" from farmers *and* merchants.

"I never heard anything so ridiculous," the fiery, Irish-born John Smilie scoffed at Paine. A farmer from Fayette County in westernmost Pennsylvania, Smilie had led farmer threats there to secede from what they called the banker-dominated "state of Philadelphia." With ambitions of becoming "president" of a new state, Smilie emerged as the most outspoken champion of charter revocation in the assembly, encouraging farmer distrust of Philadelphia's bank as a vehicle of the rich to steal the savings of the poor.

Smilie pointed at Paine in the visitors' gallery as one who "hires out his pen for pay." As farmers in the hall stood to boo Paine and cheer Smilie, sentiment against the bank—and Paine—swelled, and the assembly succumbed to mob fever by revoking the Bank of Pennsylvania's charter.

Paine called the vote an illegal breach of contract. But it was too late; the breach was a *fait accompli*; the Bank of Pennsylvania no longer existed.

As legislators prepared to follow suit by dissolving the Bank of North America, Paine stepped up his efforts to preserve what he believed to be the economic foundation of the new American republic. He wrote and published a compelling, fifty-four-page pamphlet he called *Dissertations on Government; the Affairs of the Bank; and Paper Money*.

"All laws are acts, but all acts are not laws," he explained. "An act . . . differs from a law because there are two parties [to an act]. . . . The charter of the bank . . . is to all intents and purposes . . . a contract or a joint act" that neither party can revoke unilaterally. Any assembly may alter or revoke a law passed by earlier assemblies," he asserted, but "an act of this kind [creating the Bank of North America] is "a deed or contract, signed, sealed and delivered and subject to the same general laws and principles of justice as all other deeds and contracts are. . . . The greatness of one party cannot give it superiority or advantage over the other."

> The state or its representative, the assembly, has no more power over an act of this kind after it has passed than if the state was a private person. It is the glory of a republic to have it so, because it secures the individual from becoming the prey of power and prevents might from overcoming right. . . . this is justice . . . this is the true principle of republican government.[1]

Paine displayed a remarkable depth of legal knowledge, even presaging both Article I of the US Constitution that would go into effect in 1787 and a Supreme Court decision of 1819 when New Hampshire would try to seize Dartmouth College. In a landmark decision, the Court would rule that the New Hampshire state charter that had created Dartmouth College was a contract, and Article I of the Constitution prohibited states from passing "any law impairing the obligation of contracts."[2]

Paine being Paine, he could not resist an emotional appeal to patriotism, taking readers "back to the circumstances of the country and the condition of the government . . . at the time it entered into this engagement with the bank:

> The spring of 1780 was marked with accumulations of misfortunes, the British army having laid waste the southern states, closed its ravages by the capture of Charleston. When the financial resources of Congress were dried up, when the public treasury was empty, and the army of independence paralyzed by want, a voluntary subscription for its relief was raised in Philadelphia.

Paine said he had read a letter from Washington to the House saying that the distress of the Army "from the want of every necessity . . . had risen to such a pitch" that he feared mutiny.

"On my return to the House," Paine continued, "I drew out the salary due to me as clerk, enclosed $500 to a [wealthy Philadelphia merchant] and requested him to propose a voluntary subscription." The subscription grew to 300,000 pounds (about $500,000 in 1780 currency), for which subscribers formed a bank to dispense funds as needed by the Army. "By means of this bank, the army was supplied throughout the campaign," Paine asserted, "enabling Washington to carry into execution his well-concerted plan against Cornwallis." In 1781, Congress incorporated the subscribers to the fund, under the title of the Bank of North America.

> The establishment of the bank . . . its zealous services in the public cause, its influence in restoring and supporting credit . . . are an honor to the state and what the body of her citizens may be proud to own. . . . The whole community derives benefits from . . . the bank. It facilitates the commerce

of the country. . . . It is the duty of government to give protection to the bank.[3]

Unlike their responses to *Common Sense* and *The Crisis*, however, few Americans understood, let alone applauded, *Dissertations*. Most saw the national bank as a vehicle for the wealthy to acquire control of the country's money supply and natural resources. Farmers cried "monopoly" and stepped up demands for paper money—and an end to banking. What started out as demands to close the Bank of Pennsylvania and Bank of North America expanded into demands for an end to all banking.

Although Paine's *Dissertations* had come too late to save the Bank of Pennsylvania, he believed he could still save the Bank of North America. Opponents of the bank accused him of profiting from his defense of the bank. Admitting he had been a "friend and advocate" of the bank, he nonetheless insisted that "I have never made the least use of it or received the least personal service or favor from it by borrowing or discounting notes or in any other shape or manner whatever of any person concerned with it directly or indirectly."

> I have kept cash at the bank, and the bank is at this time in account to me between eight and nine hundred pounds [$1,350–$1,525], for money which I brought from New York and deposited there ever since last September and for which I do not receive a single farthing interest. This money the country has had the use of, and I think it safer under the care of the bank until I have occasion to call for it, than in my own custody.[4]

Clearly, Paine was on the defensive, and Smilie stepped up his attacks, calling Paine a puppet of the rich "who, having reaped a recompense more adequate to his deserts, prostitutes his pen to the ruin of this country.

"I cannot conceive," Smilie wrote in a pseudonymous letter to one newspaper, "a being more deserving of our abhorrence and contempt than a writer who, having formerly vindicated the principles of freedom, abandons them to abet the cause of a faction and [devotes] his pen to the ruin of his country."[5] Smilie was relentless in his attacks, even organizing supporters to force the editor of the *Pennsylvania Packet*, Paine's publisher at the time, to cease carrying his articles.

In the autumn elections of 1786, however, bank supporters won a resounding victory—and a majority in the Statehouse. Even with independence, the power of the vote in America remained in the hands of the propertied class. Smilie lost his seat and Benjamin Franklin, a stout supporter of the bank, won the presidency of Pennsylania's Supreme Executive Council.

Nevertheless, the debate over renewal of the bank's charter continued, costing Paine many friends and supporters. His defense of the bank alienated merchants as well as farmers. Apart from their reliance on paper, many saw the Bank of North America as a replica of the Bank of England, which had concentrated that nation's wealth in the hands of a ruling oligopoly. In addition to his stand against paper money, Paine's self-righteous obsession with justice and equity and his diatribes against slavery had combined to alienate enough segments of Philadelphia's leadership to cost him consideration as a delegate to the Constitutional Convention of 1787.

Though hurt by the failure of those he considered friends to call him to the convention, he was not surprised. Paine had seen his welcome in Philadelphia all but vanish. At times he feared for his safety on the city's streets. Discouraged and disappointed by the mercurial nature of American friendships and fed up with the attacks on his commitment to liberty, Thomas Paine finally resolved to quit America.

"My Father and Mother are yet living, whom I am very anxious to see and have informed them of my coming over," he explained to Franklin. "I intend landing in France and from thence to England. . . . I am on exceeding good terms with Mr. Jefferson [by then, American minister plenipotentiary in France], which will necessarily be the first place I go to. . . . The Marquis de La Fayette I am the most known to of any gentleman in France. . . . As I have taken a part in the Revolution and politics of this country, I am not an unknown character in the political worlds."[6]

Indeed not. In contrast to the near-ignominy with which he left America, the French political world and literati of the prestigious Academy of Sciences greeted Thomas Paine as a celebrated author and philosopher. He was not only an intimate of Benjamin Franklin, whom the French deemed God-like, he was both a scholar with a master's degree (albeit honorary) from America's "Université de Pennsylvanie" and a member of the American Philosophical Society.

Although *Common Sense* had made his name central to French political discussions, Franklin's letters of introduction brought him into personal contact with every prominent political leader in Paris—Condorcet, Danton, Mirabeau, and many others. Unfortunately, Paine neither spoke nor understood a word of French and could only smile and nod amidst the shower of adulation. Jefferson tried improving Paine's social and intellectual life a bit by steering him toward English-speaking figures, among them French Finance Minister Étienne-Charles de Loménie de Brienne.

After a delay at customs, the model of his bridge finally arrived at the French Academy of Sciences in Paris, where, Paine wrote, "they unanimously gave it preference" over other proposed bridge models "as being the simplest, strongest, and lightest. . . . An arch of 4 or 5 hundred feet is such an unprecedented thing and will so much attract notice in the northern part of Europe, that the Academy is cautious."[7]

As the French Academy studied Paine's bridge, America's Constitutional Convention approved the new Constitution and sent it to individual states for ratification. Washington, as President of the Convention, sent copies to both Jefferson and Lafayette in Paris, among others. Lafayette, in turn, used it as a centerpiece to organize a French "constitutional club." His goal was to devise a comparable document with which to modernize the unpopular French royalist government and end the fiscal crisis that resulted from French involvement in the American Revolution.

Closeting with Jefferson and Paine, Lafayette emerged with a scheme that placed him among the leaders of reform-minded French noblemen. A confidante of King Louis XVI—the two had attended riding school together as boys—Lafayette proposed American-style economic, political, and social reforms that left Jefferson and Paine beaming: abolition of a salt tax, a cut in peasant income taxes from 20 percent to 10 percent, imposition of the first-ever property and income taxes on the nobility, and an end to internal interprovincial trade barriers for grain, which raised the cost of bread—a staple of French peasant life—beyond the reach of too many of the poor.

As eager as he was to participate in a second revolution, Paine had to leave for London if he was to convert into reality his vision of spanning rivers with iron bridges. He had won a unanimous endorsement for his bridge by the French Academy of Sciences, along with the enthusiastic

20. With America free and independent, Lafayette invited Thomas Paine to join him in establishing an American-style republican government in France. Their efforts ended with imprisonment for both men. (Réunion des Musées Nationaux)

support of the French Finance Minister Cardinal de Brienne. Indeed, de Brienne grew so enamored with the project he urged Paine to design an even larger "bridge of friendship" to span the Channel to England and end centuries of conflict between the two nations.

As Paine sent word of the French Academy's approval of his model bridge to the Royal Society in London, he put de Brienne's proposal in his pocket to deliver to John Adams, the American minister plenipotentiary in Britain, for transmission to the London government.

Abandoning his role as the great revolutionary, Paine left for London intent, for the moment, to assume a new role on the world stage as a bridge builder—to promote industrial growth within Europe's nations and universal peace. The Anglo-American peace treaty had made it safe for him to return to Britain.

When Paine arrived in London, however, John Adams had returned to America, leaving the United States without a diplomatic presence and forcing Paine to deliver letters from Jefferson to various British officials without formal introductions. They in turn gave him their answers, often quite abruptly, given their disdain for dealing with a commoner—and a British ex-patriot at that. Often, however, they asked him enough questions to force him into the role of de facto American minister in Britain.

"I am in as elegant style of acquaintance here as any American that ever came over," he boasted to one friend, before catching himself and resuming his role as a man of the people. "I had rather see my horse Button in his own stable or eating grass," he wrote in the next sentence, "than see all the pomp and show of Europe."[8]

Finishing his most urgent errands for Jefferson, Paine returned to his native Thetford after an absence of more than a decade—only to find that his father had died the previous year. He spent several quiet weeks with his ninety-one-year-old mother and established an annuity to ensure her comfort for the remainder of her life. She would live three more years.

Paine settled on Edmund Burke as the political leader to whom he would deliver de Brienne's proposal. Burke seemed a logical choice: as a member of Parliament, he had opposed Parliament's imposition of the stamp tax and other harsh measures against the Americans and he had tried fostering reconciliation between Britain and her colonies. He and Paine seemed to harbor enough common political views to allow the two to form a friendship of sorts—more so after the Royal Society gave Paine's iron arch its blessing and he received government patents for England, Scotland, and Ireland.

"I can raise any sum of money that I please," Paine boasted in a letter to Jefferson—and with good reason. In applying for his patent, Paine had had the foresight to envision the iron arch he had designed as "a new and important manufacture to the iron works of the nation," with applications beyond bridge building to the construction of vaulted ceilings and large interior spaces free of supporting columns. Moreover, the genius that was Paine predicted his arch would presage a new era in manufacturing—an era of revolutionary "prefabrication"—a term that had yet to be introduced into the English language.

"As the bars and parts of which it is composed need not be longer than is convenient to be towed in a vessel, boat, or wagon," he explained, "a bridge of any extent . . . may be manufactured in Great Britain and sent to any part of the world to be erected."[9]

With patents in hand after only a week, he commissioned a Yorkshire ironworks in early September 1788 to begin building the unique arch. By the end of November, the factory had completed half the arch—reduced in size, however, from 250 to 90 feet to fit within the factory's walls.

When Parliament reconvened in the winter of 1789, Jefferson pressed Paine to expand his role as an acting minister, delivering messages to government officials, sending their answers back to Jefferson, negotiating this or that trade conflict. He also visited a variety of factories—cotton mills, steel furnaces, tinplate manufacturers, and others—reporting to Jefferson that all "might be easily carried on in America."[10]

"I am in pretty close intimacy with the heads of the opposition [and] I am in some intimacy with Mr. Burke and after the new ministry are formed, he has proposed to introduce me to them."[11] Paine remained intent on promoting himself as an international peacemaker, having handed Burke the proposal of Minister de Brienne for a bridge of friendship across the Channel between Britain and France.

"When we consider . . . the calamities of war and the miseries it inflicts . . . the thousands and tens of thousands of every age and sex who are rendered wretched," Paine asserted, "surely there is something in the heart of man that calls upon him to think!"

> Surely there is a tender chord . . . to emit in the hearing of the soul a note of sorrowing sympathy. Let it then be heard, and let man learn to feel that the true greatness of a nation is founded on the principles of humanity; and that to avoid war . . . is a higher principle of true honor than madly to engage in it.[12]

Paine set forth his proposals for peace in a thirty-six-page pamphlet he had started writing in Paris after meeting with Cardinal de Brienne. He had then held extensive discussions with Jefferson about building figurative bridges of friendship between western European nations—and especially between Britain and France. Entitled "Prospects on the Rubicon," the title referred to Julius Caesar's crossing of the Rubicon as symbolic of war's initiation.

"'The Rubicon is passed' was once given as a reason for prosecuting the most expensive war that England ever knew," Paine explained in his preface to the pamphlet. "Sore with the event and groaning beneath a galling yoke of taxes, she has again been led ministerially to the shore of the same delusive and fatal river. . . . Fortunately for England, she is yet on the peaceable side of the Rubicon."

Paine reminded British leaders that "he that goeth to war should first sit down and count the costs."

> War involves in its progress such a train of unforeseen . . . circumstances that no human wisdom can calculate the end. It has but one thing certain and that is to increase taxes. . . . I defend the cause of the poor, of the manufacturer, of the tradesman, of the farmer, and of all those on whom the real burden of taxes fall—but above all, I defend the cause of humanity.[13]

Completed in his mother's house in Thetford, the pamphlet had almost as much of an impact in Britain as his startling arch, which now stood outside the ironworks of Rotherham welcoming an endless parade of amazed visitors. Engineers came from Europe, aware of the deterioration of London's famed Blackfriars' Bridge across the Thames, whose riverbed of quicksands had swallowed the bridge piers and collapsed its span.

While engineers viewed Paine's arch as a symbol of engineering progress, some political figures echoed Paine's hope that it might serve as a symbol of peace between Britain and western Europe. Edmund Burke invited him to his 600-acre estate at Beaconsfield, north of London, after which the Whig party leader, the Duke of Portland, asked him to visit his palatial estate nearby.

Hundreds upon hundreds streamed across Paine's bridge, which, according to a correspondent for America's *Gazette of the United States*, "gave infinite satisfaction."[14] Village officials and city mayors from across Britain and Ireland, along with dozens of noblemen and country gentlemen with streams running through their own estates, climbed up and over the bridge. "Mr. Fox of Derby called again on me," Paine crowed to Jefferson in Paris. "There is a project erecting a bridge at Dublin."

"I saw the rib of your Bridge," the owner of a great estate bisected by the River Don wrote to Paine. "In point of elegance and beauty it far exceeds anything I ever saw."[15]

Visitors stomped on the floorboards to test the structure's strength, peppered Paine with questions, climbed back up and over, only to return with more questions.

Built with three tons of iron, the bridge at Rotherham supported six tons placed on top of it without budging. As Paine saw Royal Society members grin with "great satisfaction," he envisioned building "a row of bridges across the Thames in London" and stuffed his pockets with calling cards of those who promised he would hear from them soon.

He never heard from any of them again.

As it had in Pennsylvania, where costs of Paine's magnificent iron bridge represented three times that state's annual budget, his bridge in Rotherham was far too expensive. No town or city, let alone estate owner, could afford it. His only hope was to ship the bridge to London to see if that city's officials would agree to buy it to span the Thames.

The ironworks that had produced the bridge agreed to dismantle it and transport it to London, but the process dragged on endlessly through the summer of 1789. With the bridge not expected to arrive in London until the middle of November, Paine decided to go to France. According to letters from Jefferson, riots had erupted across France and, as Paine put it to a friend, "My idea of supporting the liberty of conscience and the rights of citizens is that of supporting those rights in other people. For if a man supports only his own rights for his own sake he does no moral duty."[16]

And to George Washington, Paine enthused, "A share in two revolutions is living to some purpose."[17]

For the second time in a dozen years, Paine would plunge into the maelstrom of a revolution that would change the course of world history.

Chapter 7

CITIZEN PAINE

A S RIOTS BROKE OUT ACROSS FRANCE, KING LOUIS XVI CALLED ON THE nation's most illustrious figures to debate proposed social and economic reforms, but they rejected any taxes on the nobility—and sent the French economy into free fall. What Louis had called an "Assemblée des Notables" [Assembly of Notables] Lafayette mocked as an "assembly of not ables" and provoked a national debate that quickly spilled onto the streets of the nation's cities and villages.

Toward the end of June, representatives of the nobility, clergy, and the "third estate," consisting of landed gentry and illustrious commoners, amalgamated into a National Assembly. The assembly, in turn, named Lafayette to write a forward-looking constitution based on principles of Locke, Rousseau, and the American Constitution. Working closely with Jefferson and Paine, he drew up a document that drew much from the American Declaration of Independence: "Men are created . . . free and equal . . . certain unalienable rights. . . ." It abolished social classes, guaranteed rights to a fair trial, and offered Frenchmen many of the same freedoms that America's founding documents promised Americans.

"The National Assembly," Jefferson assured Paine on July 11, 1789, "are now in complete and undisputed possession of the sovereignty."[1]

As Paine would soon realize, however, Jefferson was out of touch with the French people, closeted as he was by day in the mansions of the French nobility and literati and by night in his own mansion, with a teenaged Virginia slave girl to feed his erotic needs and her older brother, a chef, to feed the rest of his body.

Most people in Paris, however, were hungry—some desperately so—and, on Sunday, July 12, thousands poured from their churches and milled about the streets and squares. Orators harangued them at street corners. In the gardens of the Palais Royal, a huge crowd had gathered in the shade of the plane trees when the cry of "Aux armes!"—"To arms!"—rang out. As some raced for refuge under the nearby arcades, the rest of the mob sprang like a great beast of prey out the garden gates onto the rue Saint-Honoré, hungering for bread, thirsting for blood. By day's end, anarchy raged in the streets, with brigands springing out of the surging mob to loot shops and homes. Ordered to fire on the mobs, army regulars—themselves mostly commoners, some with friends and relatives among the rioters—refused. Many ripped the insignias of rank and epaulettes from their uniforms and joined the mob. A huge crowd of protesters had gathered in front of the Tuileries Palace in central Paris. "On one side stood an army of nearly thirty thousand men," Paine learned, "on the other an unarmed body of citizens . . . as unarmed and as undisciplined as the citizens of London are now.

"The streets of Paris being narrow," Paine explained, "are favorable for defense."

> The night was spent in providing themselves with every sort of weapon they could make or procure: guns, swords, blacksmiths' hammers, carpenters' axes, iron crows [crowbars], pikes, halberts, pitchforks, spits, clubs. . . . The incredible numbers in which they assembled . . . astonished their enemies. Accustomed to slavery themselves, they had no idea that Liberty was capable of such inspiration.[2]

On Monday, July 13, more than 7,000 rioters invaded a government arsenal and seized 30,000 muskets. The next day, July 14, an enormous mob moved along a web of narrow Paris streets toward the forbidding walls of the huge Bastille prison. After the first rioters broke through the outer gates, the prison governor ordered his guards to fire. Ninety-eight besiegers fell dead; seventy-three others lay wounded, provoking the surviving mob to fury. Two detachments of French troops who had joined the insurrection brought up five stolen cannon and blasted through the outer walls. After setting free the only prisoners they could find—four

21. Paris mobs storm the Bastille prison on July 14, 1789, which remains the French national holiday. (Réunion des Musées Nationaux)

forgers, a libertine, and two madmen—the outraged mob massacred six prison defenders and seized the prison governor, dragging him through the streets to the city hall, where they hung his torn body by the neck from a lamppost and disemboweled him. When the mayor appeared, they seized him, disemboweled him, chopped off his limbs, then severed his head from his lifeless torso and impaled it on a pike to display along the line of march.

Twenty-five miles to the west, at the Palace of Versailles, aides informed the king of the disturbances in Paris.

When he questioned whether it was "a full-blown riot," one aide is said to have replied, "No, Sire, it is a full-blown revolution."[3]

The National Assembly responded by naming Lafayette to lead the French National Guard and take command of Paris streets. To quash rumors that he planned starving Paris into submission, he ordered military convoys to escort shipments of flour into the city's poorest neighbor-hoods. To end disorders in and around the Bastille, he ordered it razed, removing from the streetscape what had long been a mammoth symbol of royal oppression.

On August 21, the National Assembly began discussing a declaration of the rights of man, and, within a week, Lafayette and others presented—and the assembly approved—a document entitled "Declaration des droits de l'homme et du citoyen"—"Declaration of the Rights of Man and the Citizen"—which would serve as a preamble for the nation's new constitution.

But by then, riots had spread across France and although the assembly sent troops to put down rioters, the troops often tore off their insignias and joined the mobs razing prisons, chateaux, and manorial residences. Often, they left nothing but ruins and smoldering rubble where centuries of French grandeur had stood. Mutterings about staging similar revolts emanated from the Netherlands and Belgium.

It was all too much for Thomas Paine. Until then, the rioting in France had discouraged travel to France, but the same emotions that had sent him charging up King Street in Trenton, New Jersey, now inspired him to join the Paris mobs and play a part in another revolution against mo-narchic rule.

Paine arrived in France in November, however—too late for the excite-ment of what became known as the "October Days." On October 5—the first of the "October Days"—a shortage of bread and other basic foodstuffs in Paris provoked one of the most unusual popular uprisings in history, as thousands upon thousands of women—just women, no men—marched out of the city toward the seat of government at the Palace of Versailles.

Followed by Lafayette's National Guard, the mob of women swelled to 6,000 by mid-morning, when their husbands finally arrived to support them. At dawn the next day they broke through the palace gates, demand-ing that King Louis and his Queen, Marie Antoinette, follow them back to Paris to experience the food famine firsthand. Protected by Lafayette and his guardsmen, the royal family rode to Paris, stopping at City Hall for the terrified king to feign "pleasure and confidence to be among the citizens of my good city of Paris" and, under orders from his captors, declare himself a citizen of France like those peopling the mob before him. The mob responded in unison, "Du pain! Du Pain!"—"Bread! Bread! Bread! Bread!"[4]

Lafayette and his men rushed Louis and his family to the royal quarters of the Tuileries Palace, then a part of what is today's enormous Louvre Museum.* A subsequent National Assembly decree converted the king's centuries-old status as King of France to King of the French.

Although Paine had missed witnessing the ugliest elements of the popular uprising, Gouverneur Morris had not. In Paris on business, he described what he saw in his diary:

> Under the arcade of the Palais Royal . . . the head and body of Mr. Foulon† . . . an old man of seventy-five are introduced . . . the head on a pike, the body dragged naked on the earth. . . . Afterward . . . Bertier, his son-in-law‡ . . . also is put to death and cut to pieces, the populace carrying about the mangled fragments with a savage joy. Gracious God, what a People![5]

By the time Paine reached Paris, his friend Jefferson had returned to America to serve as Secretary of State in the new Washington administration. Still unable to speak or understand a word of French, Paine found himself isolated from those who had organized the uprisings and from events in which he had hoped to participate. Lafayette's National Guard had quelled street rioting and ended much of the revolutionary excitement that Paine had anticipated. The National Assembly had quieted radicals by nationalizing the properties of king and church and stripping the church of governmental power.

As an inventor, Paine made a point of examining the drawings of a new instrument for painless capital punishment—a replacement, its inventor said, for the ax or wheel. The wheel often left criminals dismembered but

---

* The Paris Commune set fire to and destroyed the Tuileries Palace in 1871.

† Joseph-François Foulon de Doué, or Foulon de Doué, a French politician and Controller-General of Finances who had urged the people of Paris to eat grass to assuage their hunger.

‡ Berthier de Sauvignon, a Paris city official.

not dead, while the executioner's ax frequently missed its mark, embedding in the chest or skull. Proposed by Dr. Joseph Ignace Guillotin, a member of the National Assembly and professor of anatomy at Paris University Medical School, the device was the invention of his medical school colleague Dr. Antoine Louis. Originally called the "Louison," its falling blade severed heads at the neck swiftly, cleanly, and accurately, with the victim feeling nothing but "a gentle caress," according to Dr. Guillotin. The assembly approved the device and despite Dr. Guillotin's howls of protest, renamed it the guillotine to honor its legislative sponsor instead of its inventor.

Jefferson's absence left Paris too lonely for the gregarious Paine to remain there long. Although Lafayette and Paine were old friends, Lafayette was now commander of the French National Guard and had little time for social activities, let alone long private conversations. Although Paine found—and tried to befriend—Gouverneur Morris, Morris used every excuse to avoid him.

22. An original guillotine. Invented by a Dr. Louison, it acquired the name of Dr. Guillotin, the lawmaker who introduced the bill in the National Assembly to make it France's official instrument of execution. (Réunion des Musées Nationaux)

With nothing better to do, Paine wrote a long letter to his British friend Edmund Burke, praising the French for completing their revolution and making progress in drawing up a new constitution. He ended his letter with hopes that the English would soon follow suit.

To Paine's astonishment, his letter incensed Burke. "Do you mean to propose that I who have all my life fought for the constitution, should devote the wretched remains of my days to conspire its destruction?" Burke snarled by way of reply. Far from being the kindred political spirit Paine had believed he was, Burke was—and had always been—an arch-conservative, but had couched his opinions in beneficent terms that Paine had confused with socially progressive beliefs.

"Do you not know that I have always opposed the things called reform?" Burke snapped at Paine. "The French have made their way through the destruction of their country to a bad constitution, when they were absolutely in possession of a good one."[6] More focused on Paine's bridge-design skills, Burke had completely misjudged Paine's social beliefs. Convinced that Paine had misled him, Burke would never write or have anything to do with Paine again. Instead, he began work on a book he would call *Reflections on the Revolution in France*, and, in early February 1790, stood in Parliament to condemn the French Revolution.

He called the "Declaration of the Rights of Man and the Citizen" that prefaced the new French constitution an "institute and digest of anarchy" and a "mad declaration . . . which may in the end produce war." He called the French Revolution part of a plan to destroy European order. Burke published his parliamentary diatribe in a pamphlet he called *Reflections . . . Concerning the Affairs of France . . . in a Letter from Mr. Edmund Burke to a Gentleman in Paris.*[7]

Recognizing that Burke's angry "letter" was aimed at him, Paine prepared to respond when the owners of the ironworks notified him his great arch was on its way to London to bridge the Thames. As Paine prepared to return to England, Lafayette embraced him and gave him a thick, seven-inch-long black iron key to the main gate of the Bastille that Lafayette had salvaged as a personal gift for George Washington from the ruins of what he called the "fortress of despotism." Lafayette invited Paine to return to Paris to carry the American flag in a huge parade the French were planning

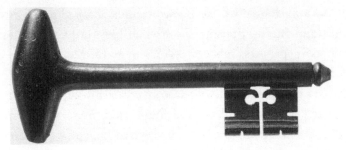

23. Lafayette salvaged a key from the wreckage of the Bastille prison to send to George Washington as one of "the first fruits of American principles, transplanted into Europe."

once they completed their new constitution. Paine, in turn, told Lafayette he believed France, rather than England, would now play the leading role in ridding Europe of "the bugbear of the divine right of kings."[8]

Paine arrived in London toward the end of March 1790 and wrote to Washington: "Our very good friend the Marquis de la Fayette has entrusted to my care the Key of the Bastille . . . as a present to your excellency—the first fruits of American principles, transplanted into Europe, to his great master and patron. . . .* The French Revolution is not only complete but triumphant."[9]

To Paine's deep disappointment—and shock—he learned that Burke's opposition to social and political reform even included defense of the notorious Test Act, a 1661 law that prohibited Church of England dissenters from holding any government office. It also banned them from working at the Bank of England or East India Company, from serving as army or navy officers, and from obtaining degrees at Oxford or Cambridge. As Paine arrived in London, Burke blocked a third attempt to repeal the Test Act, which applied to Paine's extended family and many Quaker friends. It would remain the law in Britain until 1828.

"I am the more astonished and disappointed at this conduct in Mr. Burke," Paine responded. "I had formed other expectations." By

---

*The framed key hangs on a wall in the mansion at George Washington's Mount Vernon, in Virginia.

then, Burke had published his condemnation of the French Revolution, *Reflections on the Revolution in France*, and King George III had endorsed it, declaring, "Every gentleman should read it."[10]

Burke's book so annoyed the usually affable Paine that he refused even to call on the parliamentarian. Instead, he began writing an angry rebuttal: "I saw the flagrant misrepresentations which Mr. Burke's pamphlet contains," Paine wrote, "and while it is an outrageous abuse of the French Revolution and the principles of Liberty, it is an imposition on the rest of the world."

> I had seen enough of the miseries of war to wish it might never more have existence in the world and that some other mode might be found to settle the differences . . . of nations. . . . That there are men in all countries who get their living by war and by keeping up the quarrels of nations is as shocking as it is true; but when those who are concerned in the government of a country make it their study to sow discord and cultivate prejudices between nations, it becomes the more unpardonable.

He called his new work *Rights of Man*, adding the subtitle "An Answer to Mr. Burke's Attack on the French Revolution." He inflated the importance of his pronouncements by listing beneath his name the title "Secretary for Foreign Affairs to Congress in the American War and Author of '*Common Sense*.'" Paine dedicated his work to "George Washington, President of the United States of America" and added

> Sir:—
> I present you a small treatise in defense of those principles of freedom which your exemplary virtue hath so eminently contributed to establish. That the Rights of Man may become as universal as your benevolence can wish, and that you may enjoy the happiness of seeing the New World regenerate the Old, is the prayer of
> Sir,
> Your much obliged, and
> Obedient humble Servant
> Thomas Paine

In contrast to his warm dedication, Paine followed with a vitriolic attack on Burke.

"There is scarcely an epithet with which Mr. Burke has not loaded the French nation and the National Assembly," Paine began. "Everything which rancor, prejudice, ignorance, or knowledge could suggest are poured forth in the copious fury of near four hundred pages."

Paine charged Burke with denying that people should have rights to frame their own government and choose their own governors—or powers to "cashier" them for incompetence. "That men should take up arms and spend their lives and fortunes . . . to [assert] their rights is an entirely new species of discovery . . . in the paradoxical genius of Mr. Burke."[11]

> But Mr. Burke appears to have no ideas of principles. . . . Mr. Burke . . . tells the world that a body of men who existed a hundred years ago made a law, and that there does not exist . . . nor ever will, nor ever can, a power to alter it. . . . It is difficult not to believe that Mr. Burke is extremely sorry that arbitrary power, the power of the Pope and the Bastille are pulled down. Not one glance of compassion, not one commiserating reflection that I can find throughout his book has he bestowed on those who lingered out the most wretched of lives, a life without hope, in the most miserable of prisons.[12]

Paine's assault on Burke outraged Britain's nobility and landed gentry—the very class whose financial support he would need to build his bridge. Not only did commoners like Paine seldom read or write, those who could accepted their status in British society. In an age of deference, an assault such as Paine's on a distinguished parliamentarian such as Burke was unprecedented.

As Paine scribbled his denunciations of Burke, sections of his bridge began arriving in London from the ironworks at Rotherham, where the foundry had not received a single order. Paine now hoped he might entice London officials, with their fat budgets, to let him build one or more bridges across the Thames. Putting aside his pens in favor of heavier tools, Paine went to dockside to supervise the unloading of the ribs of his bridge and their transfer onto wagons to Paddington, then a village on the edge of London. Obsessed as he was with starting revolutions, he promised Paddington officials that his bridge would produce a revolution in bridge architecture.

Paine hired three carpenters, two laborers, and a foreman to install the bridge in a field at Paddington and fence the field to keep the curious away and block their view. He intended charging visitors one ha' penny each to view his marvelous invention and had no intention of giving anyone even a wink free of charge.

After his foreman suffered a severe injury, Paine took over in his stead, lugging iron parts all day and growing too tired by nightfall to continue his written assault on Burke. Although he and his workers had completed the iron structure by the end of September 1790, he hired and worked beside six additional carpenters to slap a wooden floor on the bridge and permit visitors to walk across it before the autumn weather turned inclement. As in Pennsylvania and then in Rotherham—and as he would soon learn, even in Paris—the enthusiasm of the crowds who viewed, walked, even danced on his bridge proved meaningless, as did the words of compliment and encouragement from engineers, scientists, and city officials. The promises of orders-soon-to-come never came. In the end, Paine ordered workers to dismantle the Paddington Bridge. He paid what he owed to the Yorkshire ironworks by letting them sell the parts to build an iron bridge that would span the Wear River at Sunderland.

Opened in 1796, the Wear River Bridge was based on Paine's design and incorporated Paine's arches, but improvements by English bridge-builder Thomas Wilson lightened its weight, making it a model for dozens of subsequent iron bridges. When completed, it was the longest single-span bridge in the world, stretching 240 feet. It was more than twice as long as the world's first iron bridge over England's River Severn and only three-quarters the weight. It was only half the length of the bridge Paine had envisioned spanning Philadelphia's Schuylkill River, but, at £28,000, less than one-tenth the cost.* Although Paine would send two models of his bridge to France, the French, like the English, rejected it in favor

---

*After years of deterioration, the bridge was rebuilt from 1857 to 1859, with the ironwork reduced to only six ribs and abutments raised to flatten the span.

of less costly, lighter-weight variations. Although he would never see his bridge span the Schuylkill—or any other river, for that matter—Paine insisted to the end of his days, "Nothing in the world is as fine as my bridge, except a woman."[13]

In the end, Paine's bridge "sired many others" that spanned rivers across Europe and North America, according to the English scholar W. H. G. Armytage, and, as noted, "the Paddington model was dismantled and parts were incorporated in the bridge over the Wear at Sunderland."[14]

As fall blended into winter in 1790 and the last pieces of his Paddington bridge were carted away, Paine returned to London, where he resumed writing his *Rights of Man*, intending to stir British spirits as he had American spirits. Instead of continuing to rebut Edmund Burke, he directed his words about the French Revolution to the British people, much as he had directed the words in *Common Sense* to the American people. His style of writing was new to Britain, as it had been to America. Although beautiful—at times poetic—he used a simple vocabulary that even illiterate workmen could understand when they heard it read aloud.

"But four or five persons were seized by the populace and instantly put to death," Paine told the British in contradicting Burke's description of mass slaughter at the July 14 Paris uprising. "Their heads were stuck upon spikes and carried about the city, and it is upon this mode of punishment that Mr. Burke builds . . . his tragic scene. Let us therefore examine how men came by the idea."

> They learn it from the government they live under and retaliate the punishments they have been accustomed to behold. The heads stuck on spikes which remained for years upon the Temple Bar [in London] differed nothing in the horror of the scene from those carried about upon spikes in Paris; yet this was done by the British government. . . . Lay then the axe to the root and teach governments humanity. It is their sanguinary punishments which corrupt mankind. In England the punishment in certain cases is by *hanging, drawing and quartering*; the heart of the sufferer is then cut out and held up in the view of the populace. . . . The effect of such spectacles is to destroy tenderness . . . and governing by terror . . . become precedents.[15]

Paine then set out to incite British readers to revolution, pointing out that "every history of the creation . . . agree in establishing one point, *the unity of man* . . . that all men are born equal with equal natural right. . . . 'And God said, Let us make man in our own image. In the image of God created he him; male and female created he them.'[16]

"Man must have existed before government," Paine concluded. "Individuals themselves . . . entered into a compact with each other to produce a government." Artful men, however, created governments of priest craft, Paine continued, and were followed by a race of conquerors, whose governments, like that of William the Conqueror, were founded on power. To prevent power struggles, he said, conquerors united with priests to create "an idol they called divine right."[17]

Essential to popular rule was a constitution, Paine told the English. "A government is the creature of a constitution. The constitution of a country is not the act of government, but of the people *constituting* a government."

> It . . . contains the principles on which the government shall be established, the manner in which it shall be organized, the powers it shall have, the mode of elections, the duration of Parliaments . . . the powers which the executive shall have.[18]

England, he pointed out, had no such document. What Burke and others in power called the British constitution was, in fact, nothing but a loose-knit series of court decisions that determined the rights of individual defendants and plaintiffs, setting precedents for subsequent cases of the same type.

"A government cannot have the right of altering itself," Paine explained. "The act by which the English Parliament empowered itself to sit seven years shows there is no constitution in England." In effect, Paine sought to teach the English common man what common schools and the church had failed or refused to teach them. Few knew how to vote because they either did not have the right to vote or did not know how.

> The French Constitution says that the number of representatives for any place shall be in a ratio to the number of taxable inhabitants or

electors. . . . The county of York [England], which contains nearly a million of souls, sends two county members [to Parliament]; and so does the county of Rutland, which contains not an hundredth part of that number. The old town of Sarum, which contains not three houses, sends two members; and the town of Manchester, which contains upward of sixty thousand souls, cannot send any. Is there any principle in these things?[19]

Paine said the British government had emerged from the conquest of William the Conqueror, who imposed a government on the people "and though it has been much modified . . . the country has never yet regenerated itself and is therefore without a constitution."

He went on to explain the French and American constitutions point by point, emphasizing how the revolutions in both lands had transferred rule from the aristocracy and clergy to the common man. "A body of men holding themselves accountable to nobody," he warned, "ought not to be trusted by anybody."[20]

In addition to abolishing titles, the French constitution established the "universal right of conscience and universal right of citizenship," or freedom of worship and freedom to establish citizenship in the country of one's choice. Just as important to individual freedom, however, was the necessity that "the representatives of the nation . . . originate in and from the people by election. . . . In England it is otherwise . . . by conquest, all the rights of the people of the nation were absorbed into the hands of the Conqueror . . . who added the title of King. . . . By the French constitution, the Nation is always named before the King. . . . The Nation is the source of all sovereignty. . . . The French constitution puts the legislative before the executive; 'the Law' before 'the King'; *La Loi, Le Roi.*"[21]

Paine was not pleased by Lafayette's insistence on retaining a hereditary monarch as sole executive and giving so much power to a unicameral legislature, but he did not dwell on either point. France was, after all, Lafayette's native land, not Paine's, and the new constitution had made the nation sovereign, with the king only an official in the government.

Paine went on to cite the tenets of the French "Declaration of the Rights of Man and the Citizen," which reflected many elements of America's Declaration of Independence, including the assertion that "men are born . . . free and equal [with] rights [to] liberty, property, security, and resistance to authority."[22]

Paine did not stop there: "The revolutions of America and France have thrown a beam of light over the world, which reaches man. The enormous expense of governments have provoked people to think." Paine said he found it curious that a foreign house of kings had ruled over England for almost 125 years.* He characterized the English as "hating foreigners yet governed by them."[23]

Paine concluded his call to revolution by saying there were only two "distinctive and opposite" forms of government in the world: government by election and representation and government by hereditary succession; government by reason and government by ignorance. He called for nothing less than universal male suffrage and the abolition of monarchical sovereignty throughout Europe, citing it as the cause of wars. It was an open call to revolution across Britain, across Europe, across the world:

"When we survey the wretched condition of man under the monarchical and hereditary systems of the government, dragged from his home . . . impoverished by taxes . . . it becomes evident that those systems are bad and that a general revolution . . . is necessary. . . . Monarchical sovereignty, the enemy of mankind, and the source of misery, must be abolished."

Paine ended with a call to form a confederation of nations to abolish war and organize a European Congress "to patronize the progress of free government and promote the civilization of nations with each other. . . . It is an age of Revolutions in which everything may be looked for."[24]

The British court and parliamentary leaders called *Rights of Man* heresy and worse. Some said it was treason if the government still considered Paine a British subject, but Paine had explored British law carefully since his days as an exciseman and steered his pen on the safe sides of sedition and treason. Although the government might well have brought bogus charges that would lead to his temporary jailing, cool heads prevailed, pointing out that any persecution or prosecution of Paine would

---

*Members of the German House of Hanover—either German-born or of German descent—ruled Britain from 1714 to 1837.

martyrize him and provoke additional sales of *Rights of Man*. The government turned instead to subterfuge to try to undermine Paine's reputation, planting rumors in the press of his participation in drunken orgies, neglect of his personal hygiene, infidelity—even cruelty to his wife and neglect of his aged parents. The government-controlled press hinted at every type of immoral and evil behavior whenever Paine's name appeared.

When those efforts failed, the government hired a writer at the Board of Trade to publish (under a pseudonym) a scurrilous "biography" of Paine accusing him of plagiarizing, falsifying, and misspelling, among other faults, and of leading an immoral life. Entitled *The Life of Thomas Pain* [sic], *the Author of the Seditious Writings Entitled Rights of Man*, the twenty-six-page pamphlet enjoyed moderate success among royalists and anti-Americans, and those writers and politicians who were envious of Paine's success.

Paine, however, ignored the pamphlet, and, in fact, it had little effect on sales of *Rights of Man*. Within a month, the printer in London had sold six editions of *Rights of Man*, totaling 16,000 copies. The Irish bought upwards of 20,000 copies, and Europe absorbed another 30,000 copies.

"By what I can find," Paine wrote to William Short, the affable American chargé d'affaires in Paris, "the government have already tried all the underplots of abuse and scurrility without effect and have managed those in general so badly as to make the work and the author more famous."[25]

In America, republicans—Jefferson, Madison, and the like—hailed Paine's *Rights of Man* as a worthy sequel to *Common Sense*. "I have no doubt our citizens will rally a *second* time around the *standard* of 'Common Sense,'" Secretary of State Jefferson enthused. Jefferson personally undertook and paid for the printing of an American edition and then joined Attorney General Edmund Randolph in asking President Washington to name Paine to the cabinet as successor to Postmaster General Samuel Osgood. Congressman James Madison responded to Jefferson, "I wish you success with all my heart in your efforts for Paine. Besides the advantage to him, which he deserves, an appointment for him at this moment would do public good."[26]

Paine sent fifty copies of his new book to President Washington, noting, "The work has had a run beyond anything that has been published in this country on the subject of government, and the demand continues."

24. James Madison urged the Virginia Assembly to reward Thomas Paine for services in the Revolution with confiscated Tory land worth more than £4,000.

A letter I received from Dublin, 10th of May, mentioned that the fourth edition was then on sale . . . each edition . . . was ten thousand. The same fate follows me here as I at first experienced in America, strong friends and violent enemies, but as I have got the ear of the country, I shall go on and at least show them what is a novelty here, that there can be a person beyond the reach of corruption.

Paine told Washington he believed Britain was facing an immediate crisis and would have to decide whether the government would be "monarchical and hereditary or wholly representative. . . . The public papers will inform you of the riots and tumults at Birmingham." Misreading popular sentiment, he predicted—incorrectly—that the crisis in Britain would end with a conversion to representative government. Although he wrote in the language of commoners and had marched into battle alongside them in America, he was largely out of touch with them in England, where deference to one's betters was woven deeply into the fabric of society.

"After the establishment of the American Revolution," he explained, "it did not appear to me that any object could arise great enough to engage me a second time . . . but I now experience that principle is not confined to time or place, and that the ardor of seventy-six is capable of renewing itself."[27]

Although Washington thoroughly enjoyed *Rights of Man* and privately embraced its principles, he ignored Jefferson's suggestion to appoint Paine to the cabinet and, indeed, ignored Paine's emotional dedication to Washington in the first part of the book. With American and British negotiators still trying to settle Revolutionary War differences, Washington did not want Paine boasting to the English press how much the American President enjoyed his book condemning British monarchy.

When Paine returned to Paris, he found both city and country calm. The king and royal family had settled into the Tuileries Palace in the center of the city and, with no official duties, went unseen by government officials and the public. Paine also found a new—and unwelcome— American minister plenipotentiary sitting in Jefferson's chair.

"I have just heard of Gouverneur Morris's appointment," Paine wrote to Jefferson. "*It is most unfortunate* [his italics]." Paine called Morris an outspoken Anglophile who would "increase the dislike and suspicion" of France for America. Lafayette, who considered President Washington "my adoptive father," sent an equally strong protest to the American President.

Paine was working on *Rights of Man, Part Second*, when, on the morning of June 21, Lafayette burst into Paine's quarters shouting, "The birds are flown!"

At midnight the previous night, Lafayette related, two carriages had rolled up to the door of the palace; the king, his wife, and their three children had slipped into one, the king's brother and his wife into the other.

"'Tis well," Paine tried calming Lafayette. "I hope there will be no attempt to recall them."[28] The king's flight, Paine said, was tantamount to his abdication, "for in abandoning his throne, he has abandoned his office. The brevity of the period during which he was absent counts for nothing. . . . It is the attempt to escape that counts for everything."[29]

Both royal carriages had fled Paris toward the safety of Austrian territory in the east, then ruled by Queen Marie Antoinette's family. It was after five in the morning before servants noticed their absence and roused Lafayette, who dispatched guardsmen in every direction to recapture the royals.

Radical political leaders accused Lafayette of complicity in the flight. Cries of "traitor" followed him through the streets; later, when he reported the royal family's flight in the National Assembly, Georges-Jacques Danton, the rabble-rousing lawyer who had favored replacing monarchic with popular rule, assailed Lafayette.

"And you, Monsieur Lafayette," Danton roared. "You who guaranteed the person of the king in this assembly on pain of losing your head, are you here to pay your debt?"[30] Danton then marched out of the hall and showered the streets with leaflets accusing the French hero of the American Revolution with planning the king's escape. The National Guard had to disrupt a mob that was marching toward Lafayette's house in response to Danton's diatribe.

25. A soft *bonnet rouge*, or Phrygian cap, with the revolutionary cockade attached, was required dress in revolutionary France. Its ties to Phrygia, or eastern Europe, remain obscure, but forgetting to wear his cap and cockade almost cost Thomas Paine his head.

Although the king's brother escaped across the frontier, the French National Guard caught the king's carriage 150 miles short of the border, and three days later, Lafayette led the royal family back into Paris, where frenzied mobs milled about the Tuileries Palace demanding their royal heads—along with Lafayette's.

Later that day, as Paine relaxed on a stroll through the Tuileries gardens with two friends, a small mob appeared from nowhere, surrounding him while screaming repeatedly, "Aristocrate! À la lanterne! [Aristocrat! To the lamppost!].[31] Paine had neglected to wear his red Phrygian cap and cockade, then vivid symbols of the Revolution and required of all who favored the new national order.

All but helpless to explain himself because of his inability to speak French, Paine faced decapitation and disembowelment as the angry mob seized him and began dragging the author of *Common Sense* to the nearest lamppost to hang him by the neck.

Chapter 8

A TALE OF TWO CITIES

A FTER HIS FRENCH-SPEAKING COMPANIONS SHRIEKED AND SCREAMED Thomas Paine's identity, the mob calmed down and released him, reluctantly at first, then with profuse apologies. Several of his abusers dusted him off while others offered him their own cockades by way of apology, but the experience left Paine more than shaken. He realized he would not be able to write about the French Revolution remaining aloof as a mere witness. He would have to join it and participate, as he had in America—and wear his Phrygian cap and cockade.

He recruited four influential English-speaking friends—two members of the National Assembly—one of them a journalist—and two aristocrats who embraced republicanism. Together they formed Le Club Républicain (The Republican Club), which published a newspaper—*Le Républicain*— that translated and published most of Paine's works into French, disseminating *Common Sense* to the common man of France as he had earlier to the common man in America.

Paine issued what he called a "Republican Manifesto" and sent boys racing across Paris to post it on doors and herald the club's beginnings. "The absence of a king is more desirable than his presence," it explained to the French people. "Whether fool or hypocrite, idiot or traitor, he has proved himself unworthy. . . . The reciprocal obligation which subsisted between us is dissolved."

The history of France presents little else than a long series of public ca-
lamity, which takes its source from the vices of the kings. We have been

the wretched victims who have never ceased to suffer either for them or by them. . . . their reign is consequently at an end.

Still obsessed with repugnance for monarchy, Paine asked the French the same question he had asked Americans—again, in the language of the common man: "What kind of office must that be in a government which requires neither experience not ability to execute, that may be abandoned to the desperate chance of birth, that may be filled with an idiot, a madman, a tyrant, with equal effect by the good, the virtuous, and the wise . . . it is a place of show, not of use."

Let France . . . deliberately examine whether a king . . . may not be extremely dangerous. The thirty millions which it costs to support a king in the éclat of stupid brutal luxury presents us with an easy method of reducing taxes, which . . . would . . . stop the progress of political corruption. The grandeur of nations consists, not as kings pretend, in the splendor of the throne, but . . . in a just disdain of those barbarous follies and crimes which, under the sanction of royalty, have hitherto desolated Europe.[1]

For the first time in their years of warm friendship, Paine's stand against the monarchy put him at odds with his friend Lafayette. Despite the king's attempt to flee France, Lafayette still favored constitutional monarchy, with a government based on the American Constitution but a hereditary monarch as chief executive instead of an elected President. Much as John Adams had asserted, Lafayette believed the splendid trappings of a monarch filled ordinary men with awe, won their respect, and, therefore, their willingness to defer to his judgment. In addition, Lafayette pointed out that princes of the realm in France, like his friend Louis XVI, underwent years of rigorous mandatory training—academic, physical, and military—that few others in the nobility and no commoners could obtain.

The flight of the royal family, however, created havoc in Paris. National Assembly radicals blamed Lafayette for the king's flight and forced him to resign his command of the National Guard. Meanwhile, the remnants of the royalists raced about Paris tearing Paine's "manifesto" off walls and replacing it with demands that Paine be prosecuted for libeling the king. The demands succeeded only in elevating the impact of Paine's Republican Club far beyond its five-member base.

"I am not the personal enemy of kings," Paine responded facetiously. "Quite the contrary. No man wishes more heartily than myself to see them all in the happy and honorable state of private individuals; but I am the avowed, open, and intrepid enemy of what is called monarchy."

> And I am such by principles which nothing can either alter or corrupt—by my attachment to humanity . . . [and] the dignity and honor of the human race; by the disgust which I experience when I observe men . . . governed by brutes; by the horrors which . . . monarchy has spread over the earth . . . the calamities . . . wars . . . massacres with which monarchy has crushed mankind. In short, it is against all the hell of monarchy that I have declared war.[2]

With his declaration of war against monarchy, Paine emerged a major figure in the French Revolution, much as he had been in the American Revolution, but his revolutionary ambitions were no longer limited by national frontiers. He intended fomenting a Revolution of the World, with Britain his next target.

In the summer of 1791, he set off for London, where friends had invited him to celebrate the second anniversary of the fall of the Bastille—a celebration he saw as an opportunity to wage war against monarchy in Britain. When the owner of the establishment where the celebration was to have been held learned Paine's intent, however, he locked his doors. Paine took full advantage, issuing a "manifesto" saying, "We rejoice at the glorious event of the French Revolution. . . . As men, we rejoice in the freedom of twenty-five millions of men. . . . As Englishmen, we also rejoice, because we are immediately interested in the French Revolution."

> We congratulate the French nation for having laid the axe to the root of tyranny and for erecting a government on the sacred hereditary rights of man; rights which appertain to all and not to anyone more than another. . . . Among the blessings the French Revolution has produced . . . we enumerate the abolition of the feudal system of injustice and of tyranny.

Game laws, borough tenures, and tyrannical monopolies of numerous kinds remain. . . . The French Revolution opens . . . an opportunity . . . of promoting the general happiness of man, and to this country . . . an opportunity of reducing our enormous taxes.[3]

Paine declared the French Revolution particularly pertinent to Britain, saying it "concerns us immediately. We are oppressed with a heavy national debt, a burden of taxes, an expensive administration of government, beyond those of any people in the world. We have also a very numerous poor, and we hold that the moral obligation of providing for old age, helpless infancy, and poverty is far superior to that of supplying the invented want of courtly extravagance, ambition, and intrigue."[4]

At the time, Paine was staying with Thomas Clio Rickman, his long-time friend from Lewes who had moved to London and become a bookseller and sometime printer. The only intimate to write Paine's biography, Rickman would produce a work devoid of the vitriol found in many Paine biographies. It represents the most accurate description of Paine—despite occasional embellishment born of Rickman's deep affection for and admiration of Paine.

"Mr. Paine in his person was about five feet ten inches high, and rather athletic," Rickman described his friend in 1791. "He was broad shouldered and latterly stooped a little. His eye, of which the painter could not convey the exquisite meaning, was full, brilliant, and singularly piercing. It had in it the 'muse of fire.'"

In his dress and person he was generally very cleanly and wore his hair cued, with side curls and powdered, so that he looked like a gentleman of the old French school. His manners were easy and gracious; his knowledge was universal and boundless; in private company and among his friends his conversation had every fascination that anecdote, novelty, and truth could give it. In mixed company and among strangers he said little and was no public speaker.[5]

Rickman described Paine's life in London as "a quiet round of philosophical leisure and enjoyment. It was occupied in writing . . . in walking about with me to visit . . . enlightened friends and clever travelers from

26. After France established a constitutional monarchy, Thomas Paine set off to try to force England to do the same. Paine is seen here in an engraving by William Sharp, after a 1793 portrait in oil by George Romney. National Portrait Gallery, Washington, DC.

France and different parts of Europe and America . . . occasionally lounging at coffee houses and public places or being visited by a select few." According to Rickman, the "enlightened friends" of Paine in London at the time included, among others, artist George Romney, who painted Paine's portrait; Mrs. Mary Wollstonecraft, the pioneer of women's rights; and the brilliant scientist Dr. Joseph Priestly, who discovered oxygen.

"And, of course," Rickman went on, "as he was my inmate, the most of my associates were frequently his. At this time he read but little, took his nap after dinner and played with my family at some games in the evening, at chess, dominoes, and drafts [checkers], but never at cards; in recitations, singing, music, etc. or passed it in conversations."[6]

Although Paine's iron bridge had faded from most British memories, *Rights of Man* had captured the imaginations of far more. Sales in England alone surpassed 50,000 copies in a nation of eight million, which encouraged Paine to change its title from *Kingship* to *Rights of Man, Part Second*.

"I have so far got the ear of John Bull that he will read what I write," Paine wrote facetiously to a friend in America. "I intend to print an hundred thousand copies of each work and distribute them at six pence apiece . . . because it will alarm the wise mad folks at St. James [palace]."[7]

Despite their disagreement over a monarch's place in republican government, Paine dedicated *Rights of Man, Part Second* to "M[onsieur] De Lafayette . . . as testimony of my esteem . . . after an acquaintance of nearly fifteen years in difficult situations in America and . . . in Europe." And he signed it "Your sincere, affectionate friend."[8]

By then, the increasingly powerful, radical Jacobins had not only cost Lafayette his command, they had seized control of the National Assembly. Originally named La Société des Amis de la Constitution (Society of the Friends of the Constitution), the group derived its popular name Jacobin from the Couvent de Saint-Jacques (Saint James the Apostle monastery)* in Paris, where they held their meetings and often listened to translations of Paine's *Rights of Man, Part Second*.

More complex than the first part, *Part Second* repeated some elements of *Common Sense*, but in more complex language. It warned of a coming end to monarchy across Europe during the years immediately ahead, with England's monarchy likely to fall first. Indeed, Paine called openly for Englishmen to revolt, saying, "It is time to dismiss all those songs and toasts . . . calculated to enslave and . . . suffocate reflection. . . . To say that people are not fit for freedom is to make poverty their choice."[9]

Calling revolution "the order of the day," Paine proposed sweeping social reforms to ensure the welfare of entire societies, including state subsidies for the poor; state-subsidized universal public education; government-sponsored prenatal and postnatal care, with state subsidies at childbirth; state subsidies for all workers over fifty, doubled at sixty when man's "labor ought to be over."

---

*In French, the English name "James" is "Jacques."

27. Federalist Gouverneur Morris replaced Thomas Jefferson as ambassador to France and did nothing to obtain Paine's release from prison during the French Revolution.

"He seems cocksure of bringing about a revolution in Great Britain," Gouverneur Morris mocked Paine, "and I think it quite as likely that he will be promoted to the pillory."[10]

Paine did not disagree. Indeed, when his patron Benjamin Franklin had remarked, "Where liberty is, there is my country," Paine had retorted, "Where liberty is not, there is my country."[11]

Expecting wide acclaim for his work, Paine had given copies of *Rights of Man, Part Second* to two printers in London, only to have each of them blanch midway through the project when a "friend" warned, "If you wish to be hanged or immured in a prison all your life, publish this book."

Alarmed by the warning, both printers stopped production, and Paine had to find another to finish the job, pledging to protect him against any liabilities.

"Should any person, under the sanction of any authority, enquire of you respecting the author and publisher of the *Rights of Man*," Paine wrote to the printer, "you will please to mention me as the author and publisher . . . and show to such persons this letter."[12]

Three months later, the British government issued a summons for the printer and, a week later, for Paine. The printer pleaded guilty, surrendered all his notes and documents relating to *Rights of Man*, and was freed without further charges. The authorities did not want to martyrize an insignificant printer; they were after Paine. Until then, they had feared his arrest and trial would make a martyr out of him, but they changed their minds as they realized that all Paine's readers did not embrace his views. Many commoners as well as noblemen embraced monarchy, preferring to cling to the age-old British custom of leaving statecraft to royalty and the worldly nobility.

"I am really afraid he will be punished," Gouverneur Morris wrote to Washington. In England on private business, Morris loved England and the English and disliked Paine almost as much as Paine disliked him. "He seems to laugh at this and relies on the force he has in the nation," Morris wrote of Paine. "He seems to become every hour more drunk with self-conceit. It seems, however, that his world excites but little emotion and rather raises indignation."[13]

On May 21, 1792, King George III issued a royal proclamation against seditious writings, and his government served Paine with a summons to appear at the Court of King's Bench and face the full power and might of the British Empire:

By the King, a Proclamation.
George R[ex].

Thomas Paine, gentleman, being a wicked, malicious, seditious, and ill-disposed person, and being greatly disaffected to our Sovereign Lord the now King, and to the happy constitution and government of this kingdom . . . he, the said Thomas, wickedly, maliciously, and seditiously did write and publish and cause to be written and published a certain false, scandalous, malicious, and seditious libel . . . entitled "Rights of Man, Part the Second."[14]

The charge went on to cite specific sections of Paine's book, particularly two assertions: "All hereditary government is in its nature tyranny. . . . To inherit a government is to inherit the people as if they were flocks and herds." and "The time is not very far when England will laugh at itself for sending to Holland, Hanover, Zell, or Brunswick for men at the expense of a million a year who understood neither her laws, her language, nor her interest, and whose capacities would scarcely have fitted them for the office of a parish constable."[15]

The royal proclamation commanded all magistrates to find and identify authors and printers of "wicked and seditious writings . . . it being our determination . . . to carry out these laws vigorously against such offenders."[16]

When Paine showed up to answer the charges, the court postponed his trial for six months, until December—a tactical government error that stimulated more interest in Paine's writings and sent English sales of *Rights of Man* to more than 200,000 copies by the end of the year—the largest number of copies sold of any book in English history at the time. In France, too, *Rights of Man* captured the minds and hearts of thousands of readers.

On the second anniversary of the storming of the Bastille, the Jacobins—now with tenuous control of the National Assembly—gathered with thousands of followers on the Champs de Mars, an enormous parade ground on the Left Bank of the Seine River in front of the École Militaire, or national military academy. By then, the Jacobins had elected as their head the fiercely ambitious and stunningly glib young lawyer from Arras, in northern France, Maximilien François Marie Isidore de Robespierre, or more simply, Robespierre. He stepped forward at the gathering and proclaimed the overthrow of the king and creation of a French republic. A shot rang out. Guardsmen charged into the mob, which responded with a barrage of stones and pieces of sod. The troops fired at random into the

28. The charismatic young lawyer Robespierre seized leadership of radical Jacobins and overthrew the centuries-old absolute French monarchy. (Réunion des Musées Nationaux)

crowd, killing at least 100 men, women, and children and wounding at least that many more.

The acting mayor imposed martial law, sending Robespierre and his Jacobin radicals in full flight from Paris, while Lafayette resumed command of guardsmen and reclaimed his seat in the National Assembly. By the end of summer 1791, the assembly had pieced together a new French constitution of sorts and granted amnesty to Champs de Mars rioters.

"Their new constitution is good for nothing," scoffed Gouverneur Morris. "If this unhappy country is not plunged anew into the horrors of despotism, it is not their fault."[17]

In Britain, Paine's *Rights of Man, Part Second* inspired coal miners, shoemakers, sailors, and others to stage a series of nasty strikes. Unwilling

29. Thomas Paine faced being drawn and quartered as punishment for seditious libel in England.

to cede an iota of liberty it feared might threaten its authority, the British government responded by indicting Paine's publisher for producing a seditious book and then issuing a summons to Paine to appear for trial less than three weeks later for seditious libel.

The government, however, hoped to avoid more strikes and unpredictable street riots that Paine's trial might provoke. Hoping to frighten Paine into abandoning his activities and leaving England, the government used the captive British press to display graphic depictions of the ghastly punishments for seditious libel. *The Times*, then a willing government ally, urged "Mad Tom," as they called him, to "embark for France and there be naturalized into the regular confusion of democracy."[18]

Paine had no need for any French naturalization proceedings, however. On August 26, 1792, the French National Assembly declared Thomas Paine and sixteen others—George Washington, Alexander Hamilton, James Madison, and such, among them—honorary French citizens for having served "the cause of liberty and prepared the freedom of the people . . . by their writings and by their courage."[19] The Assembly cited *Théorie et pratique des droits de l'homme, par Thomas Paine*—a French translation of *Rights of Man*—as one of Paine's stellar contributions to freedom in France. It then followed Paine's exhortation in *Rights of Man* by abolishing monarchy and convoking a convention to write a new constitution.

To punctuate the abolition of monarchy and aristocracy, the Assembly banned the utterance or use of titles, including "monsieur" (literally, "my sire" or "my lord") and "madame" ("my dame" or "my lady"). Henceforth, citizens were to address each other as "citoyen" and "citoyenne." (Absent linguistic genders in the English language, American Jacobins adopted "citizen" and "citizenness." Mr. Paine now became Citizen Paine.

With that, delegates from across France stood to outdo each other in paying homage to Paine, with four French districts out-shouting each other to name him their deputy to the Aassembly—Aisne, northeast of Paris; Oise, due north of Paris; Puy-de-Dôme in central France, and Lafayette's home district; and Pas-de-Calais in northwestern France, the home district of the charismatic and increasingly powerful lawyer Robespierre.

"Your love for humanity for liberty and equality," read the formal invitation from Calais's mayor to Paine before Paine had even left England, "the useful works that have issued from your heart and pen in their defense, have determined our choice. Come, friend of the people, to swell the number of patriots in an assembly which will decide the destiny of a great people, perhaps of the human race. The happy period you have predicted for the nation has arrived.

"Come! Do not deceive their hope!"[20]

If Paine had ever intended deceiving their hopes, he abandoned it when poet William Blake sidled up to him at the home of a mutual friend outside London one evening and whispered, "You must not go home or you are a dead man."[21] Startled, Paine heeded Blake's advice and hurried to Dover to catch a packet to France. Twenty minutes after the boat had sailed, a pack of constables raced onto the pier with a warrant for Paine's arrest. They had good reason: in promoting *Part Second*, Paine's assertion that revolution—in Britain and elsewhere—"may be considered the order of the day"[22] constituted sedition in the minds of British prosecutors. As proof, they pointed to the "constitutional societies" that readers had formed to protest voting rights restrictions, escalating food prices and taxes, and an ever-expanding list of other grievances. Paine's *Part Second* also provoked formation of corresponding committees in various counties—similar to those that America's individual colonies had organized to coordinate their tax rebellion and, eventually, stage the American Revolution.

British authorities were not slow in recognizing the resemblance and began a concerted assault—indirectly, with anonymously written character assassinations of Paine in the press, and directly, with official encounters and detentions. When he prepared to board the ferry to Calais at Dover piers, for example, customs officials—unaware yet of the warrant for his arrest—forced him to remove every item from his grips, open every letter, read its contents, then display every note and coin on his person—and count it aloud. Only then did they permit him to repack and board the boat. The officials with the actual arrest warrant did not arrive until the ferry had left British waters.

In contrast to the humiliation he suffered leaving Dover, Paine met nothing but celebratory cannon fire when he arrived in Calais. An honor guard in dress uniforms greeted him; a crowd of hundreds cheered, shouting "Vive Thomas Paine!"—"Long live Thomas Paine!" The mayor presided over a formal banquet for him and impressed a revolutionary Gallic kiss on each of Paine's cheeks before implanting a revolutionary cockade in his hat. After the banquet, they paraded along the rue de l'Égalité (Equality Street), whose name had replaced that of the rue du Roi (King Street).

As he rode toward Paris, town after town cheered his arrival, each trying to outdo the previous one with roars of welcome, ceremonial honors (and kisses) by splendidly uniformed officials. Finally, when his carriage crossed into Paris, thunderous cheers greeted him.

"France calls you, Sir, to its bosom to perform one of the most useful and most honorable functions," the President of the National Assembly boomed by way of welcome, "that of contributing by wise legislation, to the happiness of a people whose destinies . . . are united with the welfare of all who suffer in the world. It becomes the nation that has proclaimed the *Rights of Man* to desire among her legislators he who first dared to estimate the consequences of those rights."[23]

On September 21, 1792, the French National Assembly began its deliberations by formally abolishing the monarchy and nobility and renaming the birth date of republican France as Year One of a new republican calendar.

Paine spent the next few days writing a maiden speech thanking the French for granting him honorary French citizenship and electing him to the National Assembly. For one of the few times in his life, Paine seemed at a loss for words. His good friend Lafayette was nowhere to be found to help him; deserted, they said. Impossible! Paine thought, but said nothing until he could learn more.

What Paine did not—could not—realize was that in the days and weeks before his return to Paris, his friend Lafayette had urged the able-bodied to enlist in the army and help repel invaders from nearby monarchist states. Lafayette's call to arms, based on Paine's words in *Rights of Man, Part Second*, had provoked the French people to near-madness, with many rushing to the front to reinforce the army against invading monarchist armies from Austria, Prussia, and Hesse.

Instead of luring an army of disciplined recruits and doubling army ranks to 50,000 as he had hoped, Lafayette's call echoed that of Marseille radicals—"Aux armes, Citoyens! Formez vos battaillons!" ["To arms, citizens! Form your battalions!"] Some 25,000 barefoot peasants in rags responded, desperate for food and bent on plunder. The most disciplined of the Jacobins infiltrated army ranks, encouraging disobedience, anarchy, and driving out officers, most of them sons of aristocrats.

Lafayette demanded expulsion of Jacobins from the National Assembly, calling them "a sect that has usurped the people's sovereignty, tyrannized citizens. . . . I implore the National Assembly to arrest and punish the leaders of violence for high treason against the nation."[24] His plea came too late. Led by Robespierre, a mob of Jacobin assemblymen overran that body, shouting "À bas Lafayette!" ("Down with Lafayette"), while across the gardens, a second mob of Jacobin thugs smashed their way into the Tuileries Palace and slaughtered the king's personal guardsmen—boys actually. They were largely the best of the teenaged officers' training corps, rewarded for their achievements in training school with a year's honorary duty in splendid dress uniforms at the king's side.

As the mob entered the palace, the king ordered his teenaged guards (almost all from noble families) not to fire on "his people." For their loyal

obedience, they suffered unimaginable butchery, as the mob disemboweled them one by one and planted their heads on pikes to parade through
the palace, until 600 of the young guards and 200 servants lay butchered
on the marble floors of the royal residence.

The royal family fled in desperation from their palace slaughterhouse,
slipping and sliding across the bloodied floors of their palace until they
reached the Tuileries gardens and sought sanctuary across the way in the
former royal riding academy building, where the Assembly had convened.
To save them from senseless butchery by the mob, assemblymen ordered
the royals imprisoned in the impenetrable stone "Temple," the ancient,
fortress-like seat of the Knights Templar on the northern edge of the city.

Unaware of the bloody scenes that had preceded his appearance, Paine
began the most ironic discourse of his life, casting flowery compliments at
what one Englishman called a "Convention of Cannibals."[25]

"Fellow Citizens," Paine hailed the delegates, "I receive with affectionate gratitude the honor . . . conferred upon me . . . adopting me as a
citizen of France."[26]

"The murders continue," Gouverneur Morris wrote in his diary as
Paine spoke. "The murdering continues all day," he would write the next
day. Day after day, his entries grew monotonous. "There is nothing new
this day. The murders continue. We have had one week of unchecked
murders in which some thousands have perished in this city," Morris reported to Secretary of State Jefferson.

> It began with two or three hundred of the clergy who had been shut up be-
> cause they would not take the oath prescribed by law and which they said
> was contrary to their conscience. These *Executors of speedy justice* went to
> the *Abbaye* where the persons were confin'd. . . . They were dispatched also
> and afterwards they visited the other prisons. All those confined either on
> the accusation or suspicion of crimes were destroyed. Madame [Princesse]
> de Lamballe* was, I believe, the only woman killed and she was beheaded
> and disemboweled, the head and entrails paraded on pikes through the

---

*A close friend of Marie Antoinette and member of the House of Savoy, whose hus-
band was heir to one of the great fortunes in France at the time.

30. The last known portrait of the French royal family before the execution of King Louis XVI and Queen Marie Antoinette and the kidnapping of their son and heir. (Réunion des Musées Nationaux)

streets and the body dragged after them. They continued, I am told, in the neighborhood of the Temple [prison] until the Queen looked out at this horrid spectacle.[27]

As the Prussian, Hessian, and Austrian emperors poured troops into France to free their royal relatives from prison, the National Assembly, in the days before Paine's arrival, issued a formal declaration of war against Austria, Prussia, and the various German duchies. It then imposed a draft that siphoned much of the Jacobin mob from the streets of Paris to the battlefield and left the Tuileries gardens in peace.

Faced with an army of 150,000 superbly trained, highly disciplined Austrian, Prussian, and Hessian troops, however, thousands of untrained draftees turned tail and fled the front. When French General Théodore Dillon ordered them to reverse course and fight, they slaughtered him and his aides and kept running. Old General Rochambeau, the hero at

31. A Jacobin presents the head of a Convention delegate to the French Convention President. Painting by Jean-Auguste Tellier hangs in the Museum of the Palais de Versailles. (Réunion des Musées Nationaux)

Yorktown, quit in disgust; Jacobins arrested and imprisoned him on his return to Paris and condemned him to death on the guillotine. In Paris, Jacobin thugs smashed their way past guards and disrupted proceedings of the National Assembly, thrusting spikes topped with heads of their victims into the faces of terrified deputies.

Lafayette tried restoring discipline to the army, ordering troops to stand at attention and repeat their oath to the constitution. Two battalions refused. He ordered their arrest, but, to his dismay, not a soldier or officer responded. Facing mass mutiny, he could either flee France or return to Paris, where he faced certain—and useless—execution on the guillotine. Robespierre had already filed a formal charge against him— "rebellion against the law . . . conspiracy against liberty . . . treason against the nation."[28]

Lafayette organized a cadre of officers still loyal to him and the king and led them in the night over the military front line into Austrian-occupied territory, where he presented himself to the commanding officer. The Emperor ordered his imprisonment in a dungeon cell in far-off Olmutz, Moravia,* for having provoked the Europe-wide conflict with France by introducing American-style democracy in France.

---

*Now, the Czech Republic.

"An over-ruling Providence is regenerating the old world by the principles of the new," the naïve Paine continued in his speech to the National Assembly in the wake of these events, oblivious to the river of blood rising around him or the fate of his friend Lafayette. He delivered segments of his talk in English first, before a translator stepped to the rostrum to repeat each element in French.

"It is impossible to conquer a nation determined to be free," Paine trumpeted triumphantly. "It is now the cause of all nations against the cause of all courts."[29]

Outside the hall in the streets of Paris, what had been scores of Jacobin street thugs had grown into hundreds then thousands, darting about, smashing windows, doors, and whatever else they could break, in their hunt for royalists or anyone who looked like what they imagined royalists looked like.

And still, Paine droned on, unable or unwilling to recognize the horrors abounding about him. "The same spirit of fortitude that ensured success in America will ensure it to France," he insisted. Few Jacobins in the hall understood a word of what Paine said—or cared.

"I am well aware," Paine raised his voice to the "Mountain," the metaphoric name given to the elevated section of radical Jacobins at the rear of the amphitheater, "that the moment of any great change . . . is unavoidably the moment of terror and confusion."

As Paine spoke, a mob smashed its way into a royal warehouse across the Place de la Révolution from the guillotine—not far from where Paine stood—and stole the French crown jewels.

"The scene that now opens itself to France extends far beyond the boundaries of her own dominions," Paine spoke as a self-appointed sage.

> Every nation is becoming her colleague, and every court her enemy. . . . In entering on this great scene . . . let us say to the agitated mind, "Be calm." Let us punish by instructing rather than by revenge. Let us begin the new era by a greatness of friendship and hail the approach of union and success.[30]

Two days later, the National Assembly transformed itself into a National Convention—ostensibly to write another constitution, but in fact to spread Robespierre's bloody revolution. While one division of French troops forced the celebrated Prussian army to withdraw from Verdun, another marched into Savoy to reclaim the mountainous duchy as an integral part of France.

With that, the French Revolution spread like a contagion. With little opposition, French troops occupied Nice, Mainz, and the surrounding state of the Rhineland-Palatinate; they swarmed northward like bees into Belgium, into Liège on the River Meuse and then Brussels. After the army overran Monaco, the Convention proclaimed the unity of all French-speaking peoples in Europe and called for worldwide revolution, pledging "fraternity and aid to all peoples seeking to recover their liberty. . . . We will not be satisfied until Europe—all Europe—is afire."[31] In a ghastly way, Paine's Revolution of the World was reaching fruition.

French forces soon began massing along the northern Belgian border with Holland, while the French navy sailed into Naples harbor to begin conquest of the Italian peninsula, the Vatican, and the Mediterranean world. The Convention proclaimed that "all of Europe, including Moscow, will become Gallicized, Jacobinized, Communized."[32]

The French military victories, however, came at a steep price for King Louis XVI and his family, who lost their value as hostages. With their forces in full retreat, Europe's monarchs could no longer demand release of the French royal family in exchange for sparing Paris. Recognizing the changed circumstances, Robespierre stood to announce a radical change in policy. Conceding that he had once believed capital punishment to be state-sponsored assassination—in effect, "punishing one crime with another, murder with murder"—he now announced a change of mind and heart.

"Louis must die!"[33]

He said he believed that the continued existence of the royal family represented a dangerous symbol of resistance to the Revolution and demanded the immediate trial and execution of the king for high political crimes.

The National Convention ignored Robespierre and his Mountain delegates at first and, in October 1792, elected a committee of eight moderate deputies to write a new French constitution. Most conspicuous among those named was the famous Thomas Paine, the English-born American and honorary French citizen who could neither read nor write a word of French.

A month later, on November 19, the authors of the French constitution put the finishing touches on the new document, issuing a decree that claimed for France "leadership of the free world."[34]

> The National Convention declares in the name of the French nation, that it will grant fraternity and assistance to all peoples who wish to recover their liberty and instructs the Executive Power to give the necessary orders to the generals to grant assistance to these peoples and to defend those citizens who have been—or may be—persecuted for their attachment to the cause of liberty.[35]

It was straight out of Paine's *Rights of Man, Part Second*, earning toasts to Paine at gatherings across Paris. Leaders from other lands with political dreams similar to his flocked to see him, consult with him, invite him to lead revolutions in their countries. Elected an honorary member of the revolutionary Society of United Irishmen of Dublin, Paine found himself the subject of poems and drinking songs. Inept at learning even the basics of foreign languages, he limited most of his social life in Paris to those who could claim English as their mother tongue or French intellects with command of the English language.

A few days after the Convention issued what it called the "decree of fraternity," it added a second decree using Paine's language verbatim: "All who are privileged, who are tyrants ought to be treated as an enemy in the countries we enter."[36]

Paine's words seemed to appear everywhere—in periodicals across France and, when editors and publishers dared, in England and western Europe. By 1792, he had sold an estimated 1,500,000 copies of *Rights of Man* in England (population eight million then). Paine had combined both parts in a single volume and ordered it sold at the giveaway price of three pence each. As it reached increasingly large numbers of disgruntled commoners, it spawned discussion groups with innocuous names such as the London Corresponding Society and the Society for Constitutional Information. All made revolution their central topic of discussion.

Fearing the spread of Jacobinism across the Channel, Britain's government retaliated, putting Paine on trial *in absentia* in London on December 18, 1792, as a "person of a wicked, malicious, and seditious disposition; and willing to introduce disorder and confusion and to cause it to be believed that the Crown of this kingdom was contrary to the rights of the inhabitants of this kingdom and . . . that the Bill of Rights was a Bill of Wrongs and Insults."

British authorities dedicated themselves to seeing Paine drawn and quartered—or at least silenced in some way.

Ironically, as the English king's prosecutor levelled charges against Paine in London, Jacobin delegates in the French National Convention were also turning against Paine. As in England and much of western Europe, Paine's demands for social and political reforms often monopolized the front pages of periodicals, infuriating both royalists and reformers— and especially radicals, who sought to dominate the headlines. To royalists and churchmen, Paine's charges against them constituted blasphemy. To reformers and radicals, Paine's calls for reconciliation undermined their calls for vengeance against the nobility, while his dominance in the press obscured their efforts to gain prominence and political power. His sole ambition seemed to be to philosophize and etherealize—to boast of achievements in America. France was not America, and the Convention sought answers to what a new French government should and should not do, not what America had or had not done.

On December 3, 1792, Robespierre demanded that the Convention order the trial and execution of the royal family for treason and other high political crimes. Misjudging his own influence in the Convention, Paine shot to his feet to reject Robespierre's demands outright, effectively undermining what had been a cordial, if not warm, working relationship between the two. As the debate progressed, Paine grew stubborn, even hostile, insisting that Louis XVI had been America's savior and that he and his royal family should be sentenced to a life in exile in the United States.

"It is to France alone, I know, that the United States of America owe that support which enabled them to shake off an unjust and tyrannical yoke," Paine cried out. "The ardor and zeal which she displayed to provide both men and money were the natural consequences of a thirst for liberty."

But as the nation at that time . . . could only act by means of a monarchical organ, this organ . . . performed a good, a great action. Let then those United States be the safeguard and asylum of Louis Capet. There . . . he may learn . . . that the true system of government consists not in kings but in fair, equal, and honorable representation. In submitting this proposition, I consider myself a citizen of both countries . . . as a citizen of America who feels the debt of gratitude which he owes to every Frenchman . . . as a citizen of the French republic it appears to me . . . the most politic measure that can be adopted.[37]

Paine's appeal infuriated Robespierre and the Jacobins—an American attempting to out-politic French leaders in their own assembly hall. Paine, said Robespierre to his Jacobin confidants, had not been elected to the French Assembly to defend American rights. He was there to defend French rights. Ironically, both Paine and Robespierre had opposed capital punishment when they first met, and Paine's support for Robespierre on that issue had flattered the French lawyer. Now Paine stood alone, challenging one of the most dangerous men in France, indeed, Europe.

"It is our duty as legislators," Paine declared, "not to spill a drop of blood when our purpose may be effectually accomplished without it." It was, he insisted, more important to try monarchy, the institution, than the monarch, a man.[38]

Realizing that Robespierre controlled a majority of votes, Paine yielded on the question of trying the king—hoping that Robespierre, in return, would yield on the death penalty. By then, however, Paine's tactics had infuriated Robespierre, who stunned Paine and other moderates by claiming that a search of the king's apartments had uncovered secret correspondence with other monarchs planning the assassination of revolutionary leaders.

Armed with apparently damning evidence, Robespierre demanded a vote on the king's guilt, on the advisability of a referendum, and on the range of acceptable penalties. An overwhelming majority found the king guilty, rejected a public referendum, and made royals subject to the same punishments as all citizens—death on the guillotine!

Paine rose immediately to demand that the Convention reconsider. He scribbled his words on a notepad as fast as he could, handing note after note to the translator, each with a phrase or two to read in French.

"France's sole ally is the United States of America," the translator stumbled as he translated Paine's words. Agitated by then, Paine repeated his words, all but screaming in English, "It is the only nation upon which France can depend for a supply of naval stores, because all the kingdoms of northern Europe are now waging war against her or shortly will be." Seeing that no one in the audience understood, he ceded the lectern back to the translator.

"It is my fondest desire that when an ambassador has been sent . . . to Philadelphia," the translator intoned in French, "he may carry with him the tidings from France of the respite granted by the National Convention to Louis, solely because of its friendship for America. In the name of the citizens of that republic, I beg you to delay the execution. Do not, I beseech you, bestow upon the English tyrant the satisfaction of learning that the man who helped America, the land of my love, to burst her fetters, has died on the scaffold."[39]

"The words you are reading are not those of Thomas Paine," a Jacobin delegate shouted, interrupting Paine's translator.

"It is a correct translation," the translator replied calmly.

"I deny the right of Thomas Paine to vote on such a subject," shouted a second, noticeably short delegate who rose onto his toes to be heard. "He is a Quaker!"

Suddenly, miraculously, Paine seemed to understand French and shouted back: "I have taken no inconsiderable part in the struggle for freedom during the Revolution of the United States of America!"[40]

The short delegate seemed outraged by Paine's hilariously accented response in broken French and rushed from his seat to the center aisle to repeat his accusation: "Paine's reason for voting against the death penalty is that he is a Quaker!"

"I have been influenced in my vote by public policy as well as moral reasons," Paine fired back.[41]

In London, meanwhile, Paine—had he been there—would have faced a less complex proceeding. The trial of Paine in absentia got under way on December 18, 1792, as the Master of the Crown welcomed jurors with the promise of a sumptuous dinner and two guineas cash each—if they convicted Paine. If they acquitted him, they would receive only one guinea—and no food.

Paine's attorney—a renowned orator as well as lawyer—gave an impassioned defense, arguing that freedom of speech was essential to correcting the flaws in government and, therefore, essential to maintenance of good government. Although Paine's lawyer admitted that Paine had indeed criticized the government, he had done so for what he believed were England's best interests. To find him guilty, Paine's attorney declared, it would have to prove malice, and, he insisted, there was none.

Outside the courtroom, angry gangs materialized across London burning copies of *Rights of Man*, shouting "Church and King," and smashing shop windows of printers and booksellers who carried Paine's writings. In the courtroom, the judge ignored the defense attorney's presentation, dismissed him with a wave of the hand, and turned to the jury foreman, who stood to say that, without having left the courtroom, he had deliberated with fellow jurors, and they had instructed him to announce their unanimous decision.

"Guilty!"

As spectators swarmed out of the courtroom, newsboys handed out a full-sized "newspaper" that had materialized even as the jury foreman announced the verdict. A banner headline proclaimed Paine's conviction.

The following day, London newspapers announced the imprisonment of Paine's primary book retailer. Although Paine himself had long earlier fled England, the government victory encouraged prosecutors to charge eleven publishers and booksellers of *Rights of Man* with sedition. Juries found them all guilty, and although judges could have sentenced each of the eleven to a dozen or more years of prison, they displayed mercy by imposing jail sentences of only three years each.

"Of these booksellers and publishers I was one," Paine's friend Clio Rickman recounted, "but by flying to France, I eluded this merciful sentence."[42]

The government followed its court victories against Paine's publishers by arresting thirty political radicals and trying three for high treason, but all three won acquittal.

Paine apparently laughed when he heard the verdict against him, saying, "the best way of advertising good books [is] by prosecution."[43]

In Paris, meanwhile, the National Convention began a different sort of trial to determine the fate of the French king. Each of the 721 delegates took his turn trotting down the steep incline of the amphitheater to the rostrum to announce his verdict and, if he so pleased, the reasons for that verdict.

Guilty, declared the Abbé Sieyès.

Guilty . . . Guilty . . . Guilty. . . . echoed each of the other delegates. The voting lasted into the night and through the entire next day. . . .

"Je vote . . . ," Paine stood at the rostrum speaking in slow, labored French, saying he favored imprisonment of the king until the end of the war and perpetual exile from France after the war.

Paine's defiance and haughty arguments against the death penalty—in mangled French no less—left Robespierre and his radical followers fuming at the brazen American . . . or Englishman . . . or whatever he was. But a surprisingly large number of moderate delegates voted with Paine—to their deep regrets in the bloody days that would follow.

By the end of voting, some thirty-six hours later, the Mountain won by a bare plurality, with 361 voting for the death penalty and a surprising 334 siding with Paine for imprisonment and banishment. Twenty-six voted for death with a plea for clemency, leaving Robespierre's Jacobins with an embarrassingly slim one-vote victory. It was an astonishing moral, if not political, victory for Thomas Paine. In arguing against the death penalty, however, he had, knowingly or not, humiliated Robespierre, Marat, and other radical leaders, none of whom forgave such slights. None would forgive Paine—or those who had voted with him.

Nor did Paine have the political sense to retreat while he still could. He did not or could not understand that the French Revolution had already passed him by. There was no longer any tolerance for dissent.

"The decision reached in the Convention yesterday in favor of death has filled me with genuine sorrow," Paine wrote in an address seeking to reverse the vote against the king and read by a translator to the Convention the following day.

"I deny the right of Thomas Paine to speak on such a subject," Marat's booming voice interrupted. "He is a Quaker; his religious views run counter to infliction of capital punishment."[44]

Pandemonium suddenly engulfed the proceedings; delegates stood and shouted, one after another, some demanding that Marat sit and respect Paine's right to free speech, others shouting for the foreigner Paine to stop meddling in French affairs.

"It is unfortunate," Paine's translator continued trying to read above the din, "that the individual whose fate we are now determining has always been regarded by the American people as a friend to their own revolution."

"Il n'est pas français!" shrieked a hysterical voice.[45] "He is not French!"

Paine warned that the execution of Louis would most certainly "excite the heartfelt sorrow of your ally"—and generate anger if Americans concluded that the French Revolution had replaced justice with vengeance. "If I were able to speak French, I would personally appear at the bar and, in the name of the American people, ask that Louis be respited."

Visibly outraged, one of Robespierre's radicals shouted, "Those words are not the words of Thomas Paine!"

Marat agreed twice, once on the floor of the Convention and a second time in his widely read inflammatory newspaper *L'Ami du peuple* (*The Friend of the People*). "I denounce the translator," Marat cried out. "Such opinions are not those of Thomas Paine. The translation is not correct."[46]

The translator tried continuing above the din. Paine rose from his seat and fought his way to the rostrum and standing by the translator, he called out to delegates, "Those are my words!"

Marat leaped from his seat into the center aisle and screamed hysterically, "He is a Quaker! Quaker! Quaker!" The meeting deteriorated into random shouting, some pushing and shoving, and an exodus of delegates trying to avoid injury.[47]

When the chamber came to order, Robespierre stood and, in sharp, cutting tones, refuted Paine's argument—calmly, logically. It was true, as Paine had said, that he, Robespierre, had once proposed abolishing capital punishment, but the National Assembly had rejected his proposal. Capital punishment for treason, among other crimes, remained the law of the land, and royal inviolability no longer applied. Louis himself had ridden into Paris from Versailles, accepted a republican cockade, and declared himself a citizen and, therefore, subject to the same laws and penalties for violating the laws as every other citizen.

As delegates cheered wildly in the upper tiers of the hall—on "the Mountain"—Robespierre turned and stared directly at Paine, grimacing menacingly. The cheers metamorphosed into boos and shouts of "aristocrate!" For the first time in his political life, Paine was no longer a man of the people or the people's hero.

"Tom Paine is just where he ought to be," an English spectator wrote ominously of the proceedings. "His vocation will not be complete, nor theirs either, till his head finds its way to the top of a pike, which will probably not be long."[48]

After Paine's translator had finished addressing the Convention, Robespierre had stood, demanding passage of two decrees: one, "to detect and drive out all the agents of foreign powers who . . . have introduced themselves into this society" and, two, a specific "decree against Thomas Paine."[49]

Paine's jaw dropped. Starring wide-eyed at his French antagonist, he suddenly recognized the gross error he had made equating the French and American Revolutions, an error that would not only silence his voice, but would now almost certainly cost him his head.

Chapter 9

THE TERROR

O N THE MORNING OF JANUARY 21, 1793, LOUIS XVI CLIMBED THE
steps to the guillotine on the Place de la Révolution, now the Place
de la Concorde.* The blade fell at 10:22.

"The late King of this Country has been publicly executed," American Ambassador Gouverneur Morris wrote to Secretary of State Jefferson.
"He died in a manner becoming his dignity. Mounting the scaffold, he
expressed anew his forgiveness of those who persecuted him and a prayer
that his deluded people might be benefited by his death. On the scaffold,
he attempted to speak, but the commanding officer . . . ordered the drums
to beat."[1]

After holding high the severed head by its royal hairs to display to the
cheering crowd, the executioner tossed it into a waiting cart and turned to
wipe clean the blade of his instrument and prepare it for his next client.
His assistants then tossed the king's body into the corpse-filled cart, and
guardsmen cleared a path for it to pass through the crowd and roll toward
the Madeleine Cemetery about a half-mile away. There, a gaping trench,
fifty feet wide and long, its floor lined with the previous day's grisly deposits, awaited the new arrivals.

---

*The guillotine on the Place de la Révolution stood directly in front of today's famed
Hotel de Crillon. Built in 1758 by King Louis XV as a government building, it was
the site of the signing of the 1778 treaties in which France recognized American sovereignty. The Duke de Crillon acquired it in 1788 and converted it into a palace, but
the revolutionary French government confiscated it in 1791. Returned to the de Crillon family after the Restoration, it became a luxury hotel in 1909—the first in Paris.

32. Execution of French King Louis XVI on the Place de la Révolution, now the Place de la Concorde, in Paris, on January 21, 1793. (Réunion des Musées Nationaux)

The execution of King Louis XVI outraged the civilized world. In Germany, the French king's brothers proclaimed Louis's imprisoned seven-year-old son, Louis-Charles de France, the new king. On February 1, 1793, France responded to evident British preparations for war by declaring war on Britain and Holland. Over the next month, the French annexed Belgium and Monaco, invaded Holland, and declared war on Spain. By the end of March, a huge European coalition had formed to try to crush the French Revolution and prevent its spread into neighboring countries.

Every nation in Europe, it seemed, joined an insane crusade of kings to destroy France and her Revolution. Only tiny Switzerland and far-off Russia, Sweden, and Turkey kept their armies at bay. But England, Holland, Spain, the Italian states, Austria, and Prussia—even the Papacy—sent armies pouring into France from all directions: the Spanish from the southwest along the Mediterranean, the Prussians across the Rhineland in the east, the Austrians from the north. Far more threatening, the powerful British army landed in Toulon on the French Mediterranean coast and prepared to land in the Bay of Biscay and trap southern and southwestern France in the grip of a powerful pincer of foreign armies.

France had but one ally left in the world, the United States of America, and, in a vicious display of political power, the revolutionaries leading the French government were planning to imprison a celebrated hero of its only ally and sentence him to die.

Unwilling to ride in silence to the deadly blade, Paine unsheathed his only weapon. "I now despair of seeing the great object of European liberty accomplished," his pen warned Georges-Jacques Danton. Danton had seized some reins of Jacobin power and was gradually emasculating Convention moderates and anyone else who disputed Jacobin extremism. Danton was the only French Revolution leader who could read English, allowing Paine to avoid using a translator and divulge his whereabouts.

Believing himself still a member of the Convention, Paine feigned bravado: "I am exceedingly disturbed at the distractions, jealousies, discontents and uneasiness that reign among us, and which, if they continue, will bring ruin and disgrace upon the Republic."

33. When Georges-Jacques Danton seized power in the French Convention, Thomas Paine warned that Jacobin suppression of moderate delegates would destroy the Republic and cost Danton his head. (Réunion des Musées Nationaux)

I now despair of seeing the great object of European liberty accomplished, and my despair arises not from the combined foreign powers, not from the intrigues of aristocracy and priest craft, but from the tumultuous misconduct with which the internal affairs of the present revolution is conducted. . . . I am distressed to see matters so badly conducted, and so little attention paid to moral principles. It is these things that injure the character of the Revolution and discourage the progress of liberty all over the world.[2]

In a daring challenge to Danton and the other radicals, Paine called for regulation and punishment for unfounded denunciations. Allowing every individual to denounce at random without any proof, he warned, would undermine all confidence in government. "Calumny is a species of Treachery that ought to be punished as well as any other kind of Treachery. It is a private vice productive of public evils; because it is possible to irritate men into disaffection by continual calumny who never intended to be disaffected. It is equally as necessary to protect the characters of public officers from calumny as it is to punish them for treachery or misconduct."[3]

Uncertain of his own future and unwilling to challenge so gifted a polemicist as Paine, Danton left Paine's letter unanswered and let silence mute the voice of his American critic. Danton's ploy proved effective. For the first time in his adult life, Paine's call for justice went unheard, unread—in Paris and everywhere else.

In Philadelphia, then the capital of a land at peace with France, Britain, and every other nation, the President of the United States heard and saw nothing, and, therefore, asked nothing about Thomas Paine or his whereabouts. Washington's little nation wanted nothing to do with Europe's war, had no military force to enter the conflict if it had wanted to, and had no money to pay for such an adventure. After proclaiming the United States neutral, Washington was careful not to comment on French politics or its participants, including Paine. Nor did others give much thought to the author of *Common Sense*. Americans, Englishmen, even most Frenchmen simply forgot him. In the turmoil that followed the king's execution, Paine vanished, and no one noticed. He had had his day, and it seemed to have ended.

As invading armies surrounded France, her people suffered crippling shortages of every essential—arms and ammunition to repel invaders, clothes to shield the dispossessed, food to feed defenders. Infuriated by government failures to repel enemy forces, pockets of counterrevolution developed, demanding the ouster of Jacobins from Convention leadership. Convention activities came to a halt, and Robespierre stepped in, forming a powerful Committee of Public Safety that mandated the execution of his political opponents. Most of them were either moderates who had allied themselves with Paine in the struggle to save the king from the guillotine or foreigners who might aid invading armies from their native lands.

One by one, then two by two, then by the dozens, tumbrels rumbled over Parisian cobblestones toward one or another guillotine and thence to the huge burial pits nearby. Among the most outspoken Robespierre opponents still whole in body, Paine was the most obvious—alone, however, a sad remnant of a man clutching a crumpled paper that detailed useless proposals for a constitution of the French Republic.

Like most of his supporters—even Jefferson and Franklin—Thomas Paine had failed to recognize fundamental differences between the New World and the Old, differences that made the French, English, and all peoples of the Old World incapable of governing themselves: they had never done so and any constitution that limited the role of government left them helpless and anarchic.

Americans, on the other hand, had, in effect, governed themselves for three, four, and more generations over nearly 200 years before the American Revolution. They had crossed the Atlantic, scattered across a vast untamed wilderness, alone to develop the surrounding world themselves with their bare hands—without government aid or interference. Ninety-five percent of Americans lived on farms, plantations, and woodlands, often isolated and far from any neighbors or settled communities. With no one to tell them how to survive and govern themselves and their lands, each became master of his own universe, planting what he wanted; hunting and fishing what, where, and when he chose; selling, saving, or consuming all he produced; shooting at and often killing marauding animals, Indians, or squatters who breached the borders of his land. Alone and unquestioned, he grew enraged when a government he had no say in selecting in a land he had never seen across an ocean he had never crossed demanded a share of his earnings to pay for its outrageous expenses. He—and independent men like him across America—refused and, for a moment, he and they united to form a quasi-government which they controlled to stage the American Revolution.

In contrast, the French had never governed themselves in recorded history. Indeed, most of the French were quite content living under royal rule, tilling the lands of noblemen—as long as they had enough food to eat and wine to drink. When they did not, they rebelled—not to change their government, but to make their government respond to their needs and feed them as it had in the past.

Unlike America, but very much like England, France had no constitution to define and restrict governmental powers and guarantee human rights. Heredity determined most members of the legislature as well as the executive. The French National Convention, which originally convened to write a constitution, had, in the absence of a formal government, usurped all legislative, executive, and judicial powers, exercising those powers subtly at first, but openly and ruthlessly after Jacobin extremists gained control.

"Had this revolution been conducted consistently with its principles," Paine lamented in a letter to Jefferson following the king's execution, "there was once a good prospect of extending liberty through the greatest part of Europe, but I now relinquish that hope. As the prospect of a general freedom is now much shortened . . . I shall await the event of the proposed constitution and then take my final leave of Europe."[4] Two weeks later, he wrote his fruitless letter to Danton.

As Paine saw his English-speaking French friends disappear mysteriously, he admitted:

> I saw my life in continual danger. My friends were falling as fast as the knife could cut their heads off, and as I every day expected the same fate, I resolved to begin my work. I appeared to myself to be on my death-bed, for death was on every side of me, and as I every day expected the same fate, I had not time to lose.[5]

The "work" that Paine resolved to begin had nothing to do with the French Revolution. As he testified to Jefferson, he had "relinquished" all hopes of implementing the rights of man in France and the rest of Europe. Satisfied with having ridded America of the tyranny of monarchy, he now set out to rid the nation he loved—and perhaps the world—of the tyranny of the church, its clergy, and the religions they imposed on man. Not one church, all churches; not one cleric, all clerics; not one denomination, all denominations. Just as he had sparked a revolution that upended monarchy with arguments based on logic and reason in *Common Sense*, Thomas Paine intended using similar arguments to upend organized religion. If he lived long enough to complete it, it would be his magnum opus: *The Age of Reason.*

"The most formidable weapon against errors of every kind," he wrote again and again and believed passionately, "is reason."[6]

Paine moved to a cottage beneath a grove of fruit trees in the Faubourg St. Denis, now a busy Paris neighborhood, but at the time Paine walked its lanes, a quiet rural suburb northeast of the city—in sight of the fortress-like Temple prison and window of Marie Antoinette's cell. Occasionally Paine worked his way through back-alley shadows into the city to the Convention, but found it a useless exercise. Many of his political allies in the arena had disappeared and the few still there barely acknowledged him with a silent nod and turned away. His enemies sneered.

> I went but little to the Convention, and then only to make my appearance, because I found it impossible to join in their tremendous decrees and useless and dangerous to oppose them. My having voted and spoken extensively . . . against the execution of the king had already fixed a mark upon me. . . . Pen and ink were then of no use to me . . . no printer dared to print. . . . In this retired manner, I remained about six weeks.[7]

Paine's property stood on an acre of land enclosed by a wall, shaded by fruit trees, replete with ducks, turkeys, geese, some rabbits, and two pigs, "which we used to feed out of the parlor window.

"My apartment consisted of three rooms," Paine related, "the first for wood, water, etc., the next was the bedroom, and beyond it the sitting

34. Women's rights pioneer Mary Wollstonecraft was a member of Thomas Paine's "little happy circle" of close friends in Paris.

room, which looked into the garden through a glass door." A staircase hidden by grapevines led to the garden below, where he found some relief "by walking alone . . . after dark and cursing with hearty good will the authors of that terrible system that had turned the character of the revolution I had been proud to defend."

By the end of summer, a small group of men and women—all exiled voluntarily or involuntarily from one land or another—had gathered around Paine and his turkeys, ducks, geese, rabbits, and two pigs. Among them, printers Nicolas de Bonneville and Thomas Clio Rickman had each dared print *Rights of Man, Part Second*—the former in France, the latter in England; women's rights activist Mary Wollstonecraft had written a harshly criticized work, *A Vindication of the Rights of Woman*, suggesting that women were not inferior to men. Like Bonneville and Rickman, she found a staunch friend and admirer in Paine. Like Paine they faced prison or worse if they fled to England and, again like Paine, they dared not risk capture by the British by trying to sail to the safety of American shores.

"The little happy circle who lived with him will ever remember those days with delight," Rickman recalled. "With these select friends he would talk of his boyish days, played at chess, whist, piquet [a card game], or cribbage, and enliven the moments by many interesting anecdotes. . . . Here gathered sympathetic spirits from America, England, France, Germany, Holland, Switzerland, freed from prejudices of race, rank, or nationality, striving to be mutually helpful, amusing themselves with Arcadian sports, studying nature, enriching each other by exchange of experiences. It is certain that in all the world there was no group of men and women more disinterestedly absorbed in the work of benefiting their fellow beings."[8]

In a letter to a friend, Paine recalled a macabre incident one evening, when a police captain appeared at his door and addressed Paine "in good English" about a matter that, in the end, did not concern Paine. Before he left, however, he complimented Paine for *Rights of Man*, said he had read it, admired it, and promised to help Paine if he could ever be of service.

"The man that offered me his services was no other than Charles-Henri Sanson, the public executioner who guillotined the King in Paris and who lived . . . in the same street with me."[9] Whether Sanson was sending Paine a signal or not, Paine did not ask, but simply busied himself, tapping friendly officials for passports to help his friends escape France and return safely to their homelands. Only then did he begin making queries about his own, puzzling situation.

Other political figures facing destinies similar to that of the king were, like Paine, busy writing—usually their memoirs. Not Paine, though. Paine was exposing the myths of divine right of the church and its clerics much as he had exposed the myth of divine right of kings, and the myth of divine predestination of man into different ranks of society. Although he had intended writing such a work later in life, with the realization that he might not live to see "later," he set to work writing it sooner rather than later.

"Every national church or religion has established itself by pretending some special mission from God communicated by certain individuals," Paine wrote. "The Jews have their Moses, the Christians their Jesus Christ, apostles, and saints; and the Turks their Mahomet, as if the way to God was not open to every man alike. . . . Each of those churches accuses the others of unbelief; and for my own part, I disbelieve them all."[10]

> Whenever we read the obscene stories, the voluptuous debaucheries, the cruel and torturous executions, the unrelenting vindictiveness with which more than half the Bible is filled, it would be more consistent that we called it the word of a demon than the Word of God. It is a history of wickedness that has served to corrupt and brutalize mankind, and, for my part, I sincerely detest it, as I detest everything that is cruel.[11]

Paine agreed that everyone had the right to follow the religion and the worship he preferred, but insisted that Adam—"if ever there was such a man"—had to have lived a Deist.

"I had not finished the first part of the work," Paine interrupted himself, "when I was arrested and taken to prison."[12]

Paine's arrest came as the period known as La Terreur—The Terror—was approaching its climax. It began in early October 1793, with Robespierre's Jacobins accusing almost all Convention moderates, one by one, of treason. Then, on October 16, 1793, a mob of Jacobin thugs swarmed through the prison at *Le Temple*, breaking into one cell where they stuffed a screaming seven-year-old boy, King Louis-Charles de France, into a potato sack and carried him off to no-one-knows-where. His fate remains a mystery. A second group broke into another cell and seized the diminutive Queen Marie Antoinette. Emerging from the prison gate, they lifted her like a toy doll for the mob to see, then tossed her into the tumbrel. A stunning jewel of a lady, she recovered her balance and stood, head high, looking ahead implacably, silently, almost beatifically, as the cart worked its way through the shrieking mob to the Place de la Révolution and Dr. Guillotin's killing machine. They bound the Queen to the killing board and, as the mob fell silent, the executioners lowered her to a horizontal position, placed the wooden lunette about her neck, and stepped back. Sanson released the leather ties and let the knife fall.

The mob let loose a collective gasp at the sound of the knife striking home, then a thunderous cheer as attendants disposed of the queen as they had the king nine months earlier, displaying her head to the cheering mob, then throwing it and the rest of her corpse into a tumbrel with other victims. As scavengers reached into the cart to strip its passengers of their garments and shoes, the tumbrel rolled away slowly to the huge burying pit in the Madeleine Cemetery where its gruesome cargo would rot away anonymously with thousands of other innocents.*

"Ah, France," Paine sighed as he wrote to a friend before his own arrest. "Thou hast ruined the character of a revolution virtuously begun, and destroyed those who produced it." He described having heard a "rapping at the gate, and looking out the window . . . a guard with muskets and bayonets entered. I went to bed again and made up my mind for prison, for I was the only lodger."

As it turned out, they had come to arrest two British friends whom Paine had helped flee France a few days earlier. "I thanked God they were out of their reach. . . . The guard came about a month after, in the night, and took away the landlord. . . . And the scene in the house finished with the arrestation of myself."[13]

In the early morning hours of December 28, eleven days after his trial had begun in London, five Paris policemen and two agents of the Committee of General Security, a Jacobin police agency that rooted out political enemies of the Revolution, knocked at Paine's bedroom door. Displaying an order for his arrest and imprisonment, they spent the next few hours examining all his papers, then led him off to prison. Asked the charges that had provoked his arrest, the guards shrugged their shoulders, saying they were only carrying out orders. Although most Englishmen and Frenchmen deemed Paine's arrest inevitable—all knew the dangers of criticizing authority—the audacity of arresting an American patriot of such renown, a founder of the American republic, shocked the few in Europe who learned of his arrest. Shock turned to sorrow and then fear when rumors materialized that Paine had died on the guillotine. The publication

---

*Despite years of efforts, medical examiners have never been able to identify the royal remains. A temple-like memorial, closed to the general public, stands above the burial pit alongside the Boulevard Haussmann in central Paris.

of a leaflet, "The Last Dying Words of Thomas Paine," seemed to confirm the worst fears of those who revered his works.

If Paine was dead, so was his dream and the dream of his readers for worldwide peace and establishment of a European republic based on the equality of man. Paine was still alive, of course, but even he agreed that his dream had probably died with his arrest. "There is now no prospect that France can carry revolutions through Europe," he had written to Thomas Jefferson just before his arrest, "or that the combined powers can conquer France. . . . Neither side will ask for peace though each may wish it."[14]

By the time of Paine's arrest, the Jacobins had filled conventional prisons to overflowing and they began putting English prisoners and French government officials and members of the nobility in secure areas of unused palaces and mansions to await trial. In the event they proved themselves innocent of the charges against them, they would emerge looking less brutalized than the few who emerged from stone dungeons. Instead of a prison cell, Paine found himself locked in a large, damp unheated room at the Luxemburg Palace, or, more properly, the Palais du Luxembourg, which Henry IV had built in 1615 for his queen consort Marie de Medici to inhabit after his death. It stood about a mile inland from the south, or left, bank of the Seine River, near Paris University and the French Pantheon. Its broad southern face overlooked the sparkling silver waters of an artificial lake surrounded by a wide swath of flower gardens that nestled against a small forest. On a normal day, the squeals and laughter of children at play filled the air, but their cries never reached Paine and his fellow cellmates, lodged as they were in a room that faced only a barren interior courtyard.

"The room in which I was lodged was on the ground floor," Paine recalled later, "and one of a long range of rooms under a gallery . . . I had three comrades, fellow prisoners, with me."

The state of things in the prisons was a continued state of horror. No man could count upon life for twenty-four hours. To such a pitch of rage and suspicion were Robespierre and his committee arrived that it seemed as if they feared to leave a man to live. Scarcely a night passed in which ten, twenty, thirty, forty, fifty or more were not taken out of the

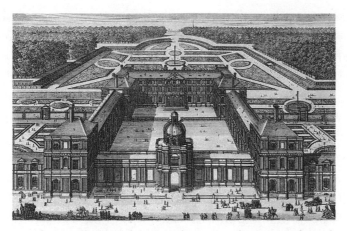

35. The grand Palais du Luxembourg on the Paris Left Bank was completed in 1645 for Marie de Medici, mother of Louis XIII. Converted into a prison during the French Revolution, it housed Thomas Paine, among others. It is now the French Senate. (Réunion des Musées Nationaux)

prison . . . and guillotined. . . . One hundred and sixty-nine persons were taken out of the Luxembourg in one night, and a hundred and sixty of them guillotined the next day.[15]

Before his arrest, Paine had been able to pass the first part of his work on religion to an American friend, Connecticut poet Joel Barlow, who managed to find a Paris publisher to print it in 1794. It bore the title *The Age of Reason, Being an Investigation of True and Fabulous Theologies.* An English printer printed it a year later.

Paine had much more to write, however, and prison guards, aware of his renown and the speed with which accusers and accused often traded places in the Revolution, brought him pencils and paper and allowed him to continue writing. In the weeks that followed, he managed to expand his original pamphlet-length essay into a book-length manuscript. Although guards also allowed him to inquire into the circumstances of his arrest, he was unable to learn any charges. In fact, there had been no formal charges. A guard said he thought it had something to do with treason, but that made no sense.

Paine petitioned the Convention President, but, again, was unable to learn the reasons for his arrest. He turned to Gouverneur Morris, the American minister plenipotentiary, naively believing Morris would provide the help and support due any American citizen. Paine had not the slightest suspicion that Morris, an appointee and friend of President George Washington, would conspire with a foreign government to injure a fellow American.

Morris, however, was still seething over the financial losses he and Robert Morris had sustained after Paine's exposure of Silas Deane's unethical transactions for arms and armaments at the start of the Revolutionary War. In addition, Morris feared that Paine was about to expose the scandalous life he had been leading in France. In addition to innumerable trysts with Parisian ladies, he had sparked the curiosity of journalists as to how he had accumulated such enormous wealth—a country home and estate outside Paris, a stable of champion horses, a sizable collection of wines—in so short a time in a country whose economy had collapsed. With Paine in prison, the American government would never learn how.

Morris, therefore, not only ignored Paine's appeal for help, he ignored his obligation as a diplomat to inform Secretary of State Jefferson or anyone in the American government of Paine's arrest. To further stifle Paine's voice, Morris sent word to Robespierre of Paine's British birth and his conviction for seditious libel. Under British law, he remained a citizen of Britain and subject to execution there.

It was, in fact, Morris's letter that provoked the President of the Convention to reject Paine's petition, insisting, "Thomas Paine is a native of England; this is undoubtedly enough to apply to him the measures of security prescribed by the revolutionary laws."[16]

With Morris's assurances concerning Paine's nationality and criminal background, Robespierre ordered Paine imprisoned indefinitely without charge under a law mandating imprisonment of foreign nationals from countries at war with France.

Having lost hope of saving the French Revolution, the usually optimistic Paine now began losing hope of saving himself. Unable at first to suspect the depths of Morris's loathing for him, Paine wrote to the American minister a second time: "You must not leave me in the situation in which this letter places me. You know I do not deserve it, and you see the unpleasant situation in which I am thrown."

> I have made an essay in answer to the Minister's letter which I wish you to make the grounds of a reply to him. They have nothing against me— except that they do not choose I should be in a state of freedom to write my mind freely upon things I have seen. Though you and I are not on terms of the best harmony, I apply to you as the Minister of America and you may add to that service whatever you think my integrity deserves. At any rate I expect you to make Congress acquainted with my situation and to send to them copies of the letters that have passed on the subject. A reply to the Minister's letter is absolutely necessary, were it only to continue the reclamation. Otherwise your silence will be a sort of consent to his observations.[17]

Paine might just as well have ended his letter, "Your silence will also be a sentence of death."

As he had done previously, Morris ignored Paine's letter and wrote to no one about Paine's plight.

A group of Americans in Paris learned of Paine's arrest and drew up an address they presented to the Convention:

> Citizens! Thomas Paine, the apostle of liberty in America, a profound and valuable philosopher, a virtuous and esteemed citizen came to France and took a seat among you. . . . Citizens! Representatives! We come to demand of you Thomas Paine in the name of the friends of liberty, in the name of the Americans your brothers and allies. . . . Do not give the leagued despots the pleasure of seeing Paine in irons.[18]

The appeal had no effect.

As Paine languished in the Luxemburg Palace, Paris guillotines chopped away almost nonstop during the day. Seizing ever-increasing powers each day, Robespierre demanded—and the Convention complied by passing—a law that allowed judges to declare suspects innocent or guilty without trial or any opportunity to defend themselves in court. The law transformed "The Terror" into "The Great Terror," with almost every Paris mansion seized and gutted, its interiors partitioned into prison cells. To supplement the guillotine on the Place de la Révolution, guillotines sprouted on the Place de la Bastille where the prison had stood, in front of City Hall (Hôtel de Ville), on the Place du Carrousel, by what is now the Louvre Museum, and on the Place du Trône (now Place de la Nation), on the east edge of Paris near Vincennes.

Each of the blades lopped off twenty or more heads a day, accommodating those whom chief executioner Charles-Henri Sanson called his "clients" from every segment of the social and political spectrum: the abolitionist Malesherbes, the scientist Lavoisier, the poet André Chenier, and King Louis XVI's younger sister, the gentle and harmless Madame Élizabeth. The retired Admiral Comte d'Estaing felt the gentle caress of the blade for having protested the execution of Marie Antoinette.

"The gods are thirsty," Jacobin journalist Camille Desmoulins scoffed—until the day arrived when the tumbrel came to carry him to the guillotine. Even Danton.

"That which you did for the happiness and liberty of your country, I tried in vain to do for mine," a repentant Danton all but sobbed to Paine on arrival at Luxemburg prison. "I have been less fortunate but not less innocent. Now they will send me to the scaffold."[19]

Terrified survivors of the Convention competed with each other to win the favor of Robespierre as the Great Terror progressed. When he demanded the President's seat, they gave it to him by unanimous vote. As it turned out, Robespierre's guillotines spared (for the moment) a small, select group he labelled "Friends of America"—including Lafayette's wife, Adrienne, and Thomas Paine—to avoid provoking American President George Washington by executing any of the American President's personal friends.

A month after Morris received Paine's letters—it was the first anniversary of King Louis XVI's execution—Morris finally got around to writing Secretary of State Jefferson. By then, the first part of *Age of Reason*—Paine's new work on religion—had appeared in print, further fueling Gouverneur Morris's loathing for Paine. Although Morris pretended to be unaware of it, Jefferson had quit his post on December 31, 1793, and had returned home to Virginia. Thus, Morris had written a letter knowing it would reach and remain on an empty desk, serving only as documentary evidence of his "concern" for Americans abroad and, therefore, to protect his own job.

"Lest I forget," Morris wrote disingenuously, "I must mention that Thomas Paine is in prison, where he amuses himself with publishing a pamphlet against Jesus Christ."

> I incline to think that if he is quiet in prison he may have the good luck to be forgotten, whereas should he be brought much into notice, the long suspended axe might fall on him. I believe he thinks I ought to claim him as an American citizen; but considering his birth, his naturalization in this country, and the place he filled, I doubt much the right, and I am sure that the claim would be, for the present at least, inexpedient and ineffectual.

Thomas Paine used the long, empty hours in prison to continue expanding *Age of Reason*. Morris had condemned the first part of *Age of Reason* in his malevolent letter to Jefferson, calling it "a pamphlet against Jesus Christ," when it actually praised Jesus and the beliefs said to have been his. What Paine was against was the deification of Jesus. Paine noted that Jesus had written nothing of himself, his birth, parentage, his life, or family.

"Not a line of . . . the New Testament is of his writing," Paine declared. "The history of him is altogether the work of other people." Centuries after he existed, mythologists brought him into the world of the New Testament "in a supernatural manner and were obliged to take him out again in the same manner or the apple in the first part of the story must have fallen to the ground.

"It is not difficult to account for . . . the story of Jesus Christ being the Son of God," Paine went on. "He was born when heathen mythology had still some fashion and repute in the world."

> Almost all the extraordinary men that lived under heathen mythology were reputed to be the sons of some of their gods . . . the intercourse of gods with women was for them a matter of familiar opinion. Their Jupiter . . . had cohabited with hundreds. . . . The Christian Church sprung out of the tail of heathen mythology.

Paine argued that ancient mythologists had gods for everything, and Christian mythologists mimicked their predecessors by creating saints for everything. "The Church became as crowded with one as the [Roman] Pantheon had been with the other . . . and Rome was the place of both. . . . The ancient mythologists tell us that the race of Giants made war against Jupiter . . . that Jupiter defeated them and confined them afterward under Mount Etna. . . . The Christian mythologists tell us that their Satan made war against the Almighty, who defeated him and confined him afterward . . . in a pit."[20]

To provide a sequel to the story of Satan's confinement in a pit, Paine went on, Christian mythologists had to release him from the pit and transform him into a serpent that slithers down a tree and calmly enters into a conversation with Eve. But, Paine added, "Eve seems in no way surprised to hear a snake talk," and the outcome of their conversation is that "he persuades her to eat an apple, and the eating of that apple damns all mankind."[21]

Calling Christian mythology absurd, Paine asserted, "When I am told that a woman called the Virgin Mary said, or gave out, that she was with child without any cohabitation with a man, and that her betrothed husband, Joseph, said that an angel told him so . . . such a circumstance required a much stronger evidence than their bare word for it; but we have not even this—for neither Joseph nor Mary wrote any such matter themselves; it is only reported by others that *they said so*—it is hearsay upon hearsay, and I do not choose to rest any belief upon such evidence."[22]

Paine emphasized that Jesus never wrote of himself, his parentage, or anything about his life. "That such a person as Jesus Christ existed, and that he was crucified, which was the mode of execution in that day, are . . . strictly within the limits of probability, but the story of Jesus . . . [in] the New Testament is entirely a compilation by others, and the supernatural elements of Christ's story—the miraculous conception, resurrection, ascension, and other miraculous events—are a fraud devised by Christian mythologists calling themselves the Christian church."

They represent this virtuous and amiable man, Jesus Christ, to be at once both God and Man and also the Son of God, celestially begotten, on purpose to be sacrificed because they say that Eve . . . had eaten an apple. Putting aside everything that might excite laughter by its absurdity . . . it is impossible to conceive a story more derogatory to the Almighty, more inconsistent with His wisdom, more contradictory to His power, than this story.[23]

Paine insisted that if Christ had wanted to start a religion, "he would have written something himself *or procured it to be written* in his life-time. . . . The probability is that he could not write, for his parents were ex-tremely poor . . . not being able to pay for a bed when he was born."[24] Yet, Paine adds, the church set up "a religion of pomp and of revenue . . . very contradictory to the character of the person whose name it bears."[25]

Thinking he would provoke Secretary of State Thomas Jefferson to turn on Paine, Gouverneur Morris miscalculated badly. He obviously did not know Jefferson well, certainly not as well as Paine knew him. Paine and Jefferson shared the same beliefs, with Jefferson—like Paine—denying that Jesus was "a member of the Godhead."[26]

But the most sinister libels Morris invented against Paine were his not being an American citizen and his having been naturalized in France. With the start of the French Revolution, the National Assembly had declared Paine—as it had Washington, Jefferson, Hamilton, and other American Founding Fathers—an "honorary" French citizen. He was no more a "naturalized" French citizen than Washington.

As for his American citizenship, the US Naturalization Act of 1790 stated, *"A free white person, who shall have resided within the limits and under the jurisdiction of the United States for the term of two years, may be admitted to become a citizen thereof."*[27] Paine had resided in the United States for twelve years, from 1775 to 1787, and was there at the founding.

Never knowing if or when the tumbrel would stop by his room, Paine wrote many premature prefaces for the parts of his manuscript he was able to complete in prison. On January 27, 1794, he wrote:

TO MY FELLOW CITIZENS OF THE UNITED STATES OF AMERICA.—I put the following work under your protection. It contains my opinion on religion. You will do me the justice to remember that I have always strenuously supported the Right of every man his opinions, however different that opinion might be to mine. He who denies to another this right makes a slave of himself to his present opinion because he precludes himself the right of changing it. The most formidable weapon against errors of every kind is Reason. I have never used any other, and I trust I never shall— Your affectionate friend and fellow citizen,

Thomas Paine.[28]

With that, Thomas Paine awaited the tumbrel he believed would carry him to the guillotine.

Chapter 10

IN THE NAME OF RELIGION

THOMAS PAINE HAD STARTED *AGE OF REASON* BY PROFESSING HIS OWN faith: "I believe in one God and no more . . . I believe in the equality of man." He asserted his disbelief in "the creeds professed by the Jewish Church . . . Roman Church . . . Greek Church . . . Turkish Church . . . Protestant Church . . . any church that I know of." He said each claimed falsely "a special mission from God" and—again falsely— that "certain books" had revealed the Word of God.

> But admitting . . . that something has been revealed to a certain person and not revealed to any other person, it is revelation to that person only. When he tells it to a second, and a second to a third, it ceases to be a revelation. . . . It is *hearsay* to every other. . . . It is a contradiction in terms . . . to call anything a revelation that comes to us at second hand, either verbally or in writing . . . it cannot be incumbent on me to believe it in the same manner, for it was not a revelation made to me, and I have only his word for it that it was made to him.[1]

From his prison room, with no distractions but death itself, Paine used pure, simple logic, often coated with biting humor, to examine and demonstrate almost every passage in the New and Old Testaments as myth born in an age of "heathen mythology." The task was not difficult for Paine, equipped as he was with an extraordinary memory. Having read both Old and New Testaments innumerable times as a Quaker youth, he could recite many of the contents of both without glancing at a page of either.

Despite the miseries of prison, Paine did not deny the existence of Christ. Indeed he asserted that a person such as Jesus not only existed but preached "most excellent morality and the equality of man," and undoubtedly died on the cross. "Crucifixion," Paine attested, was "the standard form of execution in his day. By exposing corruption . . . he undoubtedly incurred the anger and loathing of . . . priests who accused him of sedition and conspiracy against the Roman Empire—enough to get anyone executed in that era."[2]

Paine admitted he was at a loss to explain the origins of the story of the Creation, which "begins abruptly; it is nobody that speaks; it is nobody that hears; it is addressed to nobody; it has neither first, second, nor third person." Paine claimed that every nation of people at the time recounted stories of having been "world makers, and the Israelites had as much right to set up the trade of world-making as any of the rest."[3]

With that, Paine stopped writing for a moment. The damp chill of Paris spring combined with accumulated filth to provoke a sudden infection in his side. The constant terror of rumbling tumbrels added to his bodily pain by crushing his spirit. In early June 1794, he began to slip in and out of semi-consciousness. His prison roommates—three Belgians, an English physician, and an English surgeon—watched over him day and night, giving him whatever care, comfort and nourishment they could, with little or no response. As his breathing grew more labored, it seemed likely that Paine might avoid the terrifying trip on the tumbrel and go to his grave with his head as attached to his shoulders as it had been at birth.

Drifting in and out of consciousness, he emerged confronting the reality of his imprisonment at times, only to reemerge at other times raging at the defenders of religious faith. His cell mates, all of them admirers of Paine, found the wherewithal to bribe guards to continue supplying him with pencils and paper.

"People in general know not what wickedness there is in this pretended word of God," he growled as he emerged from unconsciousness one afternoon. "They take it for granted that the Bible is true, and that it is good. . . . Good heavens! . . . It is a book of lies, wickedness, and blasphemy. For what can be greater blasphemy than to ascribe the wickedness of man to the orders of the Almighty?"[4]

Paine called the biblical depiction of Moses "the most horrid that can be imagined." Under the mask of religion, Paine wrote, Moses had committed the worst atrocities in the history of any nation, ordering the officers of his conquering army to "kill every male among the little ones, and kill every woman that hath known a man by lying with him; but all the women-children that have not known a man by lying with him, keep alive for yourselves.

"Among the detestable villains that in any period of the world have disgraced the name of man, it is impossible to find one greater than Moses, if this account be true," Paine raged. "In the name of religion, here is an order to butcher the boys, massacre the mothers, and debauch the daughters."[5]

Beyond the walls of the Luxemburg Palace, Robespierre's Great Terror grew ever more terrifying, claiming 1,376 lives after only six weeks, compared to 1,251 during the previous fourteen months—all in the name of "liberté, égalité, fraternité" ("liberty, equality, and fraternity"), the Revolution's watch cry.

As blood flowed through the streets of Paris, Robespierre's paranoia became the target of Paris satirists, whose performances accelerated his descent into madness. He ordered all theaters closed to force satirists off the stages. His orders against other forms of amusement left guillotines the only entertainment in the city and the precursors of the popular, short plays of violence, horror, and sadism a century later at the Théâtre du Grand Guignol ("Theater of the Great or Grotesque Puppet"). Indeed, enterprising innkeepers turned the Great Terror into profitable enterprises by setting up clusters of tables and chairs for spectators to eat and drink while they watched the gruesome performances on the "stage" of the guillotine. In effect, they were the first and original "sidewalk cafés" of Paris. They exist to this day in the park across from where the guillotine stood on what is now the Place de la Concorde.

Street peddlers also profited from the ghastly theater, pouncing like hyenas at the base of the guillotine or onto moving tumbrels to strip shoes and salable items of clothing with professional efficiency and speed from the piles of bodies.

As prison space grew too scarce to accommodate the expanding list of suspects, the journalist Desmoulins wrote an editorial suggesting the release of women and children in the interests of justice. Infuriated by the suggestion, Robespierre confronted Desmoulins, shouting, "Terror is justice! Prompt, severe, inflexible!" With that, he ordered Desmoulins arrested and shorn by the relentless blade, leaving Robespierre himself the sole, uncontested leader of the Revolution—free to execute women and children as well as men. At his command, terrified survivors in the Convention agreed unanimously to speed the trip of suspects to the guillotine by doing away with all questioning of suspects, as well as all semblances of trials. Arrest now made death automatic.

By the end of July, Robespierre's paranoia grew too much to bear for even his most loyal supporters. After accusing members of his own Jacobin club of plotting against him, he demanded the immediate arrest of the entire Convention on suspicion of treason—every member! It was one demand too many. By then, the number of widows and orphans of Robespierre's victims had reached staggering proportions. The very women who had marched to Versailles to demand the king's head on a pike and the Jacobins who had led them now turned against Robespierre.

A mob formed outside the Convention; thousands of suspects poured from their hiding places to join them. As the mob grew, a collective cry grew into a steady menacing chant: "À bas Robespierre! À bas Robespierre!"—"Down with Robespierre! Down with Robespierre!"

Inspired by the public show of opposition, Convention delegates summoned the courage to defy him and demand that he name those he suspected of treason. He refused, and the following day, the Convention shed its timid ways and, en masse, ordered guards to arrest him. The guards seized the struggling lawyer and led him away screaming vengeance against his enemies. That evening, July 23, 1794, a pistol shot blew off half his jaw. Some claimed he had attempted suicide, but a guard insisted he had shot Robespierre trying to escape.

The source of the shot proved immaterial. With his head swathed in blood-soaked bandages, Robespierre lay in agony for but one night; the guillotine put him out of his misery the following day, followed by his brother and twenty of his closest political allies. While a mob watched in silent disbelief, seventy-one more of his followers rode the tumbrels to the relentless blade the next day in a bloody finale to The Great Terror.

Paine survived, albeit weakened by illness. The painful ulceration on his side had combined with a low-grade fever and malnutrition to leave him wavering in and out of consciousness much of the day, barely able to walk when awake. He nonetheless felt a rush of joy at news of Robespierre's death. By then, he had learned that Robespierre himself was as complicit as Morris in keeping him imprisoned without formal charges. Indeed, the two had conspired together to keep Paine locked up.

"When Robespierre had me seized and imprisoned . . . he assigned no reason for it," Paine later explained to Clio Rickman. "But when he proposed bringing me to the tribunal, which was like sending me at once to the scaffold, he assigned a reason . . . 'for the interest of America as well as France'—'pour l'intérêt de l'Amérique autant que de la France.' The words are in his own handwriting."

Paine also described his curious and narrow escape from the scaffold: "When persons by the scores and by hundreds were to be taken out of prison, it was always done at night, and those who performed that office had a private mark or signal by which they knew which rooms to go to and what number to take."

> We were four and the door to our room was marked . . . with that number in chalk. But it happened . . . that the mark was put on the door when it was open and flat against the wall and thereby came on the inside when we shut it at night—and the destroying angel passed it by. A few days after this Robespierre fell.[6]

Robespierre's papers confirmed his having written the formal decree.

"Demander que Thomas Paine soit décrété d'acccusation, pour l'intérêts de l'Amérique autant que pour la France." ("Issue a decree of accusation against Thomas Paine in the interests of America as well as of France.")

Well aware of the need to retain American military support, Robespierre had feared that Paine, once released, would expose the atrocities of The Terror in the American press and cost France her last ally. Insane in many ways, Robespierre was not so insane as to believe France could win a war against both England *and* the United States. Even the most reluctant

Robespierre followers agreed it was best if Paine remained in prison indefinitely, then be killed, quietly, without fanfare.

With Robespierre's death, Paine—as naïve in many ways as ever—believed freedom only hours away. He wrote to the Convention to remind it of his plight, noting that his eight-month loss of liberty seemed "a lifetime to a man who has been, as I have been, the unceasing defender of Liberty for twenty years. . . . But the strange power that Robespierre . . . had obtained rendered any attempt on my part to obtain justice not only useless but even dangerous."

> Citizens, when I left the United States in the year 1787, I promised . . . I would return . . . the next year, but the hope of seeing a Revolution happily established in France that might serve as a model to the rest of Europe . . . induced me to defer my return to that country. . . . This long sacrifice of private tranquility for almost eight years deserved a better fate than the long imprisonment I have silently suffered. But it is not the nation, but a faction that has done me this injustice . . . and it is to the national representation that I appeal against that injustice. . . . Citizens . . . I can have no doubt but your justice will restore me to the Liberty of which I have been deprived.[7]

Nothing but silence followed his appeal . . . incomprehensible silence, while the guillotine knives continued claiming those accused of being enemies of the nation. Although Robespierre's death had slowed the process, Parisians continued accusing anyone against whom they bore a grudge—shopkeepers, relatives, husbands, wives, brothers, and sisters—of conspiring against the Republic. Most such accusations were tantamount to death sentences.

"It is an easy thing to tell a lie, but it is difficult to support the lie after it is told," Paine mumbled incongruously as he emerged from a fitful sleep one morning. He began scribbling furiously.

> The writer of the book of Matthew should have told us who the saints were that came to life again [after the crucifixion] and went into the city and what became of them afterwards and who it was that saw them . . . whether they died again or went back to their graves alive and

buried themselves. . . . Strange indeed that an army of saints should return to life and nobody knew who they were nor who it was that saw them and that not a word more should be said upon the subject. . . . Nobody but Mathew had seen them—not Luke, not Mark, not John, though all three claimed to have been there.[8]

With each passing day, he grew more obsessive about completing *Age of Reason*: "I had neither Bible nor Testament to refer to nor could I procure any," he recalled. As the tumbrels continued collecting clients for the guillotine each day, however, he realized "my own situation, even as to existence, was becoming every day more precarious. . . . I was obliged to be quick and concise. The quotations I then made were from memory only, but they were correct." He said his opinions were based on the conviction that "the fall of man, the account of Jesus Christ being the Son of God, and of his dying to appease the wrath of God, and of salvation by that strange means, are all fabulous inventions, dishonorable to the wisdom and power of the Almighty." Paine declared "the only true religion is Deism . . . the belief in one God and . . . the practice of . . . moral virtues. So I say now—and so help me God."[9]

In comparison to the Old Testament, Paine concluded, the New Testament was "a farce in one act" with glaring contradictions which . . . are sufficient to show the story of Jesus Christ to be false."[10] The four books ascribed to Matthew, Mark, Luke, and John provided the only histories of Jesus Christ, Paine pointed out, "but each differs from the other so widely that one or all must be false." Matthew's genealogy of Jesus Christ, for example, lists forty-three generations from David through Joseph, while the third chapter of Luke shows but twenty-eight generations from David through Joseph. Only the names of David and Joseph are alike in the two lists.

"If Matthew speaks truth," Paine reasoned, "Luke speaks falsehood, and if Luke speaks truth, Matthew speaks falsehood, and as there is no authority for believing one more than the other, there is no authority for believing either, and if they cannot be believed even in the very first thing they say . . . they are not entitled to be believed in anything they say afterward."

If they cannot be believed in their account of his natural genealogy, how are we to believe them when they tell us he was the Son of God begotten by a ghost and that an angel announced this in secret to his mother. If they lied in one genealogy, why are we to believe them in the other? If his natural genealogy be manufactured . . . why are we not to suppose that the celestial genealogy is manufactured also and that the whole is fabulous?"[11]

Beyond genealogy, Paine pointed out, the apostles differed even in the inscription put above Christ on the cross at his crucifixion: "Matthew—'This is Jesus the king of the Jews'; Mark—'The king of the Jews'; Luke—'This is the king of Jews'; John—'Jesus of Nazareth the king of the Jews'. . . . We may infer from these that those writers, whoever they were and in whatever time they lived, were not present at the scene."[12]

The book ascribed to Matthew, says—*that there was an earthquake* [after the crucifixion]—*that the rocks rent.* . . . [but] the writer of the book ascribed to Mark . . . makes no mention of any earthquake. . . . The writer of the book of Luke is silent also . . . and the writer of the book of John . . . says nothing about either the darkness—the veil of the temple—the earthquake. . . . Now if it had been true that these things happened and if the writers of these books lived at the time they did happen . . . it was not possible for them . . . not to have recorded them.[13]

Growing weaker by the hour, Paine labored to write. "The Christian mythologists tell us that Christ died for the sins of the world and that he came on purpose to die. If Jesus Christ . . . came to this world to suffer . . . the only real suffering he could have endured would have been to live. . . . In fine, everything in this strange system is the reverse of what it pretends to be, and I become so tired of examining its inconsistencies and absurdities."[14]

Thomas Paine's appeal for his release from prison never reached the Convention floor. The powerful Committee of Public Safety had intercepted and rejected it. Although Robespierre was dead, as were several hundred of his rabid followers, those who feared Paine's pen were not all Jacobins. Many members of the Convention and the Committee of Public Safety saw the dangers to the Franco-American alliance of allowing ink from Paine's pen to flow across the Atlantic to American newspapers and reveal the atrocities that had accompanied the French Revolution.

"A friend of mankind is groaning in chains," a delegate from Calais and friend of Paine protested to the Committee of Public Safety. "Thomas Paine . . . was not so politic as to remain silent . . . but dared to say that Robespierre was a monster. . . . But for Robespierre's villainy this friend of man would now be free."[15]

Silence!

Weakened by infection, chills, hunger, Paine tried desperately to continue writing what he believed would be his legacy to man:

> It is because ye are sunk in the cruelty of superstition and feel no interest in the honor of your Creator that ye listen to the horrid tales of the Bible or hear them with callous indifference. The evidence I have produced . . . to prove that the Bible is without authority . . . whilst it wounds the stubbornness of a priest . . . it will free the minds of millions. . . . Could we permit ourselves to suppose that the Almighty would distinguish any nation of people by the name of his chosen people, we must suppose that people to have been an example to all the rest of the world of the purest piety and humanity and not such a nation of ruffians and cut-throats . . . as Moses and Aaron, Joshua, Samuel, and David. . . . The flattering appellation of his chosen people is no other than a lie.[16]

In mid-August, Paine learned that a new American minister, James Monroe, was replacing Morris. Paine would have leaped for joy if he had had the strength. He knew Monroe well; both had fought at Trenton, where Monroe had suffered wounds from Hessian bayonets; both were close friends of Jefferson. . . . Paine envisioned walking out of Luxemburg Palace that very day, and sent a letter that "a new minister from America is joy to me and will be so to every American in France."

> Eight months I have been imprisoned, and I know not for what except. . . . Morris has been my inveterate enemy, and I think he has permitted something of the national character of America to suffer by quietly letting a Citizen of that country remain almost eight months in prison without making every official exertion to procure him justice. . . . Wishing you happiness in your appointment, I am your affectionate friend. Thomas Paine[17]

Silence! Inexplicable, infuriating silence!

His thoughts returned to his quest for truth in the Scriptures and, as usual, he found none. "Church mythologists," he asserted, "decided by *vote* which of the books . . . should be the WORD OF GOD and which should not. . . . Who the people were that did all this we know nothing of. They call themselves by the general name of the church, and this is all we know of the matter."[18]

Monroe never received Paine's letter, of course. To Monroe's annoyance, Gouverneur Morris had received news of his replacement by disappearing—abandoning Paris for his country home thirty miles away. Unlike Morris, but like his mentor Thomas Jefferson, Monroe was an outspoken proponent of the French Revolution and disciple of Thomas Paine. Disgruntled by his recall and wanting nothing to do with revolutionary-minded Jeffersonians, the Federalist Morris not only remained out of sight for ten days, he proved less than helpful to Monroe when he returned to his Paris residence. Although he escorted Monroe to the French government's office of foreign affairs, he simply introduced Monroe, announced his own recall, and walked out, leaving Monroe to deal with French officials himself.

Monroe submitted his credentials and waited ten days without a response. In the meantime, Paine's letter sat unopened in Morris's Paris lodgings—still the official American "embassy" of sorts. Monroe never saw it.

"In addition to my letter of yesterday," Paine wrote to Monroe the following day, "I send the following memoranda." He went on to describe details of his arrest and incarceration, saying, "I was taken out of bed between three and four in the morning on the 28th of December last and brought to the Luxemburg—without any other accusations inserted in the order other than I was a foreigner; a motion having been made in the Convention to expel foreigners therefrom."

About three weeks after my imprisonment, the Americans that were in Paris went to the bar of the Convention to reclaim me, but it was miscarried. I then applied to Mr. G. Morris to reclaim me . . . and here the matter stopped. I have not heard a single line or word from any American since, which is now seven months. . . . Had it not been for the fall of Robespierre and your timely arrival I know not what fate might yet have attended me. There seemed to be a determination to destroy all prisoners without regard to merit, character, or anything else. . . . The distress that I suffered . . . is greater than it is possible for you to conceive—but thank God times are at last changed, and I hope your authority will release me from this unjust imprisonment.[19]

Silence!

Monroe did not receive Paine's second letter. Again, it fell into Morris's hands and never reached Monroe. Monroe was still unaware that Paine was in Paris, let alone in prison.

Without official French government acknowledgment of his arrival and frustrated by the disarray of the executive branch of French government, Monroe remained unrecognized as American minister. His frustration provoked a bold, if unconventional, step: he sent a letter to the President of the 700-member National Convention announcing his arrival in Paris and asserting his intention "to make known my mission immediately to the Representatives of the People. They possess the power to affix the time and prescribe the mode by which I shall be recognized as the representative of their ally and sister republic."[20]

Monroe's letter was unprecedented in the history of modern diplomacy—the representative of a new nation, born of popular revolution, stepping onto the international stage for the first time to claim a place among the world's storied kingdoms and empires—by addressing the guest nation's legislative branch rather than its executive.

The following day saw the tall Virginian lumber through the door of the Convention hall. Dramatically taller than the average European, Monroe strode to the dais, the embodiment of the American people. Most delegates had never seen an American before; they had only read mythologized descriptions of the New World, its natives, and its colonists. Awed by his stature, aware of his heroism in battle, the delegates began applauding before Monroe spoke, building up to a roar of welcome, with shouts of "Vive la République; vive les États-Unis"—"Long live the Republic; long live the United States."

"My admission into this Assembly," Monroe called out in English, "impresses me . . . as a new proof of that friendship and regard which the French nation has always shown to their ally, the United States of America."[21]

Although it understood not a word, the Convention greeted Monroe's address with "universal acclimation of joy, delight, and admiration."[22]

Not far off, in his Luxemburg Palace cell, Paine, "having nothing to do but to sit and think," wrote to Monroe a third time, "I will write to pass away time and to say that I am still here."

> I shall be very glad to receive a line from yourself to inform me in what condition the matter stands. [America] has had the services of my best days, she has my allegiance, she receives my portion of taxes for my house . . . and my farm . . . and she owes me protection both at home and through her ministers abroad, yet I remain in prison in the face of her minister at the arbitrary will of a committee. Excluded as I am from the knowledge of everything and left to a random of ideas, I know not what to think or how to act. . . . I am not out of danger till I am out of prison.

He added a P.S., saying, "I am now entirely without money . . . which I know not how to get while I am here, nor do I know how to draw for money on the rent of my farm in America."[23]

His penury forced him to beg for supplies for the first time. Other prisoners supplied him with "three or four candles, a little sugar . . . and some soap for shaving." He had exhausted his funds in France by then, and without a family to supply him, he had no one to appeal to for supplies but the American minister, who had still not replied.

Already discouraged and hurt by the failure of his wartime comrade Monroe to respond, Paine lost all hope for freedom when Peter Whiteside, the inexplicably malevolent English mechanic who had worked on Paine's bridge at Paddington, sent a note that Paine immediately forwarded to Monroe. In it Whiteside claimed Monroe had told him that "he has no orders respecting you . . . you are not considered by the government as an American citizen. You have been made a French citizen . . . and you have further made yourself a servant of the French Republic, and it would be out of character for an American minister to interfere in their internal concerns."

"This information was so unexpected by me," Paine wrote to Monroe, "that I am at a loss how to answer it. I know not on what principle it originates: whether from an idea that I had voluntarily abandoned my citizenship of America for that of France or from any article of the American Constitution as it applied to me. The first is untrue . . . and the second is without foundation."[24]

In a ten-page brief, Paine went on to disprove both arguments, concluding the first by pointing out that "I am put in arrestation because I am a foreigner" and that "I have twice taken the oath . . . of allegiance to America—once as a citizen of . . . Pennsylvania in 1776 and again before Congress, administered to me by the President, Mr. Hancock, when I was appointed Secretary of the Office of Foreign Affairs in 1777."[25]

It was clear to Paine that "it suited the purpose of both American Minister Gouverneur Morris and the French Committee of Public Safety that I should be confined. The former wished to prevent my return to America that I should not expose his misconduct, and the latter lest I should publish to the world the history of wickedness . . . of the committee, of which Robespierre was a member. . . . Painful as the want of liberty may be, it is a consolation to believe that my imprisonment proves to the world that I had no share in the murderous system that then reigned. That I was an enemy to it both morally and politically is known to all."[26]

On October 4, the French government finally recognized Monroe's credentials, and, truly surprised to learn of Paine's incarceration—Whiteside's report was pure fiction—Monroe replied to Paine immediately: "By being with us through the Revolution, you are of our country, as absolutely as if you had been born there; and you are no more of England than every native of America is."[27]

It is unnecessary for me to tell you how much all your countrymen, I speak of the great mass of people, are interested in your welfare. . . . You are considered by them as not only having rendered important services in our own revolution, but as being . . . the friend of human rights and a distinguished and able advocate . . . of public liberty. To the welfare

36. James Monroe replaced Gouverneur Morris as American minister in Paris and obtained Thomas Paine's release from prison.

of Thomas Paine the Americans are not and cannot be indifferent. Of the sense which the President has always entertained of your merits and of his friendly disposition towards you, you are too well assured to require any declaration from me. . . . I forward his wishes in seeking your safety. . . . To liberate you will be an object of my endeavors, and as soon as possible.[28]

Evidently putting credence in Paine's accusation of collusion between Morris and the Committee of Public Safety, Monroe issued a demand for Paine's release to the Committee of Public Surety, whose members agreed unanimously to release Paine.

But Paine remained in prison.

"I thank you for your very friendly and affectionate letter of 18th September," Paine answered James Monroe on October 4. "It has relieved my mind from a load of disquietude."

Still, Paine remained in prison.

"I cannot see what motive can induce them to keep me in prison," he raged a few days later. And ten days after that—by then one of the few remaining prisoners in Luxemburg Palace—he again wrote to Monroe:

"On the twenty-eighth of this month (October), I shall have suffered ten months' imprisonment, to the dishonor of America as well as of myself, and I speak to you very honestly when I say that my patience is exhausted. Had any person told me that I should remain in prison two months after the arrival of a new minister, I should have supposed that he meant to affront me as an American." Paine said his continued imprisonment now reflected on the "national character of America" and that "I no longer speak with pride of being a citizen of that country . . . when I am suffering unjust imprisonment under the very eye of her new minister? . . . When I thus see day after day and month after month and promise after promise pass away without effect, what can I conclude but that . . . the measures you take are not pursued . . . or that the American national character is without sufficient importance to the French Republic."[29]

In fact, James Monroe had tried incessantly to win Paine's release, only to receive frustrating replies from nameless French government officials and committees who said they had no authority in the matter because Paine, as a member of the French National Convention, was subject to French law. Monroe protested that Paine had been expelled from the Convention because he was a foreigner. His protest went unheeded.[30]

Paine, however, had reached another conclusion: "The Committees are secretly determined not to let me go."[31]

His mind now wandered in and out of delirium, returning some of the time to his own reality, other times to sheer fantasy, still other times to *Age of Reason.*

"The Bible-makers . . . give us in the first chapter of Genesis, an account of the Creation, and . . . demonstrated nothing but their ignorance," he scribbled with a lead stub. "They make there to have been three days and three nights . . . before there was a sun, when it is the presence or absence of the sun that is the cause of day and night. . . . Besides, it is a puerile and pitiful idea to suppose the Almighty to say, 'Let there be light.' It is the imperative manner of speaking that a conjuror uses when he says to his cups and balls, 'Presto, begone!'"[32]

Paine exposed what he called the three frauds of religion: mystery, miracle, and prophecy, and he concluded that "the most detestable wickedness, the most horrid cruelties and the greatest miseries that have afflicted the human race have had their origin in this thing called revelation."

> Whence arose all the horrid assassinations . . . of men, women, and children with which the Bible is filled and the bloody persecutions and tortures . . . and religious wars . . . that have laid Europe in blood and ashes; whence arose they but from this impious thing called revealed religion and this monstrous belief that God has spoken to man? The lies of the Bible have been the cause of one, and the lies of the Testament the other.[33]

Paine now despaired at the hopelessness of his imprisonment.

"Here we are," he concluded *Age of Reason.* "We cannot conceive how we came here ourselves, and yet we know for a fact we are here. . . . The existence of an Almighty power is sufficiently demonstrated to us, though we cannot conceive, as it is impossible we should, the nature and manner of its existence. . . . Deism teaches us, without the possibility of being deceived, all that is necessary or proper to be known. . . . I here close the subject."[34]

With that, Thomas Paine concluded it was "more agreeable . . . to contemplate an honorable destruction and to perish in the act of protesting against the injustice I suffer . . . than to remain in the wretched condition I am." In what he believed would be his last letter to Monroe—or anyone else, for that matter, he declared, "I am no longer of any use to the world or myself."[35]

Chapter 11

A LETTER TO WASHINGTON

O N NOVEMBER 6, 1794, THE SECRETARY OF THE COMMITTEE OF General Surety presented American Minister James Monroe with an order for Paine's release, and Monroe, in turn, notified the new Secretary of State Edmund Randolph that Paine "is not only released to the enjoyment of liberty but is in good spirits."[1]

But Paine was not in good spirits. The Luxemburg Palace disgorged a different Thomas Paine from the one it had swallowed ten months earlier. Benumbed by deprivation, harsh conditions, and illness, he had developed a chronic ulcerous infection on his side and wore a puzzled look on his face. He seemed on the verge of tears at the effusive greetings others now lavished on him—unable to reconcile their sudden bursts of friendship with the silence he believed they had maintained during his imprisonment. Above all, what set his heart amiss was the nonchalance with which almost all his former friends and admirers had tolerated his having been imprisoned without having been charged with a crime.

Everything about the world seemed incomprehensible to the man who believed in the equality of man. Somehow, he felt less than equal, less than a man.

Monroe tried to make amends by inviting Paine to stay at the jewel-like La Folie de la Bouexière, a luxurious estate on the rue de Clichy, just inside what were then the northern Paris city limits. Standing in a park-like oasis of splendid gardens, La Folie housed both the residence and official offices of the new American minister and his family. The main house boasted gilded bronze fixtures and statuettes and elaborately painted ceilings that transformed it into a small palace. Indeed, it was a small palace, with six principal rooms that cost the Monroes the equivalent of $15,000 a month rent in that era's dollars—not including salaries of seven servants, including a chef, coachman, and gardener. Monroe's beautiful wife, Elizabeth, filled La Folie with an extraordinary collection of Louis XIV and Louis XV chairs, tables, framed mirrors, and other furnishings, along with barrels of gold- and silver-encrusted table settings, fine Limoges china, and French silver flatware. The talented Mrs. Monroe bought a magnificent pianoforte, with which to fill the library with music, while her husband read selections from endless shelves of French and classical literature that he had collected—among others, thirty volumes of Voltaire, thirty-three of Rousseau, fifteen volumes of Plutarch, the works of Racine, Horace, Montaigne, etc. There were no works by Paine.

A stark contrast to the cold, damp quarters that had housed him at the Luxemburg Palace, La Folie gave Paine an opportunity to try to recover from the trauma of ten months of unexplained imprisonment. He had been "destitute of every necessity . . . without resource and in bad health," when the French released him, Monroe related later. "I retained him there [at La Folie] for a year and a half, supplied his wants, and furnished him afterwards with additional aid to some amount."[2] Paine took full advantage at first, working feverishly to complete what he now called *Age of Reason, Part Second.*

But Paine's imprisonment had left lasting scars on his body and mind. The sips of brandy at dinner that had once transformed him into an agreeable conversationalist rich with anecdotal humor now produced unpleasant outbursts of anger and rant.

Although Paine refused to believe it, Monroe tried convincing Paine that President Washington had been unaware of Paine's imprisonment and that he, Monroe, had been equally unaware of it, either before or after he arrived in Paris. After all, neither Robespierre nor his close allies had issued any public announcements about Paine's arrest and imprisonment. Nor had anyone witnessed it. He had simply disappeared, and, an ocean away, with no word to the contrary from Gouverneur Morris, Washington had no reason not to believe that Paine was too busy helping the French National Convention write a new constitution to write personal letters.

Paine, however, refused to believe Monroe and stung him deeply with bitter accusations. Like most Revolutionary War veterans of his generation, Monroe admired Paine as much as Washington. He had first heard Paine's words ring out in the darkness along the banks of the Delaware River eighteen years earlier on the eve of the Battle of Trenton. Paine's words had inspired Monroe's own heroism in battle then and his subsequent peacetime public service. An accomplished lawyer who had resigned his US Senate seat to serve as US minister to France, Monroe considered Paine one of America's—and the world's—great sages. When first he learned of Paine's imprisonment, he sent a long report to Secretary of State Edmund Randolph expressing his "extreme" concern "to find that our countryman . . . had been confined near nine months" and set to work immediately "to endeavor to obtain [his] enlargement."[3]

When, therefore, Paine arrived at La Folie, Monroe and his wife welcomed Paine, ill and unkempt though he was, as they would a visiting patriarch.

Paine, however, arrived a bitter man, believing that Washington was as responsible for his imprisonment as Robespierre. He believed Robespierre had interpreted Washington's failure to look into Paine's case as a signal that the American President preferred leaving Paine in prison where he would be helpless to meddle in American political and diplomatic affairs. At the time, Washington's envoy John Jay was secretly negotiating an extremely unpopular rapprochement with Britain, which elicited howls of protest from Paine and other Francophiles. "I ought not to have suspected Mr. Washington of treachery," Paine declared, "but he has acted towards me the part of a cold-blooded traitor."*[4]

Paine, however, did not realize that Gouverneur Morris had failed to notify Washington of Paine's plight. Like Monroe, Washington did not learn of Paine's imprisonment until long after Monroe had obtained his release.

Paine, however, expected some sort of message upon his release from his onetime friend and admirer—a message that never came, for good reason. President Washington, at the time, was occupied raising an army

---

* "Traitor" used in the sense of betraying another's trust.

of 15,000 troops to crush a farmer rebellion in western Pennsylvania—the so-called Whisky Rebellion to protest an excise tax on whisky stills.

Indeed, Paine received only one encouraging message following his release from the Luxemburg: an invitation from the French National Convention to reclaim his seat. One of the surviving Jacobins—a moderate—had moved for his return, saying, "I reclaim one of the most zealous defenders of liberty—Thomas Paine. . . . It was only by an intrigue that he was driven from the Convention; I demand that he be recalled to the bosom of the Convention." After thunderous applause, the Convention voted unanimously to recall Paine and award him monetary compensation disguised as a literary award. Despite his penury, Paine considered the monetary award an insult and rejected it.

"These men who were waiting in the devotion of their hearts for the joyful news of my destruction," Paine told Rickman of the National Convention members, "are the same banditti who are now hallowing all the hackneyed language . . . about humanity and piety."[5]

Paine agreed to accept only the back pay due for his months in prison and the opportunity that restored membership would give him to lecture Convention members and the rest of France on good government. The Terror had prevented the Convention from completing its original mandate to write a new constitution, and Paine now stepped into the breach with a "Dissertation on First Principles of Government."[6]

"Had a Constitution been established two years ago as ought to have been done," he scolded the Convention, "the violences that have since desolated France and injured the character of the [French] Revolution would . . . have been prevented."

He went on to recite, as he had in *Rights of Man*, the absurdities and evils of hereditary rule. "The rich have no more right to exclude the poor from the right of voting or of electing and being elected than the poor have to exclude the rich, and wherever it is attempted or proposed . . . it is a question of force not of right."[7]

He wrote to the French as if he were writing to children, realizing all too well by then that they were indeed children in terms of political maturity. Never having governed themselves, they had always been subject to whimsical commands of an absolute ruler, the man they called their "father," their king.

"The revolutions now spreading themselves in the world," he explained, "have their origin in a conflict between the representative system founded on the rights of the people and the hereditary system founded in usurpation."

> To be satisfied of the right of a thing to exist we must be satisfied that it had a right to begin. If it had not a right to begin, it has not the right to continue. By what right then did the hereditary system begin? Let a man ask himself this question, and he will find that he cannot satisfy himself with an answer. The right which any man or any family had to set himself up to govern a nation and to establish itself hereditarily was no other than the right which Robespierre had to do the same thing in France.

Paine went on to assail aristocracy, autocracy, and inequality. Again, he talked to the Convention as if to a class of children. "Inequality of rights is created by a combination in one part of the community to exclude another part from its rights . . . investing itself with powers . . . to the exclusion of the rest."

> It is dangerous and impolitic . . . and always unjust to make property the criterion of the right of voting. If the sum or value of the property . . . be considerable, it will exclude a majority of the people and unite them in a common interest against the government and against those who support it. . . . But the offensive part . . . is that this exclusion. . . . is to reduce a man to slavery, for slavery consists in being subject to the will of another. . . . The proposal therefore to disenfranchise any class of men is as criminal as to take away property.

Paine looked up momentarily as he wrote, the anger within exploding: "A declaration of rights, therefore, is not a creation of them." His words, read by a translator, puzzled the convention Delegates. "It is a manifest of the principle by which they exist . . . for every civil right has a natural right . . . rights appertain to man by right of his existence!"

Paine was exhausted.

Later, when the translator concluded reading his message, the glassy-eyed stares of delegates told him they had absorbed little of what he had written and believed none of it. None had ever heard such heresy; they could not comprehend it. They had never lived in America and, therefore, could not conceive of the freedoms he described. Paine nonetheless went on to write a second address commenting on the new French constitution then under consideration by the Convention. In effect, he called it incompatible with the original goals of the Revolution by defining citizenship in ways that "enable one part of society to destroy the freedom of the other." Various qualifications for citizenship disenfranchised almost half the nation: those who paid direct taxes to the government—that is, property owners—qualified for full citizenship, as did soldiers and veterans who had fought in at least two campaigns.[8]

As delegates shuffled in their seats uncomfortably, it was clear they wanted him to leave—to return to America and let them take the reins of power without his questioning their right to do so. None of the French wanted Paine's—or America's—republican government. Like America's southern plantation owners, those who owned most of the lands in France believed they had unalienable rights to their lands and knew what was best for their country. They did not need a British corset-maker to lecture them. Who was he, they scoffed, to restrict their powers and deny God's role in elevating them to positions of privilege?

His lecture to the French on governing themselves was the last he would make to the National Convention. In the fall elections that followed, he failed to win reappointment to his seat. French voters objected to the religious blasphemies in *Age of Reason* and had tired of his political blasphemies in the National Convention.

Nor were the French alone in rejecting Paine. The first part of *Age of Reason* had been published while he was in prison, and it left much of the Western world in disbelief—outraged as much by its incontestable logic as by its blasphemy.

"Had it been the intention of Jesus Christ to establish a new religion, he would undoubtedly have written the system himself," Paine declared, "but there is no publication extant authenticated with his name. All the books called the New Testament were written after his death."

> The first four books, called Matthew, Mark, Luke, and John, do not give a history of the life of Jesus Christ . . . only detached anecdotes. . . . In several instances they relate the same event differently. . . . They make

mention of him at the age of twelve years. . . . From this time there is no account of him for about sixteen years. . . . Jesus Christ founded no new system. He called men to the practice of moral virtues and the belief in one God.[9]

Paine called the idea that God sent Jesus to preach to all nations proof of the author's ignorance of the extent of the world and belief that the earth was flat. Jesus could speak but one language—Hebrew, or more likely Aramaic. In an age before printing in a world of several hundred languages, Paine asserted, it was impossible for Jesus to communicate "to all nations." And why, Paine asked, was no mention made of the Americas in the Bible—if, indeed, Jesus spoke to all nations?[10]

Paine insisted there was indeed "a Word of God," but it was not in the Bible. "THE WORD OF GOD" he emphasized in capital letters, "IS THE CREATION WE BEHOLD, and it is in *this word* which no human invention can counterfeit or alter, that God speaketh universally to man."[11]

Paine carried his argument into the realm of the sciences and mathematics, calling it "a fraud of the Christian system to call the sciences *human invention*," saying it was only the application of science that is human. As simple evidence, he pointed out the fallacy in calling a triangle drawn by man a human invention. "But the triangle, when drawn, is no other than . . . a delineation and from thence to the eye, of a principle that would otherwise be imperceptible."

The triangle does not make the principle any more than a candle taken into a room that was dark makes the chairs and tables that before were invisible. All the properties of the triangle existed independently of the figure and existed before any triangle was drawn or thought of by man. Man had no more to do in the formation of these properties or principles than he had to do in making the law by which the heavenly bodies move; therefore the one must have the same divine origin as the other. . . . That which man calls the *effect* is no other than the principle itself rendered perceptible to the senses.[12]

Paine called reason a divine gift that God gave man to acquire knowledge of nature, the sciences, and the structure of the universe and make the world a better place in which to live. As the world's body of scientific knowledge grew, Paine charged, Christian leaders "could not but foresee that the continually progressive knowledge that man would gain by the aid of science . . . would militate against and call into question the truth [and] assertions of their faith. . . . it would undermine the assertions of their faith." In response, he said, they restricted learning to the study of dead languages and rejected the study of sciences—even persecuting the greatest scientists and suppressing knowledge of their discoveries. Citing Galileo and his discovery and use of telescopes in 1610, Paine condemned the church for refusing to recognize the grandeur of Galileo's discoveries and forcing the great scientist to renounce them "as a damnable heresy."

"And prior to that time, Virgilius was condemned to be burned for asserting . . . that the earth was a globe and habitable in every part where there was land. . . . Had Newton or Descartes lived three or four hundred years ago . . . it is most probable that they would not have lived to finish . . . their studies; and had Franklin drawn lightening from the clouds at the same time, it would have been at the hazard of expiring for it in the flames."

Paine said the continued persecution of scientists by the church for several hundred years was proof that the church itself was a pious fraud. "The age of ignorance," he declared, "commenced with the Christian system. The Christian system was only another species of mythology and . . . a corruption of an ancient system of theism."

> The Christian story of God the Father putting His son to death or employing people to do it . . . cannot be told by a parent to a child; and to tell him that it was done to make mankind happier and better is making the story still worse—as if mankind could be improved by the example of murder; and to tell him that all this is a mystery is only making an excuse for the incredibility of it. . . . Mystery is the antagonist of truth.

Paine said he had doubted the truth of Christianity and redemption from the time he was seven or eight in Thetford, when he first heard a sermon on redemption of man and the death of Jesus. "I had a serious reflection . . . that God was too good to do such an action and also too almighty to be under the necessity of doing it," he wrote. "I believe that any system of religion . . . that shocks the mind of a child cannot be a true system. . . . How different is this to the pure and simple profession of Deism. The true Deist has but one Deity, and his religion consists in contemplating the power, wisdom, and benignity of the Deity in His works and in endeavoring to imitate Him in everything moral, scientifical [*sic*], and mechanical."[13]

As well educated, well traveled, and cultured as were the Monroes, they gradually tired of Paine's repeated rants against organized religion. Welcomed at first for his wit and erudite conversation, Paine wore out his welcome when he began writing a bitter diatribe against President Washington, and, by summer of 1795, Monroe grew exasperated.

"Upon my arrival [in France]," Monroe explained to his friend, Virginia Congressman James Madison, "I found him in prison . . . he was in extreme ill health, without resources. . . . I invited him to take a room in my house. . . . It was his intention at that time . . . October '94, to depart for America in the spring. . . . His disease continued and of course he continued in my house and will continue in it till his death or departure for America, however remote either the one or the other event may be. . . . He thinks the President winked at his imprisonment and wished he might die in jail, and bears him resentment for it."[14]

When news of Jay's Treaty with Britain became public knowledge in 1794, the French government expressed outrage. England, however, remained the world's greatest naval power, with little incentive to grant impotent America any major concessions. Jay had had to settle for what he could get: Britain agreed to pull the last of her troops from the American frontier into Canada and to stop seizing American ships not bound for France or French possessions. Britain refused, however, to stop impressing American sailors into the British navy. Impressment was the equivalent of the modern-day draft and the only way Britain could man what was the world's largest and most powerful navy with English-speaking sailors. With duties on British imports representing the American government's greatest source of revenues, the US Senate had little choice but to approve the treaty, and Washington signed it into law.

Realizing that Paine's diatribes against Washington threatened to jeopardize American relations with France, Monroe demanded that Paine write "nothing for the public upon the subject of our affairs . . . whilst in my house. I did not rest my demand upon the merit or demerit of our conduct . . . but upon the injury such essays would do me . . . if they proceeded from my house . . . Thus the matter ended."[15]

Paine, however, refused to understand why Washington, as President of the United States, had allowed him (Paine) to languish in prison for more than ten months without a word of inquiry or protest to the French or a word of support to Paine himself. Washington had called Paine "my friend," but had not sent a word of friendship while Paine languished— and faced death—in prison for no stated reason or even after his release. Paine conveniently forgot to mention that he had not written to Washington for almost two years prior to his imprisonment, and, with Gouverneur Morris refusing to write of Paine's circumstances, Washington had no way of learning that Paine was in prison. Clearly traumatized by his imprisonment, though, Paine refused to recognize that the upheavals in France and the crises Washington faced in America had made it all but impossible for the President to keep track of Paine's whereabouts.

"I was informed," Paine ranted, "that Mr. Monroe had no instructions from the President either verbally or in writing, nor any kind of authority whatever for reclaiming me as a citizen of the United States nor for taking any interest upon my account nor even enquire anything about me."

This prolonged my imprisonment from the time of Mr. Monroe's arrival at the beginning of August till the 4th of November following. . . . In the meantime from the want of everything . . . from the want of fuel in the prison, an abscess began to form . . . has continued ever since. I do not entertain much hope of being able to return to America. . . . It would be agreeable to me to live [there], but it is not to be . . . it is not agreeable to me to remember that I owe part of my present condition to the ungrateful neglect of a country, at least of its government, from which I had a right to expect better things. . . . I ought not to have suspected Mr. Washington of treachery but he has acted towards me the part of a cold blooded traitor. I trouble myself not to know [why].[16]

Paine finally wore out his welcome during the Christmas 1795 festivities, when, having consumed too much brandy, his anger toward Washington reached levels too offensive for Monroe, as Washington's appointee, to tolerate. Monroe again asked Paine to stop—"without effect"—and Paine began making plans to leave La Folie—not, however, before finishing *Age of Reason, Part Second*, and sending it off to a printer who shipped 15,000 copies to America. British authorities charged a second printer with sedition when he published *Age of Reason* the following year, and the publisher fled to America.

Although Paine tried leaving Monroe's home after their quarrel over Paine's letter to Washington, a mob blocked the rue de Clichy and forced Paine to return to the reluctant hospitality of the Monroes. The mob had formed to protest food shortages resulting in part from a strike by bakers and in part from a British blockade of French ports. As angry Parisians rioted, a mob forced its way into the National Convention, killing one delegate and assaulting dozens of others.

After five days, troops quelled the disturbances and installed a new government with a legislature called the Council of 500 and a five-man executive: the Directoire, or Directory. Made up of members of the National Convention, the Directory, in one of its first acts, named the successful Brigadier General Napoléon Bonaparte commander in chief of the Army of the Interior, to ensure order across metropolitan France.

After reviewing the Jay Treaty, the Directory declared France's nearly twenty-year-old alliance with the United States as "ceasing to exist."[17] It recalled its minister to the United States and ordered the French navy to seize all American ships and cargoes bound for England and imprison captured crews and passengers. In the year that followed, the French captured more than 300 American merchant ships and imprisoned several thousand American seamen, in what became a "quasi-war" with America. Monroe suspected Paine of having betrayed American interests and entering the employ of the Directory. In Philadelphia, the new Secretary of State William Pickering suspected Monroe of exactly the same thing, and convinced Washington to recall Monroe and replace him with an avowed Federalist.

In the spring of 1796, the Directory did indeed commission Paine to write and publish a pamphlet—not to betray American interests, but to injure British interests. Called *The Decline and Fall of the English System of Finance*, Paine's pamphlet exposed British government debts as having soared to £400 million, while cash reserves had plunged to about £1 million, leaving the Bank of England all but certain to collapse with the expansion of Britain's war with France. Issued in French and German as well as English, it found its way to banks in Holland, Switzerland, and the various German states. The Directory purchased 1,000 copies to distribute to men in finance, in and out of government, across Europe. Within days of its appearance, it provoked a run on the English pound and forced the British government to suspend conversion of pound currency and pound-denominated notes and bills into specie (i.e., gold or silver) for several months in 1797.

Monroe responded by ordering Paine to leave La Folie. Paine, in turn, retaliated by publishing his "Letter to Washington," a seventy-page polemic, much of which mirrored the objections of Patrick Henry and tens of thousands of other Americans to the Jay Treaty and the failure of the American government to end impressment of Americans into the British navy or protect American rights to navigate the Mississippi River.

But Paine's primary goal was to shame the President: "I cannot understand your silence upon . . . my imprisonment in France. . . . I therefore write you this letter to propose to you to send me copies of any letters you have written that may remove that suspicion." Paine said he was enclosing a memorandum in Robespierre's handwriting that he had imprisoned Paine for the interests of America as well as of France. "I find by the published papers of Robespierre . . . that I was designed for a worse fate. The following memorandum is in his own handwriting: 'Demander que Thomas Paine soit décrété d'accusation pour les intérêts de l'Amérique autant que de la France.'

"He [Robespierre] could have had no cause for putting America in the case," Paine charged, "but by interpreting the silence of the American government into connivance and consent, your silence in not inquiring into the cause of that imprisonment . . . was tacitly giving me up."

> I ought not to have suspected you of treachery; but whether I recover from the illness I now suffer or not, I shall continue to think you treacherous

till you give me the cause to think otherwise. . . . Whether your desertion of me was intended to gratify the English government or to let me fall into destruction in France that you might exclaim the louder against the French Revolution . . . either of these will involve you in reproach you will not easily shake off.

Paine went on to relate Washington's numerous failures on the Revolutionary War battlefield—Brandywine, Philadelphia, Germantown, etc.—and the successes attributable to others—Gates at Saratoga, Greene in the South, French General Rochambeau and the French army at Yorktown. "Nothing was done in the campaigns of 1778, 1779, 1780 in the part where General Washington commanded except the taking of Stony Point [New York] by General Wayne."[18] Paine ended his letter with a blistering assault on the President he once revered:

And as to you, Sir, treacherous in private friendship (for so you have been to me, and that in the day of danger) and a hypocrite in public life, the world will be puzzled whether you are an apostate or an imposter; whether you have abandoned good principles or whether you ever had any.[19]

Published in Philadelphia by the anti-Federalist *Aurora*, Paine's letter was republished in London and Dublin. Publicly, Washington ignored it, considering it beneath his dignity to acknowledge it or reply. Like the Federalists who supported him, Washington assumed Paine's letter was part of the French government's efforts to undermine Washington's policy of neutrality in the Franco-British war and to force Congress to abrogate the Jay Treaty. Federalists charged Paine's letter was "a tissue of lies, arrogant impudence, and disgusting egotism" and, like Washington, claimed that "the French government directed his pen."[20]

Without further protest, Paine left Monroe's lavish La Folie on the rue de Clichy and moved into the simple home of printer/editor Nicolas de Bonneville, who had published Paine's *The Decline and Fall of the English Systems of Finance* in his ground-floor print shop. Bonneville had been one of the five members of Paine's little Republican Club at the start of the French Revolution and a deeply committed Paine devotee who had published the French translation of *Age of Reason*. He also published a succession of liberal newspapers with next to no influence in France—*Le Tribune du Peuple, Bouche de Fer*, and, at the time Paine came to live with Bonneville and his family, *Bien Informé*. His adulation of Paine was such that he named his second son Thomas and made Paine godfather of all three of his sons.

"He [Paine] now indulged his mechanical turn and amused himself in bridge and ship building," Rickman recalled, "and in pursuing his favorite studies, the mathematics and natural philosophy [physics]."

> These models exhibit an extraordinary . . . skill . . . and are wrought with extreme delicacy entirely by his own hands. The largest . . . model of a bridge is nearly four feet in length: the iron-works, the chains, and every other article . . . forged and manufactured by himself. It is intended as the model of a bridge . . . to be constructed across the Delaware [River], extending 480 feet with only one arch.[21]

Although Paine longed to return to America, swarms of British ships controlled Atlantic sea-lanes and, still wanted in Britain, he dared not risk capture by venturing onto the high seas. Except for the Bonnevilles and a handful of other close friends, Paine had now tired of the French and France. He had come to France envisioning a land, a people, a nation, and a way of life that did not exist, had never existed. Paine's France was as much a myth as Camelot. Although dozens of prominent political figures had once competed for his attentions as he strolled Paris streets, his constant carping and blasphemies now made many turn away as he approached and walk in the opposite direction. He approached each as if the world awaited his opinion on every subject, and it no longer did. Only occasionally did he manage to revive interest in his views with a particularly brilliant essay that recalled the erudition and artistry of his early works. One—*Agrarian Justice*—would be his last pamphlet of consequence. Reminiscent of the younger Paine, it contained socio-economic proposals centuries ahead of their time, dealing with extremes of social and economic inequality.

"There is not, in the . . . natural and primitive state of man," Paine wrote, "any of those spectacles of human misery which poverty and want present in all the towns and streets in Europe."

Poverty, therefore, is a thing manufactured and created by that which is called civilized life. It exists not in the natural state. On the other hand, the natural state is without those advantages which flower from agriculture, arts, science, and manufactures. The life of an [American] Indian is a continual holiday compared to the poor of Europe. . . . Civilization, therefore, or that which is so-called, has operated in two ways: to make one part of society more affluent and the other more wretched than would have been the lot of either in the natural state.[22]

Introducing a concept that would be accepted in whole or in part two centuries later by a number of nations, Paine called for an end to the concept of private property as a first step in eliminating economic and social inequality. "The earth in its natural, uncultivated state," he declared, "was and ever would have continued to be the common property of the human race . . . but it is nevertheless true that it is the value of the improvement, only, and not the earth itself, that is individual property."[23]

Paine said the idea of landed property had originated when man confused his natural right to occupy land with a right to own it in perpetuity. He called cultivation "one of the greatest natural improvements ever made by human invention." But as it increased the value of the land tenfold, it "dispossessed more than half the inhabitants of every nation of their natural inheritance without providing for them . . . and created a species of poverty and wretchedness that did not exist before.

"It is necessary as well for the protection of property as for the sake of justice and humanity to form a system that, while it preserves one part of society from wretchedness shall secure the other from depredation."[24]

Using a complex series of mathematical calculations, Paine proposed a system that imposed a modicum of social and economic equality by creating a national fund from which all landowners would contribute enough to pay £15 "to every person . . . at the age of twenty-one years . . . as a compensation in part for the loss of his or her natural inheritance by the introduction of the system of landed property. After the age of fifty everyone would receive ten pounds a year until death."[25]

In the weeks, months, and years that followed, Paine often wandered the halls of French government buildings, nodding to all, greeting many by name, talking with high-level English-speaking officials such as

Talleyrand and the young General Bonaparte. All paid homage to the great sage and pretended to listen to his views, but broke away as soon as "politesse" permitted. He lived with the Bonnevilles and their three children for six years.

"He rose late," according to Madame Bonneville, "then read the newspapers from which . . . he did not fail to collect all the material information relating to politics, in which subject he took most delight." After a chat with Mr. Bonneville, Paine took a walk, returned in time for dinner—a midday affair in France—and after dinner a long nap.

"He was never idle in the house," Madame went on. "If not writing he was busily employed on some mechanical invention or else entertaining visitors." Among his regular visitors for a time were steamboat pioneer Robert Fulton and Connecticut poet Joel Barlow. Barlow later authored what became a popular epic poem, *The Columbiad*. Clio Rickman assailed Barlow for purposely omitting Paine's name from the poem "as the principal founder of the American republic . . . lest the name of Paine combined with his theological opinions and attack on Washington to injure the sale of the poem. Mean and unhandsome conduct!"[26]

To her amazement one day, Madame Bonneville answered a knock at the door and looked into the eyes of General Napoléon Bonaparte, who had come to invite Paine to dinner. Once seated at dinner, Napoléon is said to have lavished Paine with praise for *Rights of Man*, asserting that he slept with it under his pillow and wanted to see "a statue of gold" of Paine raised in "every city in the universe."[27] There is no indication that Paine disagreed.

Still harboring bitter feelings toward Britain and her king, Paine eagerly joined discussions with Napoléon on invading England. Napoléon had already spent time with Paine's friend Robert Fulton discussing Fulton's intention to build the world's first submarines. Paine subsequently published two articles, the first with a grandiose plan for a French invasion of England. He envisioned using a fleet of 1,000 gunboats, each powered by a combination of small sails and, when necessary, oarsmen. The fleet would be capable of negotiating the Channel and sailing inland along England's major rivers and landing a conquering army simultaneously on the shores and the heart of Britain.

37. A frequent visitor at Thomas Paine's house in Paris, Napoléon Bonaparte said he slept with Paine's *Rights of Man* under his pillow and wanted to see "a statue of gold" of Paine in "every city in the universe." (Réunion des Musées Nationaux)

His second article detailed the method of financing the expedition. Rather than imposing new taxes, he urged an appeal to French patriotism, saying that a mere twenty sous from only 1 percent of the nation's twenty-five million people would be enough to build the fleet. To show support for his plan, the fifty-four-year-old Paine—in typical fashion—sent the Council of 500 "a small patriotic donation" of 100 livres that he could not afford—about ten pounds sterling at the time. "With it," he sent, "all the wishes of my heart for the success of the descent and a voluntary offer of any service I can render to promote it."[28]

Although Bonaparte organized an invasion force of 50,000, the Directory's powerful Charles-Maurice de Talleyrand convinced him to forego invading England in favor of invading Egypt and seizing control of England's essential trade routes to India and the East Indies and their wealth in spices. Although Paine sought to befriend Talleyrand, Talleyrand ignored him. He was running France to his satisfaction and needed no help from Paine or America. Having visited America and lost his investments there, he loathed everything about the New World.

Snubbed by Talleyrand, Paine turned his attention to engineering projects and inventions that had often occupied his mind throughout his life. Robert Fulton now became a close friend with whom he shared his ideas for using alternative power sources such as gunpowder to drive machinery.

Somewhat skeptical of Fulton's ideas for using the power of steam to drive boats, Paine argued that "the weight of the apparatus necessary to produce steam is greater than the power of the steam to remove that weight and consequently that the steam engine cannot move itself."

> The thing wanted for purposes of this kind . . . is something that contains the greatest quantity of power in the least quantity of weight and bulk, and we find this property in gunpowder. . . . If the power which an ounce of gunpowder contains could be detailed out as steam and water, it would be the most commodious natural power because of its small weight and little bulk.[29]

Paine's mind worked incessantly, inventing imaginary machines for every conceivable use—a machine for planing wood boards, a super-efficient crane for lifting materials more quickly than was then possible, a scheme for building houses that were impermeable to dampness, and an elaborate plan to speed French industrial production and transportation by covering France with a network of canals and iron bridges.

As Paine's ideas grew flightier, however, Fulton and others interested in practical mechanics stopped visiting—as did those who had once found Paine's political and social ideas fascinating. Having repeated his views so many times, however, he became a bore to many and gradually found

38. Robert Fulton was one of many American inventors who sought Thomas Paine's friendship and ideas as they explored new means of locomotion and construction.

himself with the company of only the Bonneville children. He joined several deist groups and helped found the Theophilanthropists—a group with five or six followers who listened to lectures on science instead of sermons and celebrated four annual holidays honoring St. Vincent de Paul, George Washington, Socrates, and Rousseau, respectively. In 1801, however, Napoléon signed a concordat with the Pope re-establishing the Roman Catholic Church in France, and Paine's church had to close.

As the American presidential elections neared in October 1800, Paine invested considerable time writing extremely long letters to inform Vice

President Jefferson on "the general state of politics in Europe . . . such as are interesting to America." Jefferson, of course, had become vice president in 1797, after finishing second in the presidential election to his political opposite, then–Vice President John Adams. President Adams had sent two missions to France to attempt to negotiate an end to the "quasi-naval war" between France and America, and, when Paine tried inserting himself in the negotiations, Talleyrand reported Paine to police for "behaving irregularly." Police, in turn, warned Paine that "at the first complaint against him he will be sent back to America." Knowing the British were awaiting any opportunity to capture him on the high seas, Paine stayed away from Talleyrand and the American peace mission.[30]

In his letters to Jefferson, Paine often wrote about his longing to return to America. "If any American frigate should come to France and the direction of it fall to you," he wrote to Jefferson on October 1, 1800, "I will be glad if you would give me the opportunity of returning. The abscess under which I suffered almost two years is entirely healed of itself, and I enjoy exceeding good health."[31]

By then, of course, the second part of *Age of Reason* had been shocking American readers for five years. As a confirmed deist with views almost identical to Paine's, Jefferson remained one of the last of Paine's friends in American government who bothered answering his correspondence. *Age of Reason* had outraged the devout John Adams, who called Paine a "blackguard," insisting that Christianity was "the religion of wisdom, virtue, equity and humanity." He would never again see, let alone befriend, Paine.[32]

After writing endless pages on European political affairs, Paine told Jefferson he would "by way of relief amuse you with some account of the progress of iron bridges." He told Jefferson that his model had been erected over the River Wear at Sunderland, England, "a single arch 236 feet span," for which he received no compensation.* Undeterred, Paine said he had made two other models—"one is of pasteboard, five feet span and five inches of height from the cords. It is the opinion of every person

---

* In fact, only Paine's design and parts of Paine's model bridge from Paddington were incorporated in the bridge over the River Wear.

39. President Thomas Jefferson shared Thomas Paine's religious beliefs, but after years of close friendship, the President distanced himself in the face of popular revulsion over Paine's *Age of Reason.*

who has seen it that it is one of the most beautiful objects the eye can behold. I then cast a model in metal. . . . It is far superior in strength, elegance, and readiness. . . . I shall bring these models with me when I come home, which will be as soon as I can pass the seas safely from the piratical John Bulls."[33]

With Jefferson about to supplant John Adams as President, Paine envisioned his own return to influence in America—perhaps even a cabinet post. After six years at the Bonnevilles, they had become his family. He adored the boys, doted over them, and urged the parents to come with their children and resettle with him at his home in New Rochelle. He pledged to bequeath his New Rochelle property to the children. They would soon need it, for in November 1799, Napoléon seized power in a *coup d'état*, and Nicolas de Bonneville had the temerity to describe the new French leader as "a Cromwell" in his newspaper *Bien Informé*. Little time passed before police arrived at the Bonneville door to arrest Bonneville *père* and shut down *Bien Informé*. Bonneville's arrest left Madame Bonneville and her three boys destitute, without financial support. Paine, a tenant until then, became de facto head of household, a position of financial responsibility he soon learned would not end with Bonneville's release from prison. To punish him for his transgression, police shut Bonneville's press permanently, leaving the printer without means to feed his family. Paine interceded, embracing the Bonnevilles as his own, supporting them with the back pay he had received from the National Convention for the time he had spent in prison.*

In response to Paine's request, President Jefferson sent Paine a "very affectionate" invitation to return to America on the same government ship that had brought Robert Livingston, the new American minister, to France. As Paine made preparations to leave, Livingston—a Jeffersonian republican—is said to have given Paine a tongue-in-cheek warning: "Make out your will before sailing and bequeath the mechanics, the iron bridge . . . to America—and your religion to France."[34]

Jefferson's invitation to Paine provoked a storm of protests in America by the Federalist press and devout Christians. "What?" asked the Federalist *Mercury and New-England Palladium*. "Invite to the United States that lying, drunken, brutal infidel?" Outraged both by *Age of Reason* and Paine's "Letter to George Washington," the *Gazette of the United States* called Paine a "living opprobrium of humanity . . . the infamous scavenger of all the filth which could be raked from the dirty paths which have been hitherto trodden by all the revilers of Christianity."[35]

By then, even ordinary Frenchmen had turned on Paine. On the one hand, Napoléon's spectacular military triumphs across Europe had restored their faith in autocratic, if not monarchic, rule, and they resented the foreigner Paine criticizing their nation's military triumphs. In

---

*After Napoleon's downfall in 1815, Bonneville would be released from prison and join his wife and boys in America.

addition, a particularly savage slave rebellion had erupted in Santo Domingo (present-day Haiti cum Dominican Republic, i.e., Hispaniola), with slaves and freed blacks combining to butcher more than 10,000 French troops and 3,000 French civilians. Among the dead was the army's commander in chief in Haiti, Napoléon's brother-in-law. The rebels seized control of the entire colony and shut off the flow of sugar and coffee to mainland France, infuriating the French and all but crushing the enthusiasm Paine had promoted for emancipation.

Clearly it was time for Paine to quit the French and France. America was "the country of my heart and the place of my political and literary birth," he realized. "It was the American Revolution made me an author and forced into action the mind that had been dormant and had no wish for public life."[36]

Still a wanted felon in his native England, he had little choice but to risk the sea voyage to America, knowing that British naval vessels would scour the seas to capture him, hang him from a yardarm, and dump him into an anonymous ocean grave, to be forgotten with his blasphemous writings.

Chapter 12

FALLEN IDOL

AFTER AN ABSENCE OF FIFTEEN YEARS, PAINE STEPPED ONTO American soil in Baltimore, Maryland, on October 30, 1802, bringing with him a model of his beloved arched bridge, his planing machine, and a multitude of boxes containing his personal papers, letters, essays, half-written essays, and endless ideas for inventions that would never reach fruition. After notifying President Jefferson of his arrival and his intention to visit Washington, Paine went to inspect his properties and found them not only well cared for, but worth more than ten times their original values almost two decades earlier.

He found Americans sharply divided in their reactions to his return. "You can have no idea of the agitation my arrival occasioned," Paine wrote to Thomas Clio Rickman in London. "From New Hampshire to Georgia, every newspaper was filled with applause or abuse."[1]

Federalists had controlled the executive branch during much of Washington's second term in office and during all four years of Adams's presidency. Paine's acerbic "Letter to George Washington" in the summer of 1796 had become the most widely read Paine work, but it had infuriated almost all Federalists and, indeed, the majority of Americans. For almost all Americans—Federalist or not—Washington remained "first in war, first in peace, and first in the hearts of his countrymen," even two years after his death.[2]

Two weeks after his arrival, Paine responded to critics with a series of fierce counterattacks in seven monthly "Letters to the Citizens of the United States." Only three newspapers published them, two of them, however, national in scope: *The National Intelligencer* in Washington, the *National Aurora* in Philadelphia, and the *True American* in Trenton, New Jersey.

In the first, he warned Americans that "the luster" of the American Revolution had faded during his absence, that "a faction . . . was rising in America" which sought to seize control of government and operate it as a profitable monopoly.

"No wonder that the *Rights of Man* was attacked by that faction," he declared. Taking dead aim at the Federalists and the Adams administration, he called their principles "anti-federal and despotic . . . a dishonor to the character of the country and an injury to its reputation and importance abroad." Paine described his first letter as heralding "my arrival to my friends and to my enemies if I have any" and he ended it by stating, "I have no occasion to ask and do not intend to accept any place or office in the government. There is none it could give me that would be . . . equal to the profits I could make as an author."[3]

Four days later, Paine again lashed out at Federalists—and especially former President John Adams—for having converted federalism into "a cloak for treason, a mask for tyranny." Passage of the Alien and Sedition Act, he charged, had allowed then-President Adams to deport aliens at will and prosecute the media for publishing articles critical of the federal government. "Scarcely were they placed in a seat of power and office," Paine growled at the Adams Federalists, "than the representative system of government . . . was to be overturned."

I have had doubts about John Adams ever since the year 1776. In a conversation with me at that time, concerning the pamphlet *Common Sense*, he censured it because it attacked the English form of government. John Adams was for independence because he expected to be made great by it . . . his head was as full of kings, queens and knaves as a pack of cards.

"For what purpose could an army of twenty-five thousand men be wanted?" Paine asked of Adams's call for troops during the naval conflict with France in 1798. "It was wanted for the purpose of destroying the representative system."[4]

Paine went on to describe the evolution of The Terror during the Revolution in France, and he renewed his attack on Washington for his failure to demand Paine's liberation from prison in France. In still another letter, he assailed New York's Aaron Burr for having challenged Thomas Jefferson for the American presidency after having pledged to withdraw if the Electoral College produced a tie.

"Religion and War is the cry of the Federalists," Paine snarled in his sixth letter "To the Citizens of the United States." The voice of Thomas Jefferson's republicans, on the other hand, he said, called for "Morality and Peace." To his charges against John Adams and the Federalist government, Paine added "a continual increase of taxes and an unceasing clamor for war." In an eighth letter two years later in June 1805, Paine resumed his relentless assault while insisting, "I am not persecuting John Adams." He nonetheless continued reviling the former President for having prepared to expand into all-out war the limited naval conflict with France in Atlantic and Caribbean waters.

Although Paine insisted he wanted no role in American government affairs, his unceasing efforts to draw closer to Jefferson made his denials of political ambitions seem disingenuous. Indeed, immediately after landing in Baltimore, Paine had written to the President to say he was on his way "to pay my respects to you."[5] And on Christmas Day, when Paine learned that Spain had retroceded Louisiana to France,* Paine raced to the executive mansion to suggest that Jefferson offer to buy the territory. When Paine arrived, Jefferson told him that he had already done just that and put an end to any further discussions of government policies with Paine.

Well aware of the furor Paine's *Age of Reason* had caused, Jefferson sought ways to distance himself from Paine the public figure, without

---

* After Britain crushed France in the Seven Years' War (1756–1763), the humiliating terms of the treaty ending the war forced France to cede the Louisiana Territory to Spain, then ruled by a Bourbon family cousin of the king of France. As American settlers poured into the territory, the relatively impotent Spanish government in the territory feared the Americans might seize its Mexican silver mines, and, except for New Orleans, it retroceded the Louisiana Territory north of the Mexican border to France in hopes the powerful French army would buffer the lands between Mexico and the Americans.

wounding Paine personally or damaging their personal relationship. Indeed, he insisted on Paine's remaining several days at the White House and dining there. According to a mutual acquaintance, the President "could be seen walking arm in arm with him [Paine] on the street any fine afternoon,"[6] but the Federalist editor of the *Baltimore Republican* hurled insults at "our pious President" for his "accommodation of this loathsome reptile."[7]

With almost no opportunities to influence government, Paine spent much of his time trying to restore friendships disrupted by his years abroad, but failed for the most part. He went to Philadelphia to visit old friends at the American Philosophical Society. The oldest of these—among them Franklin, for example—were dead. As for his younger friends, Dr. Benjamin Rush, for one, was ten years younger, had been his first friend in America, had helped Paine edit *Common Sense*, but now tied Paine to *Age of Reason* rather than *Common Sense*. Stung deeply by Paine's attacks on the divinity of Christ and on the church, the devoutly religious physician wanted nothing more to do with Paine. "I did not see Mr. Paine when he passed through Philadelphia," Rush reported. "His principles avowed in his *Age of Reason* were so offensive to me that I did not wish to renew my intercourse with him."[8]

In addition to religious zealots, political fanatics used every opportunity to assail Paine. Once, when Paine sought to travel to New York, for example, Federalist owners of two stagecoaches refused to let him board. When he took his seat in a third coach, a mob of Federalists surrounded it and, while a drummer played the "Rogue's March" to scare the horses, Paine had to leave the coach and take refuge at a friend's house.

"A country, abounding in fanatics could not be a proper one for him," Clio Rickman said of Paine's return to America.

> Of all the wrath, fanatical wrath is the most intense. . . . Mr. Paine received from great numbers in America an unwelcome reception and was treated with neglect and illiberality. . . . Thousands, who had formerly looked up to Mr. Paine as the principal founder of the Republic, had imbibed a strong dislike to him on account of his religious principles. . . . The vilest calumnies were constantly vented against him in the public papers.[9]

Among the vilest of calumnies were two unauthorized biographies, one by Francis Oldys—a pseudonym for George Chalmers, a lawyer and sometime writer, whom the British government paid £500 to discredit Paine. In addition to Chalmers, newspaper editor James Cheetham would later take advantage of Paine's death to write what Clio Rickman called "a farrago of . . . trifling, false, and malicious matter . . . an outrageous attack . . . idle gossiping, and gross misrepresentation." Rickman called the Chalmers biography "so palpably written to distort, disfigure, and vilify . . . that it becomes entertaining from the excess of its labored and studied defamation."[10]

A Paine visit to New York City proved no more satisfying. Men of any consequence either revered him or detested him for his political views or his religious beliefs—and just as often both. "The letter he wrote to George Washington," Rickman opined, "estranged him from many of his old friends and has been to his adversaries a fruitful theme of virulent accusation."[11]

Whereas Paine's *Age of Reason, Part First* ran a mere 100 pages or so, it barely touched Paine's objections to the Old and New Testaments. *Part Second*, on the other hand, shredded the two books, describing their contents as outright lies, page by page, often line by line, labelling clergymen as liars, driven by lust for profits and power. *Part Second* leaves almost no phrase, word, or punctuation mark in the two Testaments untouched.

Paine attributed obvious errors in the Old Testament to its antiquity. "I know of but one ancient book that authoritatively challenged univer-sal . . . belief," he said, "and that is Euclid's 'Elements of Geometry,' and the reason is because it is a book of self-evident demonstration, entirely independent of its author and of everything related to time, place, and circumstance. The matters contained in the book would have the same authority . . . had they been written by any other person or had the work been anonymous."

Paine insisted there was no evidence that Moses existed or that he authored the book of Moses, which is "altogether the style and manner of . . . another person speaking of Moses . . . it is always, *the Lord said unto Moses,* or *Moses said unto the Lord.* . . . This is the style and manner that historians use in speaking of the persons whose lives and actions they are writing. He calls the actual author "very ignorant and stupid" for attributing to Moses such anachronistic statements as "No man knows where the sepulcher of Moses is *unto this* day."[12]

Paine points out that the author of the book of Moses failed to disclose how he obtained "the speeches which he has put into the mouth of Moses . . . since he has given in the fifth chapter a table of commandments in which the fourth commandment differed from the fourth commandment in the twentieth chapter of Exodus. The first cites origins of keeping the seventh day as, 'God . . . rested on the seventh . . .' Deuteronomy, on the other hand, makes no mention of the Creation, saying the seventh day marked the exodus of the children of Israel from Egypt and 'the Lord thy God commanded thee to keep the Sabbath day.'[13]

"There are also many things given as laws of Moses not found in any of the other books," Paine argued, "among which is that inhuman and brutal law . . . which authorizes parents, the father and mother, to bring their own children to have them stoned to death for what it is pleased to call stubbornness."[14]

Paine called the five books of Moses, Genesis, Exodus, Leviticus, Numbers, and Deuteronomy, "spurious. Neither was Moses their author," he declared, "nor were they written in the time of Moses."[15] In Genesis, for example, Abraham pursues the captors of Lot into Dan—which did not exist until more than three centuries after the death of Moses. Paine called Genesis "an anonymous book of stories, fables . . . invented absurdities, or downright lies." The story of Eve and the Serpent, of Noah and his ark, and men living to eight and nine hundred years "drops to a level with the Arabian tales, without the merit of being entertaining.[16]

"It is only in the CREATION that all our ideas and conceptions of a *Word of God* can unite," Paine insisted, appealing again to reason:

> I know I did not make myself, yet I have existence; and by searching into the nature of other things, I find no other thing can make itself; and yet millions of other things exist; therefore it is . . . by positive conclusion . . . that there is a power superior to all those things, and that power is God.[17]

Paine called reason a divine gift that God gave man to acquire knowledge of nature, the sciences, and the structure of the universe and make the world a better place in which to live. Christian leaders, he declared, "could not but foresee that the continually progressive knowledge that man would gain by the aid of science . . . would militate against and call into question the truth of their system of faith. . . . They not only rejected the study of science in Christian schools, they persecuted it. The age of ignorance commenced with the Christian system. The Christian system was only another species of mythology and the mythology . . . was a corruption of an ancient system of theism."[18]

Paine contrasted the story of the death of Christ to "the pure and simple profession of Deism!" The deist, he said, had but one deity, with a religion consisting only in contemplation of "the power, wisdom, and benignity of the Deity and His works, and in endeavoring to imitate Him in everything moral, scientifical [sic], and mechanical."[19]

Paine devoted part of *Age of Reason* to proving that far from being the Word of God, the Bible—both Old and New Testaments—was pure fiction written by men. He found it appalling that "the inhuman and horrid butcheries of men, women, and children . . . told of in these books were done, as these books say they were, at the command of God. It is a duty incumbent on every true Deist that he vindicate the moral justice of God against the calumnies of the Bible."[20]

Paine accused priests of his day of "unriddling" biblical fables in accordance with their own views and uses, with each imposing an explanation that conforms to the priest's own views. "The *whore of Babylon* has been the common whore of all the priests, and each has accused the other of keeping the strumpet to his own uses; so well do they agree in their explanations."[21]

When Paine turned to the New Testament, he outraged most Americans and much of the Christian world. Once the revered champion of individual liberty, the author of *Common Sense* became the devil incarnate to many readers. Paine did not actually dispute the existence of Mary, Joseph, and Jesus, but his words seemed to do just that. "It may be so," he comments on the nativity, "and what then? . . . It is not the existence or non-existence of the persons that I trouble myself about. It is the fable of Jesus Christ as told in the New Testament and the wild and visionary doctrine against which I contend."

> The story, taking it as it is told, is blasphemously obscene. It gives an account of a young woman engaged to be married . . . debauched by a ghost under the impious pretense that *"the holy ghost shall come upon thee and the power of the Highest shall overshadow thee."* Notwithstanding which, Joseph afterward marries her, cohabits with her as his wife, and in his turn rivals the ghost.[22]

Paine shows the story to be similar to those of Jupiter and Leda, Jupiter and Europe, and other amorous adventures of Jupiter and, therefore, proof that "the Christian faith is built upon the heathen mythology."[23]

It was Paine's next assertion that outraged all but the last of his American followers: "The story of Christ appearing after he was dead," Paine proclaimed, "is the story of an apparition, such as timid imaginations can always create . . . till it becomes a *most certain truth*. Once start a ghost and credulity fills up the history of its life . . . one tells it one way, another a second way, till there are as many stories about the ghost . . . as there are about Jesus Christ in these four books [of Matthew, Mark, Luke, John]."[24]

Paine goes on to list numerous contradictions among the four Apostles in their accounts of the resurrection and other events in the life and death of Christ. "The writers," he concluded, "could not have been eye-witnesses and ear-witnesses of the matters they relate . . . [and] the books have not been written by the persons called apostles."[25]

> The fact is . . . there was no such book as the New Testament till more than three hundred years after the time that Christ is said to have lived. . . . There is not the least shadow of evidence of who the persons were that wrote them. . . . At the time those books were written there was no printing and consequently . . . no publication. . . . About three hundred and fifty years after the time of Christ . . . as the church began to form itself into a hierarchy or church government . . . it set about collecting . . . several writings of the kind . . . into a code . . . called *The New Testament*. They decided by vote . . . which of those writing out

of the collection . . . should be the *Word of God* and which should not. The rabbis of the Jews had decided, by vote, upon the books of the Bible before . . . and nothing can present us a more strange idea than that of decreeing the Word of God by vote.[26]

Paine said there were no clues to identify the persons who wrote the New Testament or the time when it was written. "The originals are not in the possession of any Christian Church existing," he said, "any more than the two tablets of stone written on, they pretend, by the finger of God upon Mount Sinai."[27]

The only religion that man had not invented, Paine declared, was "pure and simple Deism," which, he said, did not answer the purpose of despotic governments, enhance church authority, or invent myths of mysterious church-state ties and divine rights of kings. "We can know God only through His works. . . . The principles of science lead to this knowledge, for the creator of man is the Creator of science [nature], and it is through that medium that man can see God."[28]

Most of the American press assailed Paine, with Boston's *Columbian Centinel* calling him a "notorious drunkard" and "impious buffoon," while the *New York Evening Post* described his nose as a "blazing star."*[29] In contrast, *The National Aegis*, a republican newspaper in Worcester, Massachusetts, presented a warm, glowing appraisal:

> Years have made more impression on his body than his mind. . . . He dresses plain like a farmer, and appears cleanly and comfortable in his person. . . . His address is unaffected and unceremonious. He neither shuns nor courts observation. At table he enjoys what is good with appetite of temperance and vigor and puts to shame his calumniators by the moderation with which he partakes of . . . beverage. His conversation is uncommonly interesting; he is gay, humorous, and full of anecdotes.[30]

---

*As Paine aged, he developed rhinophyma, a not uncommon condition akin to adolescent acne in which the nose becomes red and bulbous. Often mistakenly associated with excess alcohol intake, it allowed Paine's enemies to cite his rhinophyma as proof of his "drunkenness."

40. The aging Thomas Paine in this portrait belies the slander heaped on him by his enemies that he was constantly drunk, filthy, in tattered clothes, and unable to care for himself.

Thomas Clio Rickman—Paine's "Boswell"—agreed, affirming that Paine "was not in the habit of drinking to excess. He was clean in his person and in his manners polite and engaging. . . . When I was with him in France, he did not drink spirits, and wine he took moderately. . . . To give him vices he had not and seek occasions of misrepresenting and vilifying his character . . . is cruel, unkind, and unjust."[31]

Paine responded to his critics in a fourth letter "To the Citizens of the United States," in which he reported his health as "perfectly good [and] in every instance a living contradiction to the mortified Federalists."

I am now in my circumstances independent, and my economy makes me rich. . . . Had half the number of evils befallen me that the number of dangers amount to through which I have been preserved, there are those who would ascribe it to the wrath of heaven. Why then do they not ascribe my preservation to the protecting favor of heaven? My path is a right line, as straight and clear to me as a ray of light. The boldness . . . with which I speak to the reader . . . is like saying, *I treat you as a man and not as a child.* . . . And with this declaration, I take my leave for the present.[32]

His last words turned out to be prescient. At eight in the evening on Christmas Eve of 1804, as he sat silhouetted in the window writing a letter to a friend, a bullet crashed through a windowpane near his chair. Nothing but silence followed the crackling sound of falling glass.

Chapter 13

TO RESCUE MAN
FROM TYRANNY

THE BULLET AIMED AT PAINE'S HEAD MISSED ITS MARK. HE LEAPED from his chair and darted outside to try to catch or at least identify the would-be assassin, but he found and saw no one, although he had a suspect in mind.

"I directly suspected who it was, and I hallooed him by name that he was discovered . . . that the party who fired might know I was on the watch. I cannot find any ball, but whatever it was that the gun discharged hit the cottage wall about three or four inches below the window making a hole large enough for a finger to go through. The muzzle must have been very near as the place is black with the powder."[1]

Paine's suspicions proved correct, with the shooter eventually identified as Christopher Derrick, a tenant farmer whom Paine had dismissed for heavy drinking and consequent failure to tend his fields. Although constables arrested Derrick, Paine opted against pressing charges and Derrick disappeared from Paine's life.

In late summer 1803, Madame Marguerite Bonneville materialized in New York with her three boys. Fearing imminent arrest of the entire family—French police did not discriminate among men, women, and children—Nicolas de Bonneville had spent his last French sou hustling his wife and three boys onto a ship bound for America and what he assumed would be a comfortable sanctuary with his friend, the famed—and presumably well-to-do—writer Thomas Paine.

Arriving without a penny in her purse, she descended on Paine unable to speak a word of English. After failing to find a suitable haven for her and her boys, he brought them to his New Rochelle farm, with Marguerite assuming housekeeping responsibilities for the new menagerie. To ensure his solvency, Paine sold about 60 acres of meadowland for $4,020, leaving him with just over 200 acres, about 100 of which were grazing meadows and the remainder woodland. He used some of the cash to add a 34 × 32–foot annex to his house for the Bonnevilles and the rest to improve other parts of the property. He enrolled his namesake Thomas and the oldest boy Benjamin in school, hired a cook, and, at sixty-eight, seemed content to settle into a quiet life of a semi-retired family man, remaining relatively unfazed by the appearance of defamatory profiles of him in the press.

In the year that followed, Paine sent a stream of unsolicited policy papers and advice to President Jefferson as well as other American leaders. The President, in turn, made a show of welcoming Paine's counsel rather than risk alienating a once-influential political ally. Paine still had some access to the editorial pages of liberal American newspapers and an audience, albeit thinning, that revered him and had helped propel Jefferson to the White House. Paine had provoked a war against royal rule with *Common Sense*; Jefferson did not want him to provoke a war against his presidency.

As the editor of the newspaper *Aurora* explained, Paine had spent his life "devoting his time, health and talents to promote freedom" and the President "will not, by a line of conduct," open the way for a staunch ally to become an opponent.[2]

Although Jefferson had often spoken out against slavery, for example, he had refused to free his own or anyone else's slaves. Indeed, after the French had suppressed the slave rebellion in Domingo (Haiti), Jefferson acted to prevent giving asylum in America to any of the slaves and other blacks who had fled the island. Like many southern leaders, he feared they would import their rebellion onto American shores.

"If a way could be found to bring about peace between France and Domingo through the mediation and guarantee of the United States," Paine wrote to the President, "it would be beneficial to all parties. . . . All that Domingo wants of France is that France agree to let her alone . . . and withdraw her forces."

In return, he said, Domingo would give France a long-term monopoly of her commerce, which, he argued, was worth far more than conquest. "Conquest could not be accomplished without destroying the negroes, and in that case the island would be of no value." He called the United States "the Parent of the Western World" and the only power able "to put an end to this otherwise endless slaughter on both sides. . . . Such an offer, whether accepted or not, cannot but be well received and may lead to a good end."[3] The President ignored Paine's suggestion.

In subsequent policy letters to the President, Paine suggested selective restrictions for settling the American West: "Of people from abroad, the German peasantry are the best," he asserted. "The Irish in general are generous and dissolute. The Scotch turn their attention to traffic [smuggling], and the English to manufactures. These people are more fitted to live in cities than to be cultivators of new lands." He advised against bringing "poor Negroes to work the lands in a state of slavery and wretchedness. . . . Besides the immorality of it . . . I recollect when in France, you spoke of a plan of making the Negroes tenants on a plantation . . . allotting each Negro family a quantity of land for which they were to pay to the owner a certain quantity of produce. . . . A great many good things may now be done; and I please myself with the idea of suggesting my thoughts to you."[4]

When it became evident that Jefferson would not translate Paine's suggestions into executive action, Paine gradually lost interest in national affairs and focused on ensuring his own legacy. "As everything of public affairs is now on a good ground," he wrote to Jefferson, "I shall do as I did after the war: remain a quiet spectator and attend now to my own affairs."

I intend making a collection of all the pieces I have published, beginning with *Common Sense* and of what I have by me in manuscript and publish them by subscription. . . . I judge the collection I speak of will make five volumes octavo of four hundred pages each at two dollars a volume to be paid on delivery. . . . The three first volumes will be political . . . with an account of the state of affairs at the time it was written, whether in America, France, or England. . . . The two last volumes will be theological, and those who do not choose to take them may let them alone.[5]

In the fall of 1804, Paine enrolled the Bonneville boys in a boarding school, leaving Mrs. Bonneville so bored with country life, she moved to New York and took up teaching French to support herself. Left alone and friendless on his farm, Paine tried, without success, to lure city friends to visit him.

"I have six chairs and a table, a straw bed, a feather bed," he wrote to one friend in New York during the summer of 1805, "a tea kettle, an iron pot, an iron baking pan, a frying pan, a gridiron, cups, saucers, plates and dishes, knives and forks, two candlesticks and a pair of snuffers."

> I have a pair of fine oxen and an ox-cart, a good horse, a chair, and a one-horse cart; a cow and a sow and nine pigs. When you come you must take such fare as you meet with, for I live upon tea, milk, fruit pies, plain dumplings, and a piece of meat when I get it. . . . If you cannot make yourself up a straw bed, I can let you have blankets, and you will have no occasion to go over to the tavern to sleep.[6]

Without society to entertain him or a tenant farmer to produce income, Paine finally quit New Rochelle and moved to a hotel in New York. As in Philadelphia, however, many friends who had revered the author of *Common Sense* shunned the author of *Age of Reason*. Desperate for society, Paine looked to the growing deistic movement for friends. He contributed fourteen essays to the movement's journal, *The Prospect; or Views of the Moral World*.

As in *Age of Reason*, his comments tore at the belly of organized religion, even exposing the absurdities of religious classifications, including Christianity. "No two sectaries can agree what it is. It is *lo here* and *lo there*."

> The two principal sectaries, Papists and Protestants, have often cut each other's throats about it. The Papists call the Protestants heretics, and the Protestants call the Papists idolaters. . . . The word "Christian" describes what a man is not, but not what he is. When we say a "Christian," we know he is not a Jew nor a Mahometan, but we know not if he be a trinitarian or an anti-trinitarian, a believer in . . . the immaculate conception or a disbeliever, a man of seven sacraments, or of two sacraments, or of none.[7]

Paine went on to show how biblical anecdotes contradicted each other, restating his oft-repeated contention that it was a lie to call the Bible the Word of God. He cited the story of the Tower of Babel, for example, as beginning with the statement that "the whole earth . . . was of one language and of one speech"—only to contradict itself with God's assertion, "Let us go down and confound their language."[8]

And in another essay for *The Prospect*, Paine asks why Jesus never speaks of the Creation, of Adam, of the Garden of Eden and the Fall of Man. In still another, he asks, "Is the account which the Christian church gives of the person called Jesus Christ a fact or a fable? Is it a fact that he was begotten by the Holy Ghost? The Christians cannot prove it, for the case does not admit of proof . . . the story of the conception of Jesus Christ in the womb . . . did not admit of demonstration. Mary, the reputed mother of Jesus, who must be supposed to know best, never said so herself, and all the evidence of it is that the book of Matthew says that Joseph dreamed an angel told him so."[9]

As he had in *Age of Reason*, Paine questioned the very existence of Jesus Christ and other characters central to religious teachings. "Is it a fact that Jesus Christ died for the sins of the world, and how is it proved?"

If a God he could not die, and as a man he could not redeem. . . . It is said that Adam ate of the forbidden fruit, commonly called an apple, and thereby subjected himself and all his posterity for ever to eternal damnation. . . . But how was the death of Jesus Christ to affect or alter the case? . . . Many thousands of human sacrifices have since been offered on the altar of the Christian religion. . . . Did God thirst for blood? . . . That man should redeem himself from the sin of eating an Apple by committing murder on Jesus Christ is the strangest system of religion ever set up. . . . The Christian system of religion is an outrage on common sense. Why is man afraid to think?[10]

Although Paine was not the first to expose contradictions in the professions of the world's religions, even some deists feared his company. Not only had he been the target of an assassination attempt, he was often set upon by strangers in the streets, some booing and cursing him for his blasphemous attacks on their religious beliefs, others physically assaulting him. Patrick Henry started to write a bitter denunciation of Paine's work, but put it aside and simply refused to have anything more to do with Paine.

Paine fought back as only he could—with more essays and letters to Americans. "I shall continue these letters as I see occasion," he fumed, "and as to the low party prints that choose to abuse me, they are welcome. I shall not descend to answer them. I have been too much used to such common stuff to take any notice of it."[11]

In the years that followed—almost until the day he died—the prolific author of *Common Sense* wrote, and the *Aurora* published, among others, such articles as "An Essay on the Invasion of England," "On Gun-Boats," and "On the Yellow Fever" (yellow fever epidemics routinely gripped many northeast cities in summer).

Of all the public attacks on Paine and his *Age of Reason*, only one—that of Richard Watson, Bishop of Llandaff, bordered on the thoughtful. The Bishop even complimented Paine's ingenuity in uncovering "real difficulties" in the Old Testament and what he called "unsightly shrubs . . . concealed from public view . . . in the Christian grove."[12] Watson admitted that Moses had probably not written every part of the Pentateuch and that the law in Deuteronomy giving parents the right to have their children stoned to death was "improper." He admitted to the fallibility of the Bible, the discrepancies between the genealogies of Christ in Matthew and Luke, and the evidence that neither Samuel nor David wrote elements ascribed to them. But Watson then abandoned reasonable argument with a direct and specious attack on Paine.

"You profess yourself to be a deist and to believe that there is a God who created the universe and established the laws of nature by which it is sustained in existence," Watson wrote.

> You think it repugnant to his moral justice that he should doom to destruction the crying and smiling infants of the Canaanites. Why do you not maintain it to be repugnant to his moral justice that he should suffer crying or smiling infants to be swallowed up by an earthquake, drowned by an inundation, consumed by fire, starved by a famine, or destroyed by a pestilence?[13]

Far from rebutting Paine's *Age of Reason,* Watson's exposition of God's random and unrestrained cruelties to man actually planted the first seeds of atheism in America and the absence of any God—certainly any benevolent God. No one else attempted a rational, well-thought-out rebuttal of Paine's *Age of Reason.*

But the Bishop of Llandaff's inability to undermine *Age of Reason* did nothing to enhance public acceptance of it or reduce the all-but-universal contempt for Paine. The ostracism that resulted evidently affected Paine's thinking after a while. Although he continued writing essays on national and world affairs, his lines of reasoning often strayed or contradicted his earlier articles.

In one essay after Napoléon's humiliating defeats in the Middle East and subsequent seizure of absolute powers as Emperor of France, Paine heaped irrational praise on the French leader. Ignoring the slaughter of innocents by Napoléon's troops, Paine asserted that "France has for its chief the most enterprising man in Europe and the greatest general in the world. Beside these virtues . . . he is a deep and consummate politician in everything which relates to the success of his measures. He knows how to plan and execute."[14]

In another article, he criticized Pennsylvania's new state constitution unreasonably as the work of "unprincipled Federalists, who aped British customs, beliefs, and traditions" and created a Senate that was "an imitation of the House of Lords."[15]

With isolation came loneliness and a rapid depletion of his savings that provoked his writing an embarrassing letter to President Jefferson, pleading with the Virginian to remind Congress of his (Paine's) unpaid services to the nation during the Revolutionary War. "I have been a volunteer to the world for thirty years without taking profit from anything I have published in America or Europe. I have relinquished all profits that those publications might come cheap among the people for whom they were intended."[16]

When he received no response, he wrote a second time, but, again, no answer.

Paine suffered still another blow to his pride early in 1806, when he learned that Philadelphia mayor John Inskeep had refused to sell the Vine

Street wharf to the highest bidder—a Mr. Isaac Hall—because, the mayor said, "Mr. Hall was one of Paine's disciples."

"I do not know who Mr. Inskeep is," Paine assailed Mayor Inskeep, "for I do not remember the name of Inskeep in '*the time that tried men's souls.*'"

> He must be some mushroom of modern growth that has started up on the soil which the generous services of Thomas Paine contributed to bless with freedom. Neither do I know what profession of religion he is of, nor do I care. . . . As I set too much value on my time to waste it on a man of so little consequence as yourself, I will close . . . with a declaration that . . . my motive and object in all my political works, beginning with *Common Sense* . . . have been to rescue man from tyranny and false systems and false principles of government, and enable him to be free.[17]

In the fall of 1806, Paine suffered what seemed a final blow to his love of man—indeed, to his very sanity—when he returned to New Rochelle to vote and town officials refused to let him cast his ballot in the fall elections. Paine described his humiliation to Vice President George Clinton, the former governor of New York:

> Elisha Ward and three or four other Tories who lived within the British lines in the Revolutionary War . . . refused my vote . . . saying to me, "You are not an American; our Minister at Paris Gouverneur Morris would not reclaim you when you were imprisoned in the Luxemburg prison at Paris, and General Washington refused to do it." Upon my telling him that the two cases he stated were falsehoods and that if he did me injustice I would prosecute him, he got up and calling for a constable, said to me, "I will commit you to prison."[18]

Although Paine referred the case to the district attorney, he realized that even if he won his case, the victory would not come until months later and render the decision moot. It would do little or nothing to compensate for his public humiliation and deprivation of a basic right that he, Paine, had risked his life to obtain for his fellow Americans. It was the cruelest emotional blow he had ever suffered.

But more such blows were to follow, as newspaper editors turned *Age of Reason* into a profitable center of controversy among subscribers who sent letters attacking or defending it and its author.

As increasingly vicious and specious arguments battered *Age of Reason* in various newspapers, Paine grew angrier and more despondent, often wandering about aimlessly or sitting by the side of the road in the throes of what today's psychiatrists would probably call depression. Then an Englishman from happier days in Lewes showed up at Paine's door. Born and raised in Lewes, William Carver had been a stable boy when he was young, caring for, among others, Paine's horse when Paine was an exciseman. Carver later became a veterinarian and moved to New York, where he said he had become an admirer of Paine. Hoping to lift Paine's spirits, he invited the great author to his home.

Paine's stay at Carver's became the subject for Cheetham's infamous "biography" of Paine, saying Carver often found Paine drunk, disheveled, unshaved, with "the most disagreeable smell possible, just like . . . our poor beggars in England." Cheetham wrote that Carver had washed Paine "from head to foot . . . three times," then shaved him, cut his nails, which were "like birds' claws," and trimmed his toenails, some of which had "grown around his toes and nearly as far under as they extended on top."[19]

In fact, Carver was "a most strenuous advocate and supporter of Mr. Paine's political and religious principles," according to Rickman, who called Cheetham's work "nonsensical malevolence."[20]

Cheetham's tale of Carver and Paine set off a rash of similar reports of Paine's alleged degeneracy by Federalists, Tories, and defenders of almost every church. All portrayed him as the devilish author of *Age of Reason*, with one describing him as being "like other animals who delight in savage life."[21]

In contrast, Paine's admirers—mostly deists—countered with tales of Paine as "abstemious." When friends pressed Paine to drink, one admirer reported, "he usually refused with great firmness, but politely. . . . Though careless of his dress and prodigal of snuff, he was always clean and well clothed . . . patting children and humane to animals."[22]

In 1803, Vice President George Clinton's nephew Dewitt Clinton won election as mayor of New York City. A great admirer of Thomas Paine, he invited Paine to march in the following summer's "Annual Festival of Independence," as the July 4 holiday was called then.

"We were up at five o'clock and on the battery saw the cannons fired, in commemoration of liberty," the mayor described the celebration. "In the fore part of the day, I had the honor of walking with T. Paine along the Broadway."*[23]

Late in July 1806, Paine suffered a stroke that deprived him of "all sense and motion." He had been climbing the stairs to go to bed when "the fit took me . . . as suddenly as if I had been shot through the head. I had neither pulse nor breathing. The fall left me unable to get in and out of bed except by being lifted out in a blanket by two persons. . . . I consider the scene I have passed through as an experiment on dying, and I find that death has no terrors for me."[24]

There is no way of knowing the extent of the brain injury that Paine—or any other stroke victims, for that matter—may have suffered more than two centuries ago. Medicine and medical care were largely based on guess-work, superstition, or quackery. In the three years that followed his stroke, he continued writing—incessantly, passionately. But few cared what he had to say. Even the confirmed deist Thomas Jefferson—an intellectual friend for so much of Paine's life—cut short and cooled the tone of his letters to Paine, rather than risk the wrath of the nation's clergy and a growing evangelical movement and blemishing his own and his party's political future as a friend of an avowed heretic. Jefferson was already working to protect his own legacy as President and to ensure the succession to the presidency of his friend and protégé Secretary of State James Madison. He believed he would have no chance of success with Thomas Paine, the alleged blasphemer, routinely strolling in and out of the White House.

Early in 1801, when Jefferson first took office as President, he signed his letters to Paine with warmth: "That you may long live to continue your useful labors and reap the rewards in the thankfulness of nations is my sincere prayer; accept my assurances of my high esteem and affectionate attachment."[25] By the beginning of his second term when he was already

---

*As in England, it was still customary in New York to refer to avenues as proper nouns: "The Broadway," "The First Avenue," etc.

preparing for Madison's succession, Jefferson's letters to Paine grew short, even abrupt. He told his old friend he had "so small a portion of the day for answering letters that I am obliged to economize." He closed with standard, formal endings: "Accept my friendly salutations and assurances of great esteem & respect."[26]

Paine had first sensed the President's chilliness in 1803, attributing it correctly to a "fear of federal [i.e., Federalist] observation," adding, "I am not the only one who makes observations of this kind."[27]

During Paine's last years, a local baker, a young portrait painter, and a tavern keeper took turns caring for the old man, with each, however, somewhat less attentive than his predecessor. Destitute, without funds, he acceded to the demands of kindly acquaintances to sell his property in Bordentown and use the funds to pay for a proper room and board in Greenwich Village, then a separate—indeed bucolic—community north of New York City. Another stroke forced him to spend his waking hours in a chair, where he often erupted into uncontrollable tears of anger at his helplessness. In January 1809, friends hired an attendant to care for him, and he wrote a will—unusual in that he believed it necessary to preface it with a summary of his literary triumphs. "*Common Sense*," he wrote, "awaked America to a declaration of independence."[28]

Except for token bequests to his executors, he left one-half of the proceeds from the sale of his New Rochelle farm to be divided between his friend Rickman and Mrs. Elihu Palmer, the widow of the editor of *The Prospect*, which had published his last essays on deism when other publications rejected all he wrote. Paine left the rest of his estate, including the other half of the proceeds from the sale of his New Rochelle property, to Mrs. Bonneville in trust for her three sons.

Although he asked a Quaker neighbor to arrange his funeral in a nearby Quaker cemetery, the congregation rejected his request. He died at 8 o'clock in the morning of June 8, 1809, at the age of seventy-two.

Many anecdotes surfaced about the hours before his death, including one tale of an old lady who called on Paine unexpectedly. "What do you want?" he croaked.

"I come from Almighty God to tell you if you do not believe . . . in Jesus Christ, you will be damned, and. . . ."

"It is not true," he interrupted. "You were not sent with such an impertinent message. . . . He would not send such a foolish, ugly old woman with his messages. Go away and shut the door!"

"During his illness he was pestered with intrusive and impertinent visits of the bigoted, the fanatic, and the designing," biographer Rickman noted.[29] A Reverend Mr. Hargrove barged in to "explain the scripture in its true meaning," saying, "the key has been lost these four thousand years—and we have found it!"

Paine pondered before replying.

"It must have been very rusty."[30]

Not all his visitors despised him.

"I witnessed a scene last night," one of Paine's visitors wrote to Rickman, "beholding the well-known Thomas Paine . . . who had attempted to overthrow kingdoms and monarchies . . . whose works have caused a great part of mankind to think and feel as they never did before. . . . Poor Paine's body has given way before his mind, which is yet firm. . . . With respect to his principles, he will die as he lived; they are unaltered."[31]

And a newspaper in London, of all places, conceded. "No human being's efforts have done more for liberty. . . . His *Common Sense* enfranchised America. America was divided between two parties; the arguments of this little pamphlet decided the contest. His glorious *Rights of Man* had nearly a similar effect in England. He was prosecuted for his works, but they were so admired that they were in every library. . . . This apostle of liberty . . . never retracted his opinions."[32]

Biographer Mercure Daniel Conway wrote of two clergymen who approached Paine just before his death, only to have him rebuff them with what may have been his dying words: "Let me alone! Good morning!"[33]

Thomas Clio Rickman embellished the tale by citing a letter he had received claiming that Paine had twice cried out on his deathbed: "Oh, Lord Help me!" A clergyman was said to have responded appropriately to each cry, asking Paine, "Mr. Paine: Do you wish to believe that Jesus Christ is the Son of God?"

Paine replied, "I have no wish to believe in that subject."[34]

Chapter 14

WHEN THE EMPIRE
OF AMERICA SHALL FALL

E VEN AS DEATH APPROACHED, PAINE CONTINUED STRUGGLING TO
free man from what he called the "tyranny" of organized religion.

"When we consider," Paine wrote toward the end of *Age of Reason*,
"the lapse . . . between the time that Christ is said to have lived and the
time the New Testament was formed into a book, we must see, even without the assistance of historical evidence the exceeding uncertainty there is
of its authenticity."[1]

Paine said the authenticity of Homer's works, though one thousand
years older, was far better established than that of the New Testament,
as was Euclid's *Elements*, because only a great poet in the first instance
or a great geometrician in the second could have produced such majestic
works. In contrast, Paine asserted, the story in the New Testament "is most
wretchedly told. . . . Any person who could tell a story of an apparition or
of persons walking after they are dead . . . could have made such books."

> And as the people of that day were in the habit of believing such things,
> and of the appearance of angels, and also of devils, and of their getting into
> people's insides and shaking them like a fit of an ague and of their being
> cast out again as if by an emetic, it was nothing extra ordinary that some
> story of this kind should get abroad of the person called Jesus Christ and
> become afterwards the foundation of the four books ascribed to Matthew,
> Mark, Luke, and John. Each writer told a tale as he heard it . . . and gave to
> the book the name of the saint or the apostle whom tradition had given as

the eye-witness. It is only upon this ground that the contradictions in those books can be accounted for; and if this be not the case, they are downright impositions, lies, and forgeries, without even the apology of credulity.[2]

In the end, few Americans believed a word Paine wrote anymore—or cared. He had served their purpose—like a brilliant battlefield general with no leadership experience or skills in peacetime pursuits. Three decades earlier, after first arriving in America, he predicted a revolution in the system of government would be followed by a revolution in the system of religion. It seemed common sense to him but not to the rest of America or the Western world that consumed his books. Abandoned by all but confirmed deists during his last days, he went to his grave refusing to believe that religion—regardless of denomination—could actually provide as much sustenance as air, water, and food to the vast majority of Americans and millions around the world.

Viewing most mythology as mean-spirited lies, he failed to comprehend that churches successfully transported millions of his fellow beings to a different and wondrous world, bringing joy, beauty, and hope—ah, hope!—into some of the ugliest, meanest existences on earth. Dreams, fantasy, imagination, beauty, and hope seldom discriminate between truth and falsehood.

Mrs. Bonneville made the funeral arrangements for Paine. She bought a mahogany casket and attended the burial with at least one of her sons, Thomas. Some historians believe a second son, Benjamin, who later became a brigadier general in the US Army, also attended.

"Oh! Mr. Paine," biographer Conway reports Madame Bonneville as having said in French at the grave site. "My son stands here as testimony of the gratitude of America, and I for France!" Those were the only words reported at the burial. If either America or France harbored any gratitude toward Paine, neither nation expressed it. Madame Bonneville cited only "a few of Thomas Paine's friends" as having attended the burial, but a vicious report in the London *Packet* quoted what is said to have been a traveler's "letter dated June 20th from Philadelphia":

I met the funeral of Tom Paine on the road. . . . The followers were two negroes, the next a carriage with six drunken Irishmen, then a riding chair with two men in it . . . then an Irish Quaker on horseback. I stopped my sulky to ask what funeral it was; he said it was Paine, and that his friends as well as his enemies were all glad that he was gone, for he had tired his friends out by his intemperance and frailties. I told him that Paine had done a great deal of mischief in the world, and that, if there were any purgatory, he certainly would have a good share of it before the devil would let him go. The Quaker replied, he would sooner take his chance with Paine than any man in New York.[3]

In what may have been the last efforts to erase all traces of Thomas Paine and his words from the face of the earth, an English journalist, who had made a living attacking the United States and whose motive remains unclear, stole onto Paine's farm a decade later and dug up Paine's remains to take to England, where they were lost. Meanwhile, a barn in which Mrs. Bonneville's son Benjamin stored Paine's papers and possessions burned to the ground, and, as if God himself sought to cleanse the earth of Thomas Paine, a second fire—this one in York, Pennsylvania—consumed a collection of letters addressed to Paine, along with sizable piles of his books, many with his notes in the margins. Efforts by scholars have since recovered many and perhaps most of his works and letters from copies and duplicates in America, England, France, and elsewhere (see Appendix A, page 267), but church authorities, school boards, textbook publishers— even renowned historians and their publishers—have been relentless in marginalizing or eliminating Thomas Paine's name and his works—*Rights of Man* and, especially, *Age of Reason*—from the pages of American history books and the eyes and ears of Americans young and old.*

---

*Neither Jared Sparks nor Chief Justice John Marshall, both of them Washington intimates and two earliest biographers, mentioned Thomas Paine in their biographies. In the twentieth century, Douglas Southall Freeman, who won the Pulitzer Prize for his six-volume biography of Washington, also ignores Paine. After Freeman's death, his two aides finished a seventh volume to complete the work and mentioned Paine only in conjunction with Paine's "Letter to Washington," which they imply was part of French government efforts to undermine the American government. To this day, the most renowned historians—even those who mention Paine—omit mentioning *Age of Reason*.

There are only two statues and one bust of Paine in the United States. None of them are in the Hall of Fame for Great Americans or in Philadelphia or Washington. Both statues are in obscure New Jersey communities, one in Bordentown where he lived for a while, the other in Morristown. The bust of Paine sits atop a memorial column at his home in New Rochelle, New York, now a little-known "national landmark." France boasts one statue—in the Parc Montsouris on the southern edge of Paris. Its base bears the description (in English): "English by birth, French citizen by decree, and American by adoption." Although absent from Westminster Abbey for obvious reasons, two reminders of Paine do exist in England—a statue in Lewes, where he made many friends as a young exciseman, and

41. One of only three memorials in America to the forgotten Founding Father Thomas Paine, in New Rochelle, New York, on the site of Paine's farm at the Thomas Paine National Historical Association.

another statue on King Street in Thetford, his birthplace, where, to this day, there are those who consider him a traitor.

Efforts to erase Paine's name and writings from the world's literature have been constant since 1793, when George Chalmers wrote his mean-spirited biography, saying, "As a man, Paine has no moral character, and as a writer, he is entitled to no literary fame."[4]

But Paine was not only entitled to literary fame, it persisted, albeit tenuously at times, with reason overcoming superstition in the minds of the most literate. Indeed, his words continue to resonate across the American landscape among Americans with enough reason—and courage—to think independently. Essential at the founding of our republic, Thomas Paine's words remain as essential today to America's continued existence.

Listen!

A thousand years hence . . . perhaps in less, America may be what Europe now is. The innocence of her character that won the hearts of all nations in her favor may sound like a romance, and her inimitable virtue as if it had never been.

The ruins of that liberty for which thousands bled may just furnish materials for a village tale, or extort a sigh from rustic sensibility, whilst the fashionable of that day, enveloped in dissipation, shall deride the principles and deny the fact.

When we contemplate the fall of empire and the extinction of the nations of the ancient world, we see but little to excite our regret than the moldering ruins of pompous palaces, magnificent monuments, lofty pyramids and walls and towers of the most costly workmanship. But when the Empire of America shall fall, the subject for contemplative sorrow will be infinitely greater than crumbling brass and marble can inspire. It will not be said, here stood a temple of vast antiquity, here rose a Babel of invisible height, or there a palace of sumptuous extravagance; but here, ah painful thought! The noblest work of human wisdom, the grandest scene of human glory, the fair cause of freedom, rose and fell![5]

These are the times that try men's souls.

THE PRINCIPAL WORKS
OF THOMAS PAINE

Thomas Paine wrote well over 300 works, including 2 book-length works, more than 100 pamphlets and essays, at least 15 poems and songs, and more than 200 letters and memorials, many of the last being lengthy works with significant content. The most significant are listed below. More complete listings, with each work printed in full, can be found in one of two great compilations: Moncure Daniel Conway, *The Writings of Thomas Paine* (Dublin, Ireland: Merchant Books, 1896, 4 vols.), and Philip S. Foner, ed., *The Complete Writings of Thomas Paine* (Binghamton, NY: The Citadel Press, 1945, 2 vols.). More works by Paine may still be discovered.

1772

Case of the Officers of Excise

1775–1776

Pennsylvania Magazine or American Museum
The Magazine in America
Useful and Entertaining Hints
Reflections on Unhappy Marriages

1776

Common Sense
Epistle to the People Called Quakers [Appendix to 3rd edition of *Common Sense*]
The Forester's Letters [*Pennsylvania Journal*]
The American Crisis I ["These are the times that try men's souls."]

1777

Pennsylvania Journal
Retreat Across the Delaware
The American Crisis II. To Lord Howe
The American Crisis III
The American Crisis IV

1778

The American Crisis V. To Gen. Sir William Howe; To the Inhabitants of
   America
The Crisis VI. To the Earl of Carlisle, General Clinton, and William Eden, Esq.,
   British Commissioners in New York
Two Letters to Benjamin Franklin in Paris
The Crisis VII. To the People of England

1779

Pennsylvania Packet
To the Public on Mr. Deane's Affair
To the Editor: Messrs. Deane, Jay, and Gérard
Peace and the Newfoundland Fisheries

1780

The American Philosophical Society
The Crisis VIII. Addressed to the People of England
The Crisis IX
The Crisis Extraordinary
Public Good

1782

The Crisis X. On the King of England's Speech. To the People of America
The Crisis XI. On the Present State of News
A Supernumerary Crisis. To Sir Guy Carleton
The Crisis XII. To the Earl of Shelburne
Letter to the Abbé Raynal

1783

The Crisis XIII. Thoughts on the Peace and the Probable Advantages Thereof
A Supernumerary Crisis. To the People of America

1786

Dissertations on Government; the Affairs of the Bank; and Paper Money

1787

The Society for Political Inquiries
Prospects on the Rubicon

1788

Specification of Thomas Paine: Constructing Arches, Vaulter Roofs, and Ceilings [Iron Bridges]

1789

Letters to Jefferson in Paris

1791

Thomas Paine's Answer to Four Questions on the Legislative and Executive
Powers
Address and Declaration [to] Friends of Universal Peace and Liberty
A Republican Manifesto
To the Authors of *Le Républicain*
Rights of Man, Part First
To the Abbé Sièyes

1792

Rights of Man, Part Second
To the Attorney General
To Mr. Secretary Dundas
Letters to Lord Onslow
Letter Addressed to the Addressers on the Late Proclamation
Address to the People of France

Anti-Monarchal Essay (Royalty)
To the Attorney General, on the Prosecution Against the Second Part of *Rights of Man*
On the Propriety of Bringing Louis XVI to Trial

1793

Reasons for Preserving the Life of Louis Capet
Shall Louis XVI Be Respited?
Declaration of Rights
Letters to Jefferson
Letter to Danton
A Citizen of America to the Citizens of Europe

1794

Appeal to the Convention
The Memorial to Monroe
Le siècle de la raison (Paris)
The Age of Reason—Part First
Letters to James Monroe

1795

Observations on Jay's Treaty
Dissertation of First Principles of Government
The Constitution of 1795
The Age of Reason, Part Second

1796

Agrarian Justice
The Decline and Fall of the English System of Finance
Letter to George Washington

1797

Letter to Erskine on the Prosecution of *The Age of Reason*
The Existence of God
Worship and Church Bells
The Recall of Monroe

1798

Letter to the Council of Five Hundred

1800

Letters to Thomas Jefferson

1801

Letters to Thomas Jefferson
Maritime Compact: The Rights of Neutrals at Sea

1802

Proposal That Louisiana Be Purchased
Letter to Samuel Adams
Thomas Paine to the Citizens of the United States
    Letters I–V
Reply to the Bishop of Llandaff

1803

To the Citizens of the United States
    Letters VI–VII
The Construction of Iron Bridges

1804

To the French Inhabitants of Louisiana
Letters to the People of England
The Prospect Papers

1805

To the Citizens of the United States
    Letter VIII
Constitutional Reform: To the Citizens of Pennsylvania
On Constitutions, Governments, and Charters
Origin of Freemasonry

1806

Letter to Andrew Dean
On the Political and Military Affairs of Europe
Liberty of the Press
On the Cause of Yellow Fever
A Challenge to the Federalists
Liberty of the Press

1807

Observations on Gunboats
Ships of War, Gunboats, and Fortifications: Of Their Comparative Powers and
    Expense
To the People of New York
On Governor Lewis's Speech
On Mr. Hale's Resolutions
Three Letters to Morgan Lewis
On the Question, Will There Be War?
Examination of the Prophecies

1808

Memorial to the United States Senate

1809

Predestination
The Will of Thomas Paine

POSTMORTEM PUBLICATIONS

1811

Origin of Free-Masonry

1819

Songs and Rhymes [Miscellaneous Poems]. By Thomas Paine (London: R. Car-
    lisle, 1819)
Scientific Memoranda

AUTHOR'S NOTE

As of this writing, the Thomas Paine National Historical Association (TPNHA), of New Rochelle, New York, lists more than 100 additional, hitherto unknown works by Thomas Paine, and may yet discover more. The association also lists as "doubtful" at least a dozen works hitherto attributed to Paine. The association's determinations result from studies by a computer-driven "automatic authorship attribution" system devised by four scholars at the Institute for Thomas Paine Studies at Iona College, New Rochelle, who raised the accuracy of identifying authorship to nearly 90 percent, significantly improving results from previous author attribution methods.

Paine's use of pseudonyms, of course, makes it difficult—at times impossible—to determine with 100 percent certainty the authorship of all works attributed to him and the published articles yet to be identified as his. Computer programs will surely help, but they are only as accurate as the data put into them and the objectivity of the people who construct the programs and select the data. Developed in 2013 and improved in succeeding years, the automated authorship identification system of the Institute for Thomas Paine Studies has proved the most valuable tool available at this time for identifying documents that Thomas Paine did and did not write. Indeed, their arguments for "attributing" and "de-attributing" Paine works are convincing and difficult to refute. Among the most famous essays once thought to have been written by Paine but "deattributed" by the TPNHA are "African Slavery in America," "An Occasional Letter on the Female Sex," "Duelling," and "Thoughts on Defensive War."

The association's valuable work goes on.

Appendix B

THE AGE OF REASON
Contents and Summary

THE AGE OF REASON, PART FIRST

Chapter I—The Author's Profession of Faith [1]

"I believe in one God, and no more; I believe in the equality of man. . . . I do not believe in the creed professed . . . by any church. . . . My own mind is my own church. All churches appear to me no other than human inventions to terrify and enslave mankind and monopolize power and profit."

Chapter II—Of Missions and Revelations [2]

"Every national church or religion has established itself by pretending some special mission from God, communicated to certain individuals. The Jews have their Moses; the Christians their Jesus Christ, their apostles and saints; and the Turks their Mahomet. When Moses told the children of Israel that he received the two tablets of the commandments from the hand of God . . . they had no other authority for it than some historian telling them so; and I have no authority for it than some historian telling me so. . . . When I am told that the Koran was written in Heaven and brought to Mahomet by an angel, the account comes near the same . . . second hand authority as the former. I did not see the angel myself, and therefore I have a right not to believe it. When also I am told that a woman, called the Virgin Mary said, or gave out that she was with child without any cohabitation with a man and that her betrothed husband, Joseph, said that an angel told him so, I have a right to believe them or not; such a circumstance required a much stronger evidence than their bare word for it; but we have not even this; for neither Joseph nor Mary wrote any such matter themselves. It is only reported by others that *they said so*. It is hearsay upon hearsay, and I do not choose to rest my belief on such evidence. . . . Something revealed to a certain person and not . . . to any other . . . is revelation to that person only. When he tells it to a second, and a second to a third, it ceases to be a revelation. . . . It is *hearsay*."

Chapter III—Concerning the Character of Jesus Christ, and His History [3]

"Not a line of . . . the New Testament is of his writing. The history of him is altogether the work of other people. Historians who wrote of Jesus, centuries after he existed . . . brought him into the world of the New Testament in a supernatural manner. . . . That such a person as Jesus Christ existed and that he was crucified, which was the mode of execution at that day, are historical relations strictly within the limits of probability. He preached excellent morality and the equality of man. . . . But the resurrection of a dead person from the grave and his ascension through the air is a thing very different. . . . Not more than eight or nine . . . say they saw it, and all the rest of the world are called upon to believe it. . . . Thomas did not believe the resurrection. . . . So neither will I."

Chapter IV—Of the Bases of Christianity [4]

"The Christian mythologists, calling themselves the Christian Church, have erected their fable, which for absurdity and extravagance is not exceeded by anything . . . found in the mythology of the ancients. The ancient mythologists tell us that the race of Giants made war against Jupiter, and that one of them threw a hundred rocks against him . . . that Jupiter defeated him and confined him afterwards under Mount Etna. . . . The Christian mythologists tell that their Satan made war against the Almighty, who defeated him and confined him . . . in a pit . . . . the ancient and the Christian mythologists differ very little from each other."

Chapter V—Examination in Detail of the Preceding Bases [5]

"Putting aside everything that might excite laughter by its absurdity or detestation by its prophaneness [*sic*] . . . it is impossible to conceive a story more derogatory to the Almighty, more inconsistent with his wisdom, more contradictory to his power than this story is. [The Scriptures are] derogatory to the Almighty . . . The inventors call Satan a power equally as great, if not greater than ... the Almighty. ... They represent him as having compelled the Almighty to the *direct necessity* ... of coming down upon earth and exhibiting himself upon a cross in the shape of a man. Had the inventors of this story told it the contrary way, that is, had they represented the Almighty as compelling Satan to exhibit *himself* on a cross in the shape of a snake, as a punishment for his transgression, the story would have been less absurd, less contradictory. But, instead, they make the transgressor triumph and the Almighty fall."

Chapter VI—Of the True Ideology[6]

"Can our gross feelings be excited by no other subjects than tragedy and suicide? Or is the gloomy pride of man become so intolerable that nothing can flatter it but a sacrifice of the Creator?"

Chapter VII—Examination of the Old Testament[7]

"These books ... are, we are told, the word of God. It is, therefore, proper for us to know who told us so. The answer is ... nobody can tell. ... The church mythologists collected all the writings they could find ... added, altered, abridged, or dressed them up ... [and] decided by *vote* which of the books of the collection they had made should be the WORD OF GOD."

Chapter VIII—Of the New Testament[8]

"Had it been the object ... of Jesus Christ to establish a new religion, he would ... have written the system himself ... but there is no publication ... with his name. All the books called the New Testament were written after his death. He was a Jew by birth and ... in like manner that every other person is ... he was the son of God ... for the creator is the father of All. ... If Jesus Christ was the being which these mythologists tell us he was, and that he came into this world to *suffer* ... the only real suffering he could have endured would have been *to live*."

Chapter IX—In What the True Revelation Consists[9]

"The idea that God sent Jesus to publish ... the glad tidings to all nations from one end of the earth to the other is consistent only with the ignorance of those who know nothing of the extent of the world and who believed ... that the earth was flat ... and that a man could walk to the end of it. How was Jesus Christ to make anything known to all nations? He could speak but one language, which was Hebrew, and there are in the world several hundred languages. . . . As to translations, it is impossible to translate from one language to another . . . without losing a great part of the original. And besides all this . . . printing was wholly unknown at the time of Christ."

Chapter X—Concerning God, and the Lights Cast on His Existence[10]

"The only idea man can affix to the name of God is that of a first cause, *the cause of all things.* . . . It is only by the exercise of reason that man can discover God. . . . Every man is an evidence to himself that he did not make himself . . . and it is . . . from this evidence that carries us . . . to the belief of a first cause . . . and this first cause, man calls God. . . . Belief of first cause [arises] from the . . . difficulty of disbelieving it. It is difficult to conceive that space can have no end . . . but it is more difficult to conceive an end. It is difficult . . . to conceive an eternal duration of what we call time . . . but it is impossible to conceive a time when there shall be no time."

Chapter XI—Of the Theology of the Christians, and the True Theology[11]

"The Christian system of faith [is] a species of atheism, a . . . religious denial of God. It professes to believe in a man rather than in God. It introduces between man and his maker an opaque body which it calls a redeemer. . . . It has put the whole orbit of reason into shade. The effect of this obscurity has been that of turning everything upside down. . . . That which is called natural philosophy [physics], embracing the whole circle of science, of which astronomy occupies the chief place, is the study of the works of God . . . and is the true theology."

Chapter XII—The Effects of Christianism on Education; Proposed Reforms[12]

"Learning does not consist . . . in the knowledge of languages, but in the things to which language gives names. . . . The schools of the Greeks were schools of science and philosophy, and not of languages; and it is the knowledge of the things that science and philosophy teach that learning consists. . . . Supporters . . . of the Christian system . . . incessantly opposed and not only rejected the sciences, but persecuted the professors. . . . The age of ignorance commenced with the Christian system."

Chapter XIII—Comparison of Christianism with the Religious Ideas Inspired by Nature[13]

"The Christian story of God the father putting his son to death . . . cannot be told by a parent to a child; and to tell him that it was done to make mankind happier and better is making the story still worse; as if mankind could be improved by the example of murder; and to tell him that this is a mystery is only making an excuse for the incredibility of it. How different is this to the pure and simple profession of Deism! The true deist has but one Deity; and his religion consists in contemplating the power, wisdom, and benignity of the Deity in his works, and in endeavoring to imitate him in everything moral, scientifical, and mechanical."

Chapter XIV—System of the Universe[14]

"The Christian system that this world we inhabit is the whole of the habitable creation . . . [is] at once little and ridiculous. . . . Our solar system . . . immense as it is, is only one system of worlds. Beyond this . . . the immensity of space will appear . . . to be filled with systems of worlds."

Chapter XV—Advantages of the Existence of Many Worlds in Each Solar System[15]

"As the Creator made nothing in vain, so also must it be believed that he organized the structure of the universe . . . for the benefit of man."

Chapter XVI—Application of the Preceding to the System of the Christians[16]

"From whence could arise the solitary and strange conceit that the Almighty, who had millions of worlds equally dependent on his protection, should quit the care of all the rest and come to die in our world, because, they say, one man and one woman had eaten an apple! And . . . are we to suppose that every world . . . had an Eve, an apple, a serpent, and a redeemer? In this case, the person who is irreverently called the Son of God . . . would have nothing else to do than to travel from world to world in an endless succession of deaths, with scarcely a momentary interval of life. It has been by rejecting the evidence . . . that so many wild and whimsical systems of faith and of religion have been fabricated."

Chapter XVII—Of the Means Employed in All Time, and Almost Universally, to Deceive the Peoples[17]

"Those three means are Mystery, Miracle, and Prophecy. The first two are incompatible with true religion, and the third ought always to be suspected. Though every created thing is . . . a mystery, the word mystery cannot be applied to *moral* truth. . . . Mystery is the antagonist of truth. It is a fog of human invention that obscures truth. . . . When men, whether from policy or pious fraud, set up systems of religion . . . they were under the necessity of inventing or adopting a word that should serve as a bar to all questions, inquiries, and speculations. The word *mystery* answered this purpose. . . . As mystery . . . served to bewilder the mind, *miracle* followed to puzzle the senses. But unless we know the whole extent of . . . the powers of nature, we are not able to judge whether anything that may appear to us wonderful [is] miraculous. . . . As mystery and miracle took charge of the past and present, prophecy took charge of the future and rounded the tenses of faith. It was not sufficient to know what had been done, but what would be done. The supposed prophet was the supposed historian of times to come; and if he happened . . . to strike within a thousand miles of a mark, the ingenuity of posterity could make it point-blank; and if he happened to be directly wrong, it was only . . . that God had . . . changed his mind. What a fool do fabulous systems make of man!"

THE AGE OF REASON, PART SECOND

Preface[18]

Chapter I—The Old Testament[19]

"There are matters in that book, said to be done by the *express command* of God, that are . . . shocking to humanity and to every idea we have of moral justice. When we read in the books ascribed to Moses, Joshua, etc., that they (the Israelites) came by stealth upon whole nations of people, who . . . had given them no offense; *that they put all those nations to the sword; that they spared neither age nor infancy; that they utterly destroyed men, women, and children; that they left not a soul to breathe*; expressions that are repeated over and over again in those books and that too with exulting ferocity; are we sure these things are fact? Are we sure the Creator of man commissioned those things to be done? Are we sure that the books that tell us so were written by his authority?"

Chapter II—*The New Testament*[20]

"The New Testament, they tell us, is founded upon the prophecies of the Old. If so, it must follow the fate of its foundation. . . . The New Testament compared with the Old is like a farce of one act, in which there is not room for very numerous violations of the unities. There are, however, some glaring contradictions, which . . . are sufficient to show the story of Jesus Christ to be false. . . . We know from history that one of the principal leaders of this church, Athanasius [of Alexandria], lived at the time the New Testament was formed, and we know also from the absurd jargon he has left us . . . the character of the men who formed the New Testament; and we know also from the same history that the authenticity of the books . . . was denied at the time. It was upon the vote of such as Athanasius that the Testament was decreed to be the word of God; and nothing can present to us a more strange idea than that of decreeing the word of God by vote."

Chapter III—*Conclusion*[21]

"I here close the subject. I have shown in all the foregoing parts of this work that the Bible and the Testament are impositions and forgeries. . . . I leave the evidence I have produced (extracted from the books themselves) as proof of it to be refuted, if anyone can do it; certain as I am that when opinions are free, either in matters of government or religion, truth will finally and powerfully prevail."

Notes

Abbreviations used in the Notes below:

Thomas Paine	TP
The Complete Writings of Thomas Paine (Philip S. Foner, editor)	Foner
Moncure Daniel Conway, *The Life of Thomas Paine*	*TP Life*
Moncure Daniel Conway, *The Writings of Thomas Paine*	*TP Writings*
The Papers of George Washington, Revolutionary Series	PGWR
Thomas Clio Rickman, *The Life of Thomas Paine*	Rickman, *Life of TP*

INTRODUCTION

1. John Adams to Benjamin Waterhouse, October 29, 1805, Founders Online.

CHAPTER 1: CRIES OF PAINE

1. Thomas Paine [henceforth TP], *The Age of Reason*, in Moncure Daniel Conway, *The Writings of Thomas Paine* (Dublin, Ireland: Merchant Books, 1896, 4 vols.), 4:21–22. [Henceforth, *TP Writings*].

2. Moncure Daniel Conway, *Life of Thomas Paine* (New York: G. P. Putnam's Sons, 1892, 2 vols.), 1:11. [Henceforth, *TP Life*].

3. TP, *Rights of Man* (Mineola, NY: Dover Publications, 1999), 151.

4. *Notes and Queries, A Medium of Communication for Literary Men, General Readers. Etc.* (London, September 27, 1873), cited in *TP Life*,1:9.

5. TP, *Common Sense, Addressed to the Inhabitants of America* (Philadelphia: R. Bell, 1776), 6. [Henceforth, *Common Sense*].

6. *Common Sense*, 11.

7. TP, *The Crisis III* in *The Political Works of Thomas Paine* (Springfield, MA: Tannatt & Co., 1826), 253.

8. Ibid., 14.

9. *Common Sense*, 38.

10. Ibid.

11. *TP Writings*, 4:67–68.

12. Thomas Clio Rickman, *Life of Thomas Paine* (London: Thomas Clio Rickman, 1819), 36. [Henceforth, *Life of TP*].

13. Ibid., 37.

14. *TP Life*, 1:18.

15. Rickman, *Life of TP*, 41–42.

16. Ibid., 31.

17. Ibid., 45.

18. Ibid., 38.

19. Ibid.

20. Ibid.

21. "Farmer Short's Dog Porter: A Tale," Philip S. Foner, ed., *The Complete Writings of Thomas Paine* (New York: Citadel Press, 1945, 2 vols.) 1:1084–1088 [Henceforth, Foner].

22. "Rules by Which a Great Empire May Be Reduced to a Small One," *Public Advertiser*, London, September 11, 1773.

23. Benjamin Franklin to Richard Bache, September 30, 1774, in Benjamin Franklin, *The Life of Benjamin Franklin By Himself* (Cambridge: Cambridge University Press, 3 vols., 1874), 2:248.

24. TP to Benjamin Franklin, March 4, 1775, *The Papers of Benjamin Franklin* (New Haven, CT: Yale University Press, 1978– [multiple volumes, in progress]), 21:515–518.

25. TP to Benjamin Franklin, March 4, 1775, Founders Online.

26. Benjamin Rush, M.D., to Thomas Clio Rickman, July 17, 1809, Rickman, *Life of TP*, 49–55.

27. "African Slavery in America," *TP Writings*, 1:4–9.

28. *TP Life*, 1:41.

29. Rickman, *Life of TP*, 1.

30. TP to Benjamin Franklin, March 4, 1775, Founders Online.

31. "An Occasional Letter on the Female Sex," *TP Writings*, 1:59–64.

32. "Dueling," *TP Writings*, 1:40–45.

33. Rickman, *Life of TP*, 56–57.

34. A Lover of Peace [Thomas Paine], "Thoughts on a Defensive War," *Pennsylvania Magazine*, July 1775, 328–329.

35. Ibid.

36. Ibid.

37. Benjamin Rush, M.D., to Thomas Clio Rickman, July 17, 1809, Rickman, *Life of TP*, 49–55.

CHAPTER 2: *COMMON SENSE*

1. *Common Sense*, 27.

2. Benjamin Rush, M.D., *The Autobiography of Benjamin Rush* (Philadelphia: American Philosophical Society, 1948), 112.

3. *Common Sense*, 22, 34.

4. Ibid., 72.

5. Rush, *Autobiography*, 113–114.

6. *Common Sense*, 83.

7. Mark Puls, *Samuel Adams, Father of the American Revolution* (New York: Palgrave Macmillan, 2006).

8. Rush, *Autobiography*, 114.

9. *Common Sense*, 2.

10. Ibid., 10.

11. Ibid., 9.

12. Ibid., 14.

13. Ibid., 15.

14. TP, *Rights of Man*, 53.

15. Ibid., 83.

16. Ibid., 73.

17. Ibid., 123, 104.

18. *TP Life*, 1:304.

19. "The Magazine in America," *TP Writings*, 1:14–19.

20. *Common Sense*, 19.

21. Ibid., 20.

22. Benjamin Franklin to James Parker, March 20, 1750, *Papers of Benjamin Franklin*, 4:117–121.

23. Ibid.

24. Ibid., 95, 72.

25. George Washington to Lieutenant Colonel Joseph Reed, January 31, 1776; W. W. Abbott, Dorothy Twohig, Philander D. Chase, and Theodore J. Crackel, eds., *The Papers of George Washington: Revolutionary Series* (Charlottesville: University Press of Virginia, 1985– [multiple volumes, in progress], 18 vols. to date), 3:225–229. [Henceforth, PGWR].

26. *Common Sense*, 20.

27. Ibid., 35.

28. Ibid., 36.

29. Ibid., 40.

30. Ibid., 33.

31. Ibid., 54.

32. Ibid., 55–56.

33. John Durand, ed., *New Materials for the History of the American Revolution . . . from Documents in the French* [government] *Archives* (New York: Henry Holt, 1889), 169.

34. Ibid.

35. Teresa O'Neill, ed., *Opposing Viewpoints: The American Revolution*, American History Series (San Diego: Greenhaven Press, 1992), 151; see also Sidney Kobre, "The Revolutionary Colonial Press—A Social Interpretation," *Journalism Quarterly* 20 (1943): 194, 202; and *Development of American Journalism* (Dubuque, Iowa: W. C. Brown, 1969), 53–100.

36. TP, "The Forester," *Pennsylvania Journal*, March 28, 1776.

37. John Adams to James Warren, May 12, 1776, Founders Online.

38. John Adams, *Thoughts on Government: Applicable to the Present State of the American Colonies* (Philadelphia: John Dunlop, 1776).

39. Harlow Giles Unger, *First Founding Father: Richard Henry Lee and the Call for Independence* (Boston: Da Capo Press, 2017).

40. Joseph Reed, in Douglas Southall Freeman, *George Washington* (New York: Charles Scribner's Sons, 1951, 7 vols.), 4:198.

CHAPTER 3: THE TIMES THAT TRY MEN'S SOULS

1. Freeman, *George Washington*, 4:194n.

2. Thomas Paine, "Retreat Across the Delaware," *Pennsylvania Journal*, January 29, 1777. [The newspaper editor printed a note with Paine's article, attributing its late appearance to the suspension of publication in the face of the British threat to Philadelphia.]

3. George Washington to John Hancock, November 19–21, 1776, PGWR, 7:180–186.

4. Frank Moore, *Diary of the American Revolution from Newspapers and Original Documents* (New York: Charles Scribner, 1860, 2 vols.), 1:350.

5. TP, "Retreat Across the Delaware," *Pennsylvania Journal*, January 29, 1777.

6. TP Writings, *The Crisis II* (New York: G. P. Putnam's Sons, 1906, 4 vols.), 1:185.

7. TP, "The American Crisis Number I, by the Author of COMMON SENSE," in *TP Writings*, 1:178.

8. George Washington to John Augustine Washington, November 16–19, 1776, PGWR, 7:102–105.

9. TP, "Retreat Across the Delaware."

10. George Washington to Lund Washington, December 10–17, 1776, PGWR, 7:289–292.

11. TP, *Crisis I*, *TP Writings*, 1:170–179.

12. Foner, 1:17.

13. Robert Morris to Silas Deane, August 11, 1776, *The Deane Papers*, Collections of the New-York Historical Society for the year 1886 (1887), 19:174.

14. Louis de Loménie, *Beaumarchais et son temps: Études sur la société en France au XVIIIe siècle* (Paris: Michel Lévy Frères, 2 vols., 1856.), 97.

15. Loménie, *Beaumarchais et son temps*, 266.

16. Henri Doniol, *Histoire de la participation de la France à l'établissement des États-Unis d'Amérique* (Paris: Imprimerie Nationale, 1886, 5 vols.), 1:407.

17. TP, *Crisis I*, *TP Writings*, 1:176–177.

18. Ibid., 171.

19. Ibid., 178.

20. Ibid.

21. Ibid., 173–174.

22. Colonel Joseph Reed to George Washington, December 22, 1776, PGWR, 7:414–417.

23. TP, *Crisis I*, *TP Writings*, 1:176.

24. Ibid., 170.

25. Ibid.

26. Ibid., 170–179.

27. *TP Writings*, 1:180.

28. Ibid., 189.

29. George Washington to Colonel Joseph Reed, December 23, 1776, PGWR, 7:423–424.

30. John Adams to James Warren, May 12, 1776, Founders Online.

31. John Adams, *The Diary and Autobiography of John Adams*, L. H. Butterfield, ed. (New York: Atheneum, 1964, 4 vols.), 3:334.

32. Rickman, *Life of TP*, 64, 66.

33. Ibid., 68.

CHAPTER 4: AMERICAN CRISIS

1. "Proclamation Concerning Persons Swearing British Allegiance [Morristown, January 25, 1777], By His Excellency George Washington . . . ," PGWR, 8:152–153.

2. *TP Writings*, 1:196–229.

3. Thompson Westcott, *A History of the "Test Laws" of Pennsylvania* (Philadelphia: John Campbell, 1865), xviii.

4. *TP Writings*, 1:196–229.

5. George Washington to John Hancock, February 20, 1777, PGWR, 8:381–383.

6. George Washington to Richard Henry Lee, May 17, 1777, PGWR, 9:453–454.

7. Francis Wharton, ed., *Revolutionary Diplomatic Correspondence of the United States* (Washington, D.C.: Government Printing Office, 1889, 6 vols.), 2:250.

8. Richard Henry Lee, *The Life of Arthur Lee, LL.D.* (Boston: Wells and Lilly, 1829, 2 vols.), 2:124, 127–128.

9. Wharton, *Revolutionary Diplomatic Correspondence*, 2:424.

10. *TP Writings*, 1:229–232.

11. TP to Benjamin Franklin, May 16, 1778, Foner, 1:1143–1154.

12. Adams, September 18, 1777, *Diary*, 2:265.

13. Adams, *Diary*, 4:1.

14. TP to Benjamin Franklin (two letters), May 16, 1778, Founders Online.

15. Ibid.

16. Ibid.

17. Ibid.

18. Thomas Conway to Horatio Gates, January 4, 1778, Robert Douthat Meade, *Patrick Henry, Practical Revolutionary* (New York: Lippincott, 1969), 185.

19. George Washington to Patrick Henry, March 27, 1778, ibid., 328–329.

20. Ibid., March 28, 1778, 336–337.

21. *TP Writings*, 1:233–252.

22. Ibid.

23. TP to George Washington, January 1779, Founders Online.

24. Harlow Giles Unger, *Lafayette* (Hoboken, NJ: John Wiley, 2002), 72.

25. George Washington to John Augustine Washington, July 4, 1778, PGWR, 16:25–26.

26. "The American Crisis VI," Foner, 2:133; *TP Writings*, 1:261–271.

27. *TP Writings*, 1:261–271.

28. Ibid., 271–293.

29. Ibid.

30. Ibid.

31. Thomas Paine, "The Affair of Silas Deane," in the *Pennsylvania Packet*, December 15, 1778; "To the Public on Mr. Deane's Affair, *Pennsylvania Packet*, December 31, 1778, *TP Writings*, 1:395–408, 409–437.

32. Ibid.

33. Statement of Robert Morris "To the Public," *The Deane Papers* (New York: Collections of the New-York Historical Society for the year 1888 (1889) 3:260–266. See also Charles Rappleye, *Robert Morris, Financier of the American Revolution* (New York: Simon & Schuster, 2010), 170–171.

34. Ibid.

35. George Washington to Benjamin Harrison, December 18, 1778, PGWR, 18:447–452.

36. Benjamin Franklin to Robert Morris [undated], *The Works of Benjamin Franklin* (New York: G. P. Putnam's Sons, 1904, 12 vols.), 9:14.

37. *Pennsylvania Packet*, December 24, 1778.

38. Francis Lightfoot Lee to Richard Henry Lee, December 22, 1778, Lee Family Digital Archive.

39. Worthington Chauncy Ford et al., ed., *Journals of the Continental Congress, 1774–1789* (Washington, D.C.: US Government Printing Office, 1904–1937, 34 vols.), 13:31–36.

40. Rickman, *Life of TP*, 69.

41. W. T. Sherwin, *Memoirs of the Life of Thomas Paine* (London: R. Carlile, 1819), 69.

42. TP to Congress, January 7, 1779, *TP Life*, 1:151.

43. Ford et al., *Journals of the Continental Congress*, January 8, 1779, 13:54.

44. Beatrix Cary Davenport, ed., *A Diary of the French Revolution by Gouverneur Morris, 1752–1816* (Boston: Houghton Mifflin, 1939, 2 vols.), 2:370, 159.

45. James Madison, *Debates on the Adoption of the Federal Constitution in the Convention Held at Philadelphia in 1787* (Philadelphia: J. B. Lippincott, 1901), 283.

46. Ibid., 13:75.

CHAPTER 5: CAN NOTHING BE DONE FOR POOR PAINE?

1. TP to Henry Laurens, September 14, 1779, *TP Life*, 1:168–171.

2. Ibid.

3. George Washington to the President of Congress, January 5, 1780, *The Writings of George Washington, from the Original Manuscript Sources, 1745–1799*, John C. Fitzpatrick, ed. (Washington, D.C.: U.S. Government Printing Office, 1931–1944, 39 vols.), 17:355–358.

4. TP to Blair McClenaghan [?], [Philadelphia], May 1780 [?], Foner, 2:1183–1185.

5. *TP Life*, 1:176–177.

6. *The Crisis VIII*, *TP Writings*, 293–300.

7. *The Crisis IX*, *TP Writings*, 301–306.

8. Ibid., *The Crisis Extraordinary*, 1:306–323, esp. 308–312.

9. Ibid.

10. TP to Gen. Nathanael Green, *TP Life*, 191–193.

11. Ibid.

12. Foner, 2:1234–1235.

13. TP to Jonathan Williams, November 26, 1781, *The Deane Papers*, Collections of the New-York Historical Society for the year 1889 (1890), 22:543–544.

14. TP to George Washington, November 30, 1781, *TP Life*, 1:199–202.

15. *TP Life*, 203–204.

16. *The Crisis XIII*, *TP Writings*, 370–376.

17. Ibid.

18. TP "To a Committee of the Continental Congress," *Journals of Congress*, October 2, 1783, 2:1242.

19. George Washington to TP, September 10, 1783, *The Writings of George Washington*, 27:146–147.

20. "A Representation of the Services of Thomas Paine, 1783," *Mss.*, New-York Historical Society, in Foner, 1:xxiii.

21. TP to George Washington, April 28, 1784, Foner, 2:1248–1249. [Eighteen of Paine's poems and song lyrics may be found in *TP Writings*, 2:477–498 and Foner, 2:1083–1106.]

22. George Washington to Richard Henry Lee, June 12, 1784, *The Writings of George Washington*, 27:422–423.

23. George Washington to James Madison, June 12, 1784, ibid., 27:420–421.

24. "To the People of America, December 9, 1783, *TP Life*, 1:223.

25. TP to Benjamin Franklin, December 31, 1785, ibid., 1:238–239.

26. Ibid., June 6, 1786, 1:242.

27. *Rights of Man*, 73.

28. Ibid., 82–88.

29. TP to My Dear Father and Mother, New York, September 11, 1785, *TP Writings*.

30. Maj. Gen. Henry [Light-Horse Harry] Lee, Jr., to GW, October 1, 1786, PGWR Confed., 4:281–282.

31. Madison, *Debates on the Adoption of the Federal Constitution*, 283.

CHAPTER 6: MONEY IS MONEY; PAPER IS PAPER

1. TP, *Dissertations on Government; the Affairs of the Bank; and Paper Money*, Foner, 2:376ff.

2. Harlow Giles Unger, *John Marshall: The Chief Justice Who Saved the Nation* (Boston: Da Capo Press, 2014), 323.

3. TP, *Dissertations on Government; the Affairs of the Bank*, 2:369–414, esp. 369; Rickman, *Life of TP*, 81–82.

4. TP, "Letters on the Bank," June 20, 1786, *TP Writings*, 2:432.

5. Smilie, writing pseudonymously as "Atticus," in *Freeman's Journal*, May 3, 1786.

6. TP to Benjamin Franklin, March 31, 1787, Foner, 2:1260–1261.

7. TP to George Clymer, August 15, 1787, Foner, 2:1264.

8. TP to Kitty Nicholson Few, January 6, 1789, Foner, 2:1274.

9. Specification of Thomas Paine, A.D. 1788, No. 1667, "Construction Arches, Vaulted Roofs, and Ceilings, *TP Writings*, 2:227–230.

10. TP to Jefferson, June 17, 1789, Foner, 2:1292.

11. Ibid., December 23, 1788; Julian P. Boyd, ed., *The Papers of Thomas Jefferson* (Princeton, NJ: Princeton University Press, 1960– [multiple volumes, in progress]), 14:14:454.

12. TP, "Prospects on the Rubicon," *TP Writings*, 2:191–226, esp. 194–195.

13. Ibid.

14. Article carrying an October dateline, published in *Gazette of the United States*, January 5, 1791.

15. TP to Thomas Jefferson, February 26, 1789, *TP Life*, 1:259.

16. TP to Thomas Walker, April 14, 1790, W. H. G. Armytage, "Thomas Paine and the Walkers: An Early Episode in Anglo-American Co-operation, *Pennsylvania History: A Journal of Mid-Atlantic Studies* 18, no. 1 (University Park: Pennsylvania State University Press, 1951), 16–30.

17. TP to George Washington, October 16, 1789, *Papers of George Washington, Presidential Series*, Dorothy Twohig, ed. (Charlottesville: University Press of Virginia, 1993– [multiple volumes, in progress]), 4:196–198.

CHAPTER 7: CITIZEN PAINE

1. Thomas Jefferson to TP, July 11, 1789, Boyd, *Papers of Thomas Jefferson*, 15:266.

2. TP, "Rights of Man," *TP Writings*, 291–292.

3. Unger, *Lafayette*, 236–237.

4. Jean Tulard, Jean-François Fayard, Alfred Fierro, *Histoire et Dictionnaire de la Révolution Française, 1789–1799* (Paris: Robert Laffont, 1987), 54.

5. Davenport, *A Diary by Gouverneur Morris*, 1:158–159.

6. Edmund Burke to TP [undated], David Freeman Hawke, *Paine* (New York: Harper & Row, 1974), 201.

7. R. R. Fennessy, *Burke, Paine, and the Rights of Man: A Difference of Political Opinion* (The Hague, Holland: Martinus Nijhoff, 1963), 103 ff.

8. TP to Anonymous, March 16, 1790, Foner, 2:1285–1286.

9. TP to George Washington, May 1, 1790, *TP Life*, 1:273–275.

10. Hawke, *Paine*, 216.

11. *TP Writings*, 275 ff., esp. 275–276.

12. Ibid.

13. *TP Life*, 2:445.

14. Armytage, "Thomas Paine and the Walkers," 29 n163.

15. *TP Writings*, 2:295.

16. Ibid., 305.

17. Ibid., 308.

18. Ibid., 312, 313–314.

19. Ibid.

20. Ibid., 323.

21. Ibid., 316.

22. Ibid., 351–353.

23. Ibid.

24. Ibid.

25. TP to William Short, November 12, 1791, Foner, 2:1320–1322.

26. James Madison to Thomas Jefferson, July 13, 1790, *TP Life*, 1:299.

27. TP to George Washington, July 21, 1791, *TP Life*, 1:302.

28. Rickman, *Life of TP*, 84.

29. Ibid.; TP, "A Republican Manifesto," July 1, 1791, *TP Life*, 1:308–310.

30. Danton, June 21, 1791, Proceedings of *La Société de Jacobins*, in Étiènne Charavay, *Le Général La Fayette, 1757–1834* (Paris: Société de la Révolution Française, 1898), 269–270.

31. Hawke, *Paine*, 227.

CHAPTER 8: A TALE OF TWO CITIES

1. *TP Writings*, 3: 1–3.

2. TP, "Letter to the Abbé Sièyes," in *Le Moniteur* , July 8, 1791; *TP Writings*, 3:9–10.

3. *TP Life*, 1:315–319.

4. Rickman, *Life of TP*, 87–88.

5. Ibid., xv.

6. Ibid., 100–101.

7. TP to John Hall, November 25, 1791, Foner, 2:1321–1322.

8. *TP Writings*, 2:392–393.

9. Ibid., 398.

10. Davenport, *A Diary by Gouverneur Morris*, 2:367–368.

11. Rickman, *Life of TP*, 179.

12. TP to Mr. Jordan, February 16, 1792, *TP Life*, 335–336.

13. *TP Life*, 1:337. [Au. Note: Unable to authenticate; letter is *not* included in *Papers of George Washington, Presidential Series* or Davenport, *A Diary by Gouverneur Morris*.]

14. *TP Life*, 1:342.

15. *TP Writings*, 2:415 ff.

16. Fennessy, *Burke, Paine*, 243.

17. Gouverneur Morris to George Washington, December 27, 1791, Davenport, *A Diary by Gouverneur Morris*, 2:332–333.

18. *The Times*, July 12, 1792.

19. *Le Moniteur*, August 28, 1792.

20. Hawke, *Paine*, 252, citing Archives Nationales, C 180.

21. Alexander Gilchrist, *Life of William Blake* (London: John Lane, 1907), 94.

22. Foner, 1:352.

23. Marie-Jean Hérault de Seychelles to TP, *TP Life*, 2:438–439.

24. Lafayette to the National Assembly, June 16, 1792 (read on June 18), George-Washington Lafayette [Gilbert Motier, Marquis de Lafayette], *Mémoires, Correspondence et Manuscrits du Générale Lafayette, publiés par sa famille* (Paris: H. Fournier, ainé, 6 vols., 1837), 1:450–452.

25. Lord Fortescue to William Augustus Miles, September 26, 1792, *The Correspondence of William Augustus Miles on the French Revolution* (London: Longmans, Green and Co., 1890, 2 vols.), 1:334.

26. Paine to the National Assembly, Foner, 2:537–540.

27. Davenport, *A Diary by Gouverneur Morris*, 2:540

28. Tulard et al., *Histoire et Dictionnaire de la Révolution Française*, 348–350.

29. TP, "Address to the People of France," Foner, 2:537–540.

30. Ibid., 540.

31. Tulard et al., *Histoire et Dictionnaire de la Révolution Française*, 348–350.

32. Ibid.

33. Robespierre to the Convention, M. J. Mavidal and M. E. Laurent, eds., *Archives parlementaires de 1787 à 1860, première série, 1787–1799* (Paris: Dupont, 1879–1913, 82 vols.), 5356:32426.

34. Decree of Fraternity, November 19, 1792. *Archives Parliamentaire de 1784–1860, Receuil Complet des Débats Politiques des Chambres Françaises, Première Série (1787–1799)* (Paris: Société de l'Imprimerie et Librairie Administratives et de Chemins de Fer, Paul Dupont, 1879), Tome 53, 838.

35. Ibid.

36. Ibid.

37. TP, "Address to the People of France," September 25, 1792, Foner, 2:537–540.

38. Ibid.

39. Ibid.

40. Ibid.

41. Ibid.

42. Rickman, *Life of TP*, 124.

43. Ibid., 127.

44. TP, in Thomas Clio Rickman, "An Address Delivered Before the Convention," *The Life and Writings of Thomas Paine* (New York: Vincent Parke, 1908, 8 vols.), 5:812.

45. Ibid.

46. Lisa Plummer Crafton, ed., *The French Revolution Debate in English Literature and Culture* (Westport, CT: Greenwood Press, 1997), 27.

47. "Shall Louis XVI Be Respited," Proceedings of the French National Convention, January 19, 1793, Foner, 2:555–558.

48. Lord Fortescue to W. A. Miles, September 26, 1792, *TP Life*, 2:17.

49. *The Age of Reason, Part Second*, "Preface," Foner, 1:516.

CHAPTER 9: THE TERROR

1. Morris to Jefferson, January 25, 1793, Davenport, *A Diary by Gouverneur Morris*, 2:601–602.

2. TP to Danton, May 6, 1793, Foner, 2:1335–1338.

3. Ibid.

4. TP to Jefferson, April 20, 1793, Foner, 2:1330–1332.

5. TP to Samuel Adams, January 1, 1802, Foner, 2:1434–1438.

6. *TP Life*, 2:130.

7. TP to Lady Smyth, "Forgetfulness, from the Castle in the Air to the Little Corner of the World" [undated, ca. 1794], Foner, 2:1120–1126.

8. *TP Life*, 2:69.

9. "Forgetfulness," Foner, 2:1124.

10. Foner, 1:465–467.

11. Ibid., 474.

12. Ibid.

13. TP to Samuel Adams, January 1, 1802, Foner, 2:1434–1438.

14. TP to Thomas Jefferson, April 20, 1793, Foner, 2: 1330–1332.

15. TP to George Washington, July 30, 1796, Foner, 2:691–723, esp. 698–699.

16. *TP Life*, 2:109.

17. Thomas Paine to Gouverneur Morris, February 24, 1794, Foner, 2:1338–1339.

18. Rickman, *Life of TP*, 162–163.

19. Mémoires sur les prisons, qui concernent les prisons de Port-Libre, du Luxembourg, de la rue de Sèvres, etc., etc. (Paris: Baudouin Frères, 1823, 2 vols.), 2:153.

20. *TP Life*, 25.

21. Ibid., 29.

22. Ibid., 6–7.

23. Ibid., 15.

24. Ibid., 29, 30.

25. Ibid.

26. Thomas Jefferson, *Syllabus of an Estimate of the Merit of the Doctrines of Jesus Compared with Those of Others*, Washington, April 21, 1803, enclosed with letter to Benjamin Rush, *The Letters of Thomas Jefferson, 1743–1826* (Electronic Textcenter of University of Virginia).

27. Statutes at Large, First Congress, Session II, p. 103.

28. *TP Life*, 2:130.

CHAPTER 10: IN THE NAME OF RELIGION

1. *TP Writings*, 4:24.

2. Ibid., 34.

3. Ibid., 34.

4. *TP Writings*, 4:103.

5. Ibid., 102–103.

6. Rickman, *Life of TP*, 158.

7. TP to the National Convention, August 7, 1794, Foner, 2:1339–1341.

8. *TP Writings*, 4:167.

9. Ibid.

10. Ibid., 153.

11. Ibid., 571–572.

12. Ibid., 574–575.

13. Ibid., 158–159.

14. *TP Writings*, 4:40.

15. Achille Audibert to Citizen Thuriot of the Committee of Public Safety, August 20, 1794, *TP Life*, 2:139–140.

16. *TP Writings*, 4:113.

17. TP to James Monroe, August 17, 1794, Foner, 2:1341–1342.

18. *TP Writings*, 4:32–33.

19. Ibid., August 18, 1794, 2:1342–1343.

20. James Monroe to the president of the National Convention, August 13, 1794, James Monroe, *The Writings of James Monroe*, Stanislaus Murray Hamilton, ed. (New York: G. P. Putnam's Sons, 1898–1903, 7 vols.), 2:11–12.

21. Ibid., James Monroe to the National Convention, August 14, 1794, 2:13–15.

22. Ibid., 34n.

23. Ibid., August 25, 1794, 2:1343–1344.

24. TP to Monroe, Foner, 2:1345–1354.

25. Ibid.

26. Ibid.

27. Monroe to TP, ibid., September 18, 1794, Daniel Preston, *A Comprehensive Catalogue of the Correspondence and Papers of James Monroe* (Westport, CT: Greenwood Press, 2001, 2 vols.), 1:34; *TP Life*, 2:147.

28. *TP Life*, 2:147.

29. TP to James Monroe, October 13, 1794, Foner, 2:1357–1363.

30. James Monroe to James Madison, January 20, 1796, *Writings of James Monroe*, 2:440–447.

31. Ibid.

32. *TP Writings*, 4:192n–193n.

33. Ibid., 4:185.

34. Ibid., 4:194.

35. Ibid.

CHAPTER 11: A LETTER TO WASHINGTON

1. James Monroe to Edmund Randolph, November 7, 1794, *Life of TP*, 2:151.

2. James Monroe, *The Autobiography of James Monroe* (Syracuse, NY: Syracuse University Press, 1959), 72.

3. James Monroe to the Secretary of State Edmund Randolph, November 7, 1794, *Writings of James Monroe*, 2:98–108.

4. TP to James Madison, September 24, 1795, Foner, 2:1378–1381.

5. Ibid., 155.

6. TP, *Dissertation on First Principles of Government*, July 1795, Foner, 2:570–588.

7. Ibid.

8. TP, Speech in the French National Convention, July 7, 1795, on the Constitution of 1795, Foner, 2:588–594.

9. *TP Writings*, 4:39–40.

10. Ibid., 4:34–45.

11. Ibid., 4:45–50.

12. Ibid., 4:51–65.

13. Ibid.; Rickman, *Life of TP*, 191.

14. James Monroe to James Madison, January 20, 1796, *Writings of James Monroe*, 2:440–447.

15. Ibid.

16. TP to James Madison, September 24, 1795, Foner, 2:1378–1381.

17. James Monroe to the Secretary of State, February 16, 1796, *Writings of James Monroe*, 2:454–456.

18. Letter to George Washington, July 30, 1796, Foner, 2:691–723, esp. 720.

19. Ibid.

20. George Washington to David Stuart, January 8, 1797, Fitzpatrick, *Writings of Washington*, 35:357–360.

21. Rickman, *Life of TP*, 164–165.

22. *Agrarian Justice*, January-February, 1796, Foner, 1:609–623.

23. Ibid.

24. Ibid.

25. Ibid., 320.

26. Rickman, *Life of TP*, 132–133.

27. Ibid., 164n.

28. TP to the Council of Five Hundred, January 28, 1798, Foner, 2:1403.

29. TP, "Of Gunboats," in Foner, 2:1067–1072.

30. *Archives Nationales*, cited in Hawke, 338.

31. TP to Thomas Jefferson, October 1, 1800, Foner, 2:1406–1412.

32. Adams, *Diary & Autobiography*, July 26, 1796, 3:244.

33. TP to Thomas Jefferson, October 1, 1800, Foner, 2:1406–1412.

34. Robert Livingston to TP [original source missing], cited in *TP Life*, 2:446.

35. William Woodward, *Paine: America's Godfather* (New York: E. P. Dutton, 1945), 309; *Gazette of the United States*, July 21, 1801.

36. Rickman, *Life of TP*, 166–167.

CHAPTER 12: FALLEN IDOL

1. TP to Thomas Clio Rickman, March 8, 1803, Foner, 2:1439–1440.

2. Major-General Henry Lee, *Funeral Oration on the Death of General Washington* (Boston: Joseph Nancrede and Manning & Loring, 1800).

3. TP, "To the Citizens of the United States and Particularly to the Federal Faction, Letter I, *The National Intelligencer*, November 15, 1802, Foner, 2:909–912.

4. TP, "To the Citizens of the United States and Particularly to the Federal Faction, Letter II, *The National Intelligencer*, November 19, 1802, Foner, 2:912–918.

5. TP to Thomas Jefferson, November 1802, Foner, 2:1429–1430.

6. *TP Life*, 2:309n.

7. *Baltimore Republican*, October 18, 1802.

8. Benjamin Rush to Thomas Clio Rickman, July 17, 1809, in Rickman, *Life of TP*, 49–55.

9. Rickman, *Life of TP*, 6–7.

10. Ibid., 4.

11. Ibid., 7.

12. Ibid.

13. Ibid., 120–121.

14. Foner, 2:524.
15. Rickman, *Life of TP*, 112, 114.
16. Ibid.
17. Ibid., 40–42.
18. Ibid., 60–61.
19. Ibid., 70.
20. *Age of Reason, Part Second*, 89.
21. Foner, 2:532.
22. Ibid., 570–571.
23. Ibid., 571.
24. Ibid., 584.
25. Ibid., 239.
26. Rickman, *Life of TP*, 170.
27. Ibid.
28. Foner, 2:601–602.
29. *Columbian Centinel*, August 22, 1801; *New York Evening Post*, January 10, 1803.
30. *The National Aegis*, December 15, 1802.
31. Rickman, *Life of TP*, 12.
32. TP "To the Citizens of the United States, Letter IV," December 3, 1802, Foner, 2:927–928.

CHAPTER 13: TO RESCUE MAN FROM TYRANNY

1. *TP Life*, 2:341–342.
2. [Philadelphia] *Aurora*, December 9, 1802.
3. TP to Thomas Jefferson, January 1, 1805, Foner, 2:1453–1455.
4. Ibid., January 25, 1805, Foner, 2:1456–1464.
5. Ibid.
6. TP to John Fellows, July 31, 1805, Foner, 2:1469–1471.
7. *TP Writings*, 4:309.
8. "The Tower of Babel," Foner, 2:795–796.
9. *TP Writings*, 4:307.
10. *TP Writings*, 4:307–308.
11. Rickman, *Life of TP*, 172.
12. Ibid., 4:243.
13. *TP Writings*, 4:249.
14. TP, "Remarks on English Affairs," *Baltimore Evening Post*, July 9, 1805.
15. TP, "Constitutional Reform," Foner, 2:999.
16. TP to Thomas Jefferson, September 30, 1805, Foner, 2:1472–1473.

17. TP to John Inskeep, Mayor of the City of Philadelphia, [Philadelphia] *Aurora*, February 10, 1806.

18. TP to George Clinton, May 4, 1807, Foner, 1:1487–1488.

19. William Carver to TP, December 2, 1806, Keane, 514.

20. Rickman, *Life of TP*, 181.

21. [George Chalmers] Francis Oldys, A. M., *The Life of Thomas Pain* [sic], *the Author of the Seditious Writings, Entitled Rights of Man* (London: John Stockdale, 1793), 17.

22. *TP Life*, 2:390–391.

23. Diary of Daniel Constable, in Rickman, *Life of TP*, 388.

24. TP to Andrew Dean, August 15, 1806, Foner, 2:1483–1485.

25. Thomas Jefferson to TP, March 18, 1801, Founders Online.

26. Ibid., October 9, 1807.

27. TP to Thomas Jefferson, January 12, 1803, Foner 2:1439.

28. Foner, 1:1498–1501.

29. Rickman, *Life of TP*, 182.

30. Ibid., 183–185.

31. Rickman, *Life of TP*, 195–196.

32. Ibid., 197–198.

33. *TP Life*, 2:416.

34. Rickman, *Life of TP*, 289.

CHAPTER 14: WHEN THE EMPIRE OF AMERICA SHALL FALL

1. *TP Writings*, 4:173.

2. Ibid., 174–175.

3. *TP Life*, 2:417, citing *London Packet* (or *New Lloyd's Evening Post*), August 7, 1809.

4. George Chalmers, *The Life of Thomas Pain*, 165.

5. Rickman, *Life of TP*, 172–173.

APPENDIX B: CONTENTS OF *THE AGE OF REASON*

1. *TP Writings*, 4:21–23.

2. Ibid., 23–25.

3. Ibid., 26–28.

4. Ibid., 28–30.

5. Ibid., 30–31.

6. Ibid., 31–32.

7. Ibid., 32–38.

8. Ibid., 38–44.

9. Ibid., 45–46.

10. Ibid., 47–50.

11. Ibid., 50–55.

12. Ibid., 55–62.

13. Ibid., 62–68.

14. Ibid., 68–71.

15. Ibid., 72–73.

16. Ibid., 73–75.

17. Ibid., 75–82.

18. Ibid., 85–88.

19. Ibid., 89–151.

20. Ibid., 152–182.

21. Ibid., 183–195.

Primary Research Resources
and Bibliography

MANUSCRIPT COLLECTIONS

Archives du Ministère des Affaires Etrangères, Paris, France
Bibliothèque de l'Institut de France, Paris, France
Bibliothèque Historique de la Ville de Paris, Paris, France
Bibliothèque Nationale de France, Paris, France
The Bodleian Library, Oxford University, Oxford, England
Founders Online
Lee Family Digital Archive
Library of Congress [*Annals of Congress*, 42 vols.]
The (British) National Archives, Kew, Richmond, Surrey
Thomas Paine National Historical Association

CORE BIBLIOGRAPHY

W. W. Abbott and Dorothy Twohig, *The Papers of George Washington, Confeder-ation Series, January, 1784–September, 1788* (Charlottesville: University Press of Virginia, 1992–1997, 6 vols.).

W. W. Abbott, Dorothy Twohig, Philander D. Chase, and Theodore J. Crackel, eds., *The Papers of George Washington, Presidential Series, September, 1788–May 1793* (Charlottesville: University Press of Virginia, 1987– [multiple volumes, in progress]).

———, *The Papers of George Washington, Revolutionary War Series, June 1775–April 1778* (Charlottesville: University of Virginia Press, 1984– [multiple volumes, in progress]).

Charles Francis Adams, ed., *The Works of John Adams* (Boston: Little, Brown, 1840, 10 vols.).

John Adams, *The Diary and Autobiography of John Adams*, L. H. Butterfield, ed. (New York: Atheneum, 1964, 4 vols.).

John R. Alden, *History of the American Revolution* (New York: Alfred A. Knopf, 1969).

Henry Ammon, *The Genet Mission* (New York: W. W. Norton, 1973).

Archives Parliamentaire de 1784–1860, Receuil Complet des Débats Politiques des Chambres Françaises, Première Série (1787–1799) (Paris: Société de l'Imprimerie et Librairie Administratives et de Chemins de Fer, Paul Dupont, 1884).

J. Ayer, *Thomas Paine* (London: Secker and Warburg, 1988).

Carl Binger, *Revolutionary Doctor: Benjamin Rush, 1746–1813* (New York: W. W. Norton, 1966).

Julian P. Boyd, ed., *The Papers of Thomas Jefferson* (Princeton, NJ: Princeton University Press, 1960– [multiple volumes, in progress]).

Edmund Burke, *The Philosophy of Edmund Burke: A Selection from His Speeches and Writings* (Ann Arbor: The University of Michigan Press, 1960).

———, *Reflections on the French Revolution* (London: James Dodsley, 1790).

Lester J. Cappon, ed., *The Adams-Jefferson Letters* (Chapel Hill: University of North Carolina Press, 1959).

Gerald M. Carbone, *Nathanael Greene* (New York: Palgrave Macmillan, 2008).

George Chalmers, *Life of Thomas Paine . . . by Francis Oldys* (London: John Stockdale, 1793).

Étiènne Charavay, *Le Général La Fayette, 1757–1834* (Paris: Société de la Révolution Française, 1898).

James Cheetham, *The Life of Thomas Paine* (London: A. Maxwell, 1809). [The first TP biography but deeply biased emphasis on Paine's alleged drinking habits and debaucheries.]

Clifford D. Conner, *Jean Paul Marat: Tribune of the French Revolution* (London: Pluto Press, 2012).

Moncure Daniel Conway, *The Life of Thomas Paine* (New York: G. P. Putnam's Sons, 1892, 2 vols.).

———, *The Writings of Thomas Paine* (New York: G. P. Putnam's Sons, 1894–1896, 4 vols.).

Edward S. Corwin, *French Policy and the American Alliance of 1778* (Princeton, NJ: Princeton University Press, 1916).

Lisa Plummer Crafton, ed., *The French Revolution Debate in English Literature and Culture* (Westport, CT: Greenwood Press, 1997).

Beatrix Cary Davenport, ed., *A Diary of the French Revolution by Gouverneur Morris, 1752–1816* (Boston: Houghton Mifflin, 1939, 2 vols.).

Alexander DeConde, *Entangling Alliance* (Durham, NC: Duke University Press, 1958).

——, *The Quasi-War: The Politics and Diplomacy of the Undeclared War with France, 1797–1801* (New York: Charles Scribner's Sons, 1966).

——, *This Affair of Louisiana* (New York: Charles Scribner's Sons, 1976).

Henri Doniol, *Histoire de la Participation de la France à l'Établissement des États-Unis d'Amérique* (Paris: Imprimerie Nationale, 1886, 5 vols., quarto).

John Durand, ed., *Documents of the American Revolution* (New York: Henry Holt, 1889).

——, *New Materials for the History of the American Revolution . . . from Documents in the French* [government] *Archives* (New York: Henry Holt, 1889).

R. R. Fennessy, *Burke, Paine, and the Rights of Man: A Difference of Political Opinion* (The Hague, Holland: Martinus Nijhoff, 1963).

Eric Foner, *Tom Paine and Revolutionary America* (New York: Oxford University Press, 1977).

Philip S. Foner, *The Complete Writings of Thomas Paine* (Binghamton, NY: The Citadel Press, 1945, 2 vols.).

Worthington Chauncey Ford, ed., *Journals of the Continental Congress, 1774–1789* (Washington, DC: Library of Congress, 1904–1937, 34 vols.).

Benjamin Franklin, *The Life of Benjamin Franklin by Himself* (Cambridge: Cambridge University Press, 3 vols., 1874).

——, *The Papers of Benjamin Franklin* (New Haven, CT: Yale University Press, 1978– [multiple volumes, in progress]).

Douglas Southall Freeman, *George Washington* (New York: Charles Scribner's Sons, 1951, 7 vols.).

Alexander Gilchrist, *Life of William Blake* (London: John Lane, 1907).

Richard Gimbel, *Thomas Paine's Fight for Freedom* (New Haven, CT: Yale University Press, 1961).

Terry Golway, *Washington's General: Nathanael Greene and the Triumph of the American Revolution* (New York: Henry Holt, 2006).

Louis Gottschalk, *Lafayette Between the American and the French Revolution (1783–1789)* (Chicago: University of Chicago Press, 1950).

David Freeman Hawke, *Paine* (New York: Harper & Row, 1974).

Walter Isaacson, *Benjamin Franklin, An American Life* (New York: Simon & Schuster, 2003).

[Thomas Jefferson], *The Papers of Thomas Jefferson*, Julian P. Boyd et al., eds., (Princeton, NJ: Princeton University Press, 1950– , multiple volumes, in progress]).

Merrill Jensen, *The New Nation: A History of the United States During the Confederation, 1781–1789* (New York: Alfred A. Knopf, 1950).

Malou Julin, *Thomas Paine: Un intellectual d'une Révolution à l'autre* (Paris: Éditions Complexe, 2004).

John Keane, *Tom Paine: A Political Life* (London: Bloomsbury Publishing, 1995).

George-Washington Lafayette [Gilbert Motier, Marquis de Lafayette], *Mémoires, Correspondence et Manuscrits du Générale Lafayette, publiés par sa famille* (Paris: H. Fournier, ainé, 6 vols., 1837).

David Lawday, *The Giant of the French Revolution: Danton, A Life* (New York: Grove Press, 2009).

Major-General Henry Lee, *Funeral Oration on the Death of General Washington* (Boston: Joseph Nancrede and Manning & Loring, 1800).

Richard Henry Lee, *The Letters of Richard Henry Lee*, James Curtis Ballagh, ed. (New York: Macmillan Company, 1911, 2 vols.).

———, *The Life of Arthur Lee, LL.D.* (Boston: Wells and Lilly, 1829, 2 vols.).

Georges Lemaitre, *Beaumarchais* (New York: Alfred A. Knopf, 1949).

Jean Lessay, *Thomas Paine, l'américain de la Convention* (Paris: Perrin, 1987).

Louis de Loménie, *Beaumarchais et son temps: Études sur la société en France au XVIIIe siècle* (Paris: Michel Lévy frères, 2 vols., 1856).

James Madison, *Debates on the Adoption of the Federal Constitution in the Convention Held at Philadelphia in 1787* (Philadelphia: J. B. Lippincott, 1901).

Pauline Maier, *The Old Revolutionaries: Political Lives in the Age of Samuel Adams* (New York: Alfred A. Knopf, 1980).

Dumas Malone, *Jefferson and His Time* (Boston: Little, Brown, 1948–1977, 6 vols.).

Jean-Clémant Martin, *La Révolution française, 1789–1799: Une histoire sociopolitique* (Paris: Belin, 2004).

———, *Nouvelle histoire de la Révolution* (Paris: Éditions Perrin, 2012).

———, *Robespierre: La fabrication d'un monstre* (Paris: Éditions Perrin, 2016).

André Maurois, *Adrienne: The Life of the Marquise de la Fayette* (New York: McGraw-Hill, 1961).

Peter McPhee, *Robespierre: A Revolutionary Life* (New Haven, CT: Yale University Press, 2012).

Mémoires sur les prisons, qui concernent les prisons de Port-Libre, du Luxembourg, de la rue de Sèvres, etc., etc. (Paris: Baudouin Frères, 1823, 2 vols.).

William Augustus Miles, *The Correspondence of William Augustus Miles on the French Revolution* (London: Longmans, Green and Co., 1890, 2 vols.).

John C. Miller, *Crisis in Freedom: The Alien and Sedition Acts* (Boston: Little, Brown, 1951).

———, *The Federalist Era, 1789–1801* (New York: Harper & Brothers, 1960).

James Monroe, *The Autobiography of James Monroe* (Syracuse, NY: Syracuse University Press, 1959).

———, *The Writings of James Monroe*, Stanislaus Murray Hamilton, ed. (New York: G. P. Putnam's Sons, 1898–1903, 7 vols.).

Frank Moore, *Diary of the American Revolution from Newspapers and Original Documents* (New York: Charles Scribner, 1860, 2 vols.).

Gouverneur Morris, *A Diary of the French Revolution*, Beatrix Cary Davenport, ed. (Cambridge, MA. The Riverside Press, 1939, 2 vols.).

Teresa O'Neill, ed., *Opposing Viewpoints: The American Revolution*, American History Series (San Diego: Greenhaven Press, 1992).

Thomas Paine, *Paine: Collected Writings*, Eric Foner, ed. (New York: The Library of America, 1995).

Daniel Preston, *A Comprehensive Catalogue of the Correspondence and Papers of James Monroe* (Westport, CT: Greenwood Press, 2001, 2 vols.).

Mark Puls, *Samuel Adams, Father of the American Revolution* (New York: Palgrave Macmillan, 2006).

Charles Rappleye, *Robert Morris, Financier of the American Revolution* (New York: Simon & Schuster, 2010).

Thomas Clio Rickman, *Life of Thomas Paine* (London: Thomas Clio Rickman, 1819). [The only Paine biography by a Paine intimate. Hagiographic but, next to Conway (q.v.), the most important Paine biography.]

Ted Ruddock, *Arch Bridges and Their Builders, 1735–1835* (Cambridge: Cambridge University Press, 1979).

Benjamin Rush, *The Autobiography of Benjamin Rush* (Philadelphia: The American Philosophical Society, 1948).

———, *Letters of Benjamin Rush*, L. H. Butterfield, ed. (Philadelphia: American Philosophical Society, 1951, 2 vols.).

W. T. Sherwin, *Memoirs of the Life of Thomas Paine* (London: R. Carlile, 1819).

Étiènne Taillemite, *La Fayette* (Paris: Libriarie Athème Fayard, 1989).

Jean Tulard, Jean-François Fayard, and Alfred Fierro, *Histoire et Dictionnaire de la Révolution Française* (Paris: Éditions Robert Laffont, 1987).

Harlow Giles Unger, *First Founding Father: Richard Henry Lee and the Call for American Independence* (Boston: Da Capo Press, 2017).

———, *John Marshall: The Chief Justice Who Saved the Nation* (Boston: Da Capo Press, 2014).

———, *Lafayette* (Hoboken, NJ: John Wiley & Sons, 2002).

———, *The Last Founding Father: James Monroe and a Nation's Call to Greatness* (Cambridge, MA: Da Capo Press, 2009).

Bernard Vincent, *Thomas Paine ou la réligion de la liberté* (Paris: Aubier, 1987).

———, *Thomas Paine ou la république sans frontiéres* (Nancy: Presses de l'université de Nancy, 1993).

George Washington, *The Writings of George Washington, from the Original Manuscript Sources, 1745–1799*, John C. Fitzpatrick, ed. (Washington, D.C.: U.S. Government Printing Office, 1931–1944, 39 vols.).

Thompson Westcott, *A History of the "Test Laws" of Pennsylvania* (Philadelphia: John Campbell, 1865).

Francis Wharton, ed., *The Revolutionary Diplomatic Correspondence of the United States* (Washington, D.C.: 1889, 6 vols.).

Mary Wollstonecraft, *A Vindication of the Rights of Woman* (Boston: Peter Edes, 1792).

Gordon Wood, *The Creation of the American Republic, 1776–1787* (New York: Norton, 1969).

James Woodress, *A Yankee's Odyssey: The Life of Joel Barlow* (Philadelphia: Lippincott, 1958).

William Woodward, *Paine: America's Godfather* (New York: E. P. Dutton, 1945).

NEWSPAPERS

(Philadelphia) *Aurora*
Baltimore Evening Post
Baltimore Republican
Columbian Centinel
Freeman's Journal
Gazette of the United States
London Packet
The National Aegis
The National Intelligencer
New Lloyd's Evening Post
New York Evening Post
Pennsylvania Journal
Pennsylvania Magazine
Pennsylvania Packet
The Public Advertiser
The Times
True American

Index

Page references in *italics* indicate illustrations.